VOLUNTEER VACATIONS

Eleventh Edition

SHORT-TERM ADVENTURES
THAT WILL BENEFIT YOU
AND OTHERS

Bill McMillon, Doug Cutchins,
and Anne Geissinger

Foreword by Ed Asner

CHICAGO
REVIEW
PRESS

Copyright © 2012 by Bill McMillon, Doug Cutchins, and Anne Geissinger
Foreword copyright © 2009 by Ed Asner
All rights reserved
Eleventh edition
Published by Chicago Review Press, Incorporated
814 North Franklin Street
Chicago, Illinois 60610
ISBN 978-1-56976-841-9

Many of the personal vignettes included in this edition were provided courtesy of the sponsoring organizations and permissions are their responsibility.

The authors have made every effort to ensure that all the listing information is correct and current at the time of publication.

Library of Congress Cataloging-in-Publication Data
McMillon, Bill, 1942–
  Volunteer vacations : short-term adventures that will benefit you and others / Bill McMillon, Doug Cutchins, and Anne Geissinger. — Eleventh ed.
    p. cm.
  Includes indexes.
  ISBN 978-1-56976-841-9
 1. Voluntarism—Directories. 2. Associations, institutions, etc.—Directories.
 3. Vacations—Directories. I. Cutchins, Doug. II. Geissinger, Anne. III. Title.
  HN49.V64M35 2012
  302'.14—dc23
                                2011039139

Cover and interior design: Scott Rattray
Cover and interior layout: Jonathan Hahn
Cover photos: (top) Landscape at Madeira island, Portugal © Dhoxax/Shutterstock; (bottom) Volunteer teaching in Goa, India, courtesy of Robert Lyon

Printed in the United States of America
5 4 3 2 1

For Grinnell College

VOLUNTEER
VACATIONS

Eleventh Edition

Contents

Indexes

Foreword

Ed Asner

IT'S BEEN SAID that "man would rather spend himself for a cause than live idly in prosperity." I'm sure that upon uttering that axiom in a group, you'd see everyone nodding wisely—agreeing that hard work for a cause is preferable to the good life unfulfilled. It's a noble thought during a philosophical discussion. When everyone's in accord on that point, pull out some airline tickets to Perryville, Arkansas, and ask who's willing to give up their Bermuda vacation in order to work with livestock. Any takers?

It's a hard sell. Public service is an antiquity in today's society. In the 1930s, the Civilian Conservation Corps instilled in the minds of young men and women the notion that national service is an obligation, indeed, a privilege: putting something back into the country in exchange for all the benefits derived from living in a free and democratic society. It was a wonderful setup and one that should have been perpetuated.

Since that time, however, our country's military bent has made national service an anathema—national service has come to mean the draft, the military, risk of life and limb on some foreign shore. Some states, to supplement low budget allocations, use public service as punishment for misdemeanors. In Oregon, for instance, DWI offenders can be seen picking up highway litter.

In short, the notion of a "volunteer vacation" sounds like a disciplinary measure akin to assigning extra household chores to a balky teenager.

Happily, there are people like Bill McMillon, Doug Cutchins, and Anne Geissinger (along with the hundreds of people who have taken volunteer vacations) to set us straight: volunteering for a worthy cause can be fun, fulfilling, and an adventure you'll anticipate year after year. Maybe working with livestock isn't your thing, but there's plenty of variety: go on archaeological expeditions, assist with health care in remote villages, maintain trails in beautiful mountain climes, or build homes for the homeless. Some programs encourage you to bring the kids; some pay part of your expenses.

Best of all, you'll be helping people who need you. These days our local, state, and federal government budgets (and many government budgets around the world) have cut "people programs" in favor of big business and the military. More and more, our nation and our world must look to volunteers to fill the gaps that governments are unwilling or unable to fill—in health care, education, and programs for the disabled and underprivileged.

Read this book . . . try a volunteer vacation. The world will be a better place and so will you.

Preface

YOUR COMMUNITY IS growing. Whether or not you want it to, whether or not you are aware of it, the bounds of where you can go, what you can do, and who you can meet grow almost every day. As technology improves, communities and countries that were once geographically and culturally isolated are coming into close contact with other cities and nations. We recall walking into a village in the middle of the rain forest of Suriname, commenting on how remote the village was and how little contact it had with the outside world, and then noticing a Nike swoosh shaved into the back of a villager's haircut. The fact that this icon of American corporate culture had made its way to a village that lacked roads, running water, and electricity demonstrated what we already knew but had forgotten: there are very few communities left on Earth that you can't reach, and soon we'll all be friends on Facebook and follow one another on Twitter.

This process of globalization has had both positive and negative aspects. More people have access to better health care. More children are being educated. More communities are getting basic services, such as clean drinking water and electricity. But these same communities are under attack from outside influences both cultural and economic. Is it a good thing when a child learns to read . . . but not in the language of her parents? What happens to a rural family who finally gets electricity . . . but the husband has to work—and live—in the nearest city in order to afford it? And why do so many people around the world seem to love American products, sports, and popular culture but profess a disdain for our country?

There are no easy answers to these questions. But, as the definition of your community changes and more people become your "friends," you have a level of responsibility to try to answer these and other questions.

We would argue that volunteering is one of the best ways to start finding these answers. As a volunteer, you can begin to halt the tide of the nastier effects of globalization and instead promote the benefits of international understanding and cooperation. Through personal, one-on-one exchanges and dialogues, individuals around the world—including people from different communities in the United States—will better understand and appreciate the people in their national and global neighborhoods.

Why turn a vacation into a volunteer vacation? After researching this book, we're hard-pressed to see why you wouldn't! First, the opportunities presented here are amazing. We challenge you to read this book and not find organizations that make you want to get on the next plane to Nepal, France, or California. Second, your help is desperately needed. The 150 organizations listed in this book exist for a reason—there is a lot of need in the world, and the skills that you have can be put to tremendously good use in helping to fulfill that need.

We hope that you'll take advantage of the chance that you have to turn a regular vacation into an experience that will truly benefit yourself, others, and your community. Almost everyone who undertakes these projects returns home proclaiming that their vacations benefited them at least as much as they did the people being served. And when this happens to you, we hope that you'll then take the next step: share the experience. Invite friends over to see pictures of your trip. (We promise they'll be more interested in these pictures than those of your last trip to the beach!) Talk to a group at your place of worship about what you did. Write a column for the local newspaper. Call an elementary school and ask if you can come speak to a class. The medium isn't crucial; what's most important is that you share the lessons that you learned with a wider audience, because then your understanding of a new community is spread to more people.

Volunteer vacations can change your perspective on the world, teach you new skills, and greatly affect the lives of others. We hope that you are inspired to make an ordinary vacation extraordinary and to use your talents to better yourself and your community.

—Doug Cutchins and Anne Geissinger

Acknowledgments

for Doug Cutchins and Anne Geissinger

OUR FIRST THANKS have to go to the organizations that form the heart of this book. For months, they put up with our requests, reminders, and questions, spending time and resources on e-mails and phone conversations. Each organization was truly outstanding to work with. In addition to their cooperation, though, we are also thankful for the work they do, the opportunities they create, and the assistance they give to volunteers, all in order to help improve the planet and the human condition.

We are also thankful for the help and cooperation of the authors and photographers whose work appears in this book and helps bring volunteer experiences to life. None of these artists received compensation; all agreed to have their work published as a way to help promote the volunteer organizations and to inspire others. We are indebted to them for their kindness and generosity.

It is one of the greatest oddities of our lives that we have never met Bill McMillon, or even talked to him on the phone. Yet we are deeply impressed and inspired by the years of work he put into the early editions of this book. There are many people about whom we can say, "This book would not be what it is without you." Without Bill, though, this book simply would not be at all.

We sometimes wonder what we did to deserve the faith that our friends at Chicago Review Press have shown in us. Cynthia Sherry recruited us out of the blue to take over authorship of this book, and she has always been there to answer our questions and give helpful, timely advice. Our publicists—Catherine Bosen, Elizabeth Malzahn, and Jen Wisnowski—have surprised us with their incredible resourcefulness and tenacity in finding new audiences and media outlets for the book and delighted us with their marvelous senses of humor. This eleventh edition was immensely improved by the watchful eyes of our editor, Devon Freeny, and our copyeditor, Kendra Millis. We are indebted to and thank them all.

On more personal notes, we would like to recognize the huge influence that all of our friends in Grinnell and beyond have in our lives every day, and how enriched we are by all of them. We'd also like to thank the members of the Grinnell College DC Posse 6—Greg, Imani, Javon, Lana, Matheos, Mekdes, Milton, Nicole, Rocio, and Vilma—for working hard and achieving every day.

Emma and Bea, our daughters, have been our ongoing sources of inspiration and joy throughout the four editions of this book that we've written.

We dedicate the book to Grinnell College—where we met, where we were educated, and the place that has become our home. Any young people who are interested in volunteer vacations and want to combine that passion for doing good, internationalism, and top-flight academics ought to come join us on the prairie.

Introduction

SEE A NEW part of the United States or a completely different country.

Help other people.

Relax.

Make new friends.

Learn a few words in a new language or resurrect the Spanish that you haven't used since high school.

Change your perspective on what it means to be rich or poor, first world or third world, developed or underdeveloped. Consider what it might mean to be "overdeveloped."

How? Take a volunteer vacation.

"A volunteer vacation?" you might say. "Doesn't that imply work? But isn't that why I'm going on vacation, to get away from work?"

Yes and no. If you take advantage of one of the opportunities in this book, you'll certainly work. You'll build bridges and blaze trails (both real and metaphorical), teach people how to read, take care of injured wildlife, play with kids in an orphanage, or do any of a hundred other jobs that will make a real difference on our planet. That's work—hard work.

But it's completely different from what most of us do to bring home a paycheck every week.

You'll be in a new place, surrounded by people you don't know. You'll be using parts of your brain and body that haven't gotten good workouts in years. You're likely to experience some kind of paradigm shift and to look at yourself, your country, or the world in a new way. Not only will you come home refreshed and rejuvenated, as you would after any vacation, but you'll also have the knowledge that you've made a difference in someone's life or in the world.

Sounds good—what's next?

There are two ways to go about using this guide. The first is to open it up and begin to dream, to allow yourself to exclaim, "That's it, honey—pack your bags for Belem, Brazil! I hear it's beautiful this time of year." If you're open to new places to go and new things to do, this is the approach for you; start reading and dreaming. Some people, though, need to be a little more intentional in their planning. If you know that you want to go to Europe, for example, or that you really want to work with kids, or that you can't spend more than $500, then you need to be more selective in your reading. Make good use of the indexes in the back of this book and frequently check the websites of the organizations you're considering, since information can and does change over time.

What This Guide Does and Doesn't Do

This is a resource guide; it is not a review book. We provide basic information about select organizations that we have vetted and that we feel good about recommending in order to allow you to begin to make decisions about what organizations are right for you and the experience that you want to have. Given that well over 100 organizations run thousands of programs in scores of countries, we wouldn't want to try to make a judgment call for you as an individual; what is perfect for some people is horrible for others. Instead, we give you excellent information that you need to know about these organizations so that you can begin to make an informed decision. We've made a trade-off in doing so: instead of focusing on giving you a little bit of information on as many organizations as possible, we've been very selective and pared down our list, but have given you in-depth information about each organization. Even with this additional information, though, we hope that nobody goes on a volunteer vacation without first talking with a staff member of the organization and, if at all possible, with people who have volunteered with the organization in the past. Every organization's listing in this book has extensive contact information, including e-mail addresses and website URLs. Use a quick Google blog search to turn up several journals from volunteers who traveled with an organization you are considering. Check the organization's Facebook page to find "fans" of that organization and ask them about their experiences. Research and evaluate organizations the same way you would go about making any other decision about how to use your time and money. (Speaking of money, it's important for you to know that none of the organizations listed in this book had to pay anything to be included. This book is free publicity for them, and they deserve it. We hope that their inclusion in *Volunteer Vacations* helps them to recruit volunteers like you.)

We've given you another valuable tool to start with in addition to this expanded information. Sprinkled throughout this book you'll find volunteer vignettes, stories written by past volunteers about their experiences with some of these organizations, as well as photos of volunteers in action. These more personal glimpses into the daily lives of volunteers will give you a better sense of what your experience might be like, and they can help you to imagine yourself in the volunteers' places.

How Do I Evaluate an Organization to See If It Is Right for Me?

Here are ten questions you should get answers to before signing on with a volunteer organization.

1. Does the work involved mesh with what I want to do on my vacation? Will it allow me to develop or use skills that are important to me?
2. Will the project take me to a place that I want to go?
3. Do I have the same goals and values as those of the organization? (This is especially important for organizations that have overt political or religious goals; you don't want to end up promoting a cause, directly or

indirectly, that you don't believe in. Read the mission statement carefully in each entry.)

4. What do past volunteers say about their experiences with this organization?
5. What are living conditions at the site like?
6. What will my exact job responsibilities be? How much scut work (cooking, cleaning, filing, and so on) will I be expected to do? Keep in mind that someone has to do this work, and it is often divided among all of the employees and volunteers, from top to bottom.
7. How much does it cost to participate? What exactly is included in the program fee?
8. When does the project take place, how long does it last, and does it fit with my schedule?
9. Will I be working in a group? What is the profile of the average volunteer? Age range? What are the motivations of the other people in the group?
10. What kind of training or orientation is offered? (This information is crucial for international organizations, where you might be working in a culture very different from your own.)

Always check the US State Department's lists of countries under travel warnings and public announcements to better understand the security situation in the places where you might be traveling. We would strongly discourage anyone from volunteering in a country that is under a travel warning, and we would caution you to do more research before volunteering in a country under a public announcement.

Getting the Most Out of This Book

Each listing in this book contains up to twelve sections:

- *General contact information,* including (as available) postal address, phone and fax numbers, e-mail addresses, and website URLs.

- *Project Type:* We asked each organization to place itself in several of approximately 25 categories so that you can tell at a glance what an organization does, broadly speaking. You can use this section (in addition to the indexes) if you are glancing casually through the book looking for, say, opportunities to volunteer with orphans, or another specific type of opportunity.
- *Mission Statement Excerpt:* This statement gives you an idea of how each organization defines itself.
- *Year Founded* and *Number of Volunteers Last Year:* Though numbers can certainly be misleading, you can get a sense of the scope of an organization's work by looking at how long it has been in existence and how many people it is used to serving. That said, don't reject small or recently founded organizations out of hand; some of our favorite organizations are young but have passionate, go-getter administrators behind them.
- *Funding Sources:* To borrow the old dictum from the movie *All the President's Men*, "Follow the money." This step is important, as knowing where an organization's funding comes from helps you know more about its reason for being and who supports its work. Luckily, most organizations are very up-front about this information; they don't want disaffected volunteers who don't share their mission. Assume that the funding sources that are listed here are in addition to the program fees that organizations charge to volunteer with them.
- *The Work They Do:* Here's where we get into the meat of the description. This part describes, in broad terms, what the work of the organization is, as well as how volunteers help with that work. Look for specifics on volunteer jobs and examples of how you'll be spending your time with this organization.
- *Project Location:* The location can be incredibly specific for some of our smaller organizations, or "around the world" for organizations that operate a large number of ever-changing global operations. Also included in this

section are details, as we know them, about lodging accommodations so that you can be sure you'll be comfortable with the arrangements.

- *Time Line:* Information here includes when applications are accepted, when volunteer positions begin, and how long positions last (minimum, maximum, and average time lengths).
- *Cost:* Yes, virtually all of these opportunities cost money (the few that do not usually require very specialized skills or a long-term commitment). This section tries to detail as best it can what those costs will be, as well as what is included in the organizations' fees and what additional expenses you will need to bear. Pay close attention to insurance coverage; if the organization does not provide insurance, check with your insurance provider before departure to make sure that you will be covered overseas. If not, please consider purchasing a short-term supplemental policy.
- *Getting Started:* This section gives information about how best to contact the organization or obtain an application and whether or not an interview is required, as well as details on training and orientation programs.
- *Needed Skills and Specific Populations:* If an organization requires that you have mastered specific skills before volunteering with it, that information will be noted here. Also found here is information regarding age minimums and maximums, as well as information for volunteers with disabilities and families.

Expectations: What Is Reasonable and What Is Unreasonable

Be nice to the organizations that offer these services. Remember that many of them operate on extremely lean budgets with underpaid and overworked staff. Please don't request printed information from a group unless you are seriously considering volunteering with them. Make ample use of the vast resources of the Internet—all of the organizations in this book have websites that you can access for basic information. Be polite and understand that your request is one of many that the organization is dealing with at any given time. Act as a partner, not as a consumer. Remember: the more money these organizations spend on administration, the less they have to spend on what they're working to achieve.

That said, organizations have a responsibility to their volunteers as well. Organizations should live up to their promises and advertising. They should answer your questions fully, honestly, and in a timely manner. There is also some truth to the phrase "you get what you pay for." In other words, if you are paying thousands of dollars for an experience, you have a right (within limits) to expect more service than someone whose experience is wholly sponsored by the organization.

Last, don't expect to change the world overnight. Have reasonable expectations of the organization, yourself, and your ability to create long-term change. Recognize that the work you do is important, but that it is just one piece of the larger puzzle of improving global conditions. Let the process, not the product, be your measure of success.

VOLUNTEER VACATIONS

Eleventh Edition

ACDI/VOCA

50 F Street NW, Suite 1075
Washington, DC 20001
(800) 929-8622; Fax: (202) 469-6257
E-mail: volunteer@acdivoca.org
Website: www.acdivoca.org; volunteer-specific information at
www.acdivoca.org/volunteer

Project Type: Agriculture; Community Development; Economic
Development; Professional/Technical Assistance; Rural
Development; Women's Issues

Mission Statement Excerpt: "ACDI/VOCA's worldwide mission
is to promote economic opportunities for cooperatives, businesses, and communities worldwide through the innovative
application of sound business practices."

Year Founded: 1963

Number of Volunteers Last Year: Approximately 250

Funding Sources: ACDI/VOCA receives government funding
from the US Agency for International Development and the
US Department of Agriculture, Millennium Challenge
Corporation/Millennium Challenge Account, Bill &
Melinda Gates Foundation, and World Bank, as well as
gifts, grants, and donations from private sources

The Work They Do: ACDI/VOCA creates short-term volunteer
opportunities for experts in agriculture, business, finance,
cooperative development, and community development.
ACDI/VOCA volunteers are typically mid- to late-career
professionals with significant experience who provide
expertise to host organizations in economically developing
countries. Some volunteers are members of teams, and many
conduct repeat assignments. ACDI/VOCA is driven by the
needs of its host countries, not by the desires of volunteers;
as such, they only place volunteers after receiving requests
from their offices around the world. Examples of specific
project assignments might include spending three weeks in
Ghana addressing issues producers are having with postharvest handling and storage of crops, vegetables, or fruits, or a

1

volunteer might go on a two-week assignment to Lebanon to work with a food processor to help them develop a plan for quality control, safety, and sanitation.

Project Location: Projects are located around the world, including the Middle East, Africa, Latin America, the former Soviet Union, Asia, and Southeast Asia. Accommodations vary from country to country; in urban areas, volunteers are typically housed in moderate-quality hotels, guesthouses, or apartments leased by the project. In rural areas, volunteers may be asked to stay with the host or in more rustic settings.

Time Line: Volunteers are placed year-round. Placements are typically two to six weeks in length.

Cost: ACDI/VOCA pays and arranges for all assignment-related expenses, including round-trip coach airfare, passport, visas, lodging, meals and incidentals, required immunizations, emergency medical evacuation, and supplemental health insurance. Volunteers are met at the airport and receive staff support (including, as needed, an interpreter) throughout the assignment.

Getting Started: Applications are accepted year-round via the ACDI/VOCA website. Volunteers are interviewed at the time of selection for an assignment, and briefings are provided before volunteers travel to their assignments.

Needed Skills and Specific Populations: ACDI/VOCA volunteers are typically mid- to late-career and senior professionals with a minimum of ten years of experience in one of the following areas: accounting; agricultural extension and education; banking and finance; business management; community development; cooperative and association development; domestic and international marketing; enterprise development; entrepreneurship; farm management; food and meat processing; food storage and handling; fruit, vegetable, and plant production and protection; grain and commodity inspection and storage; information technology and e-commerce; livestock production and disease control; ecotourism and agrotourism; policy reform; postharvest handling; rural credit; sustainable agriculture; and training of trainers. Many retired experts have volunteered with ACDI/VOCA. Because some work sites are in rural areas in economically developing countries, ACDI/VOCA may have problems accommodating volunteers with disabilities. Some programs require US citizenship. ACDI/VOCA does not recruit families. Volunteers are required to submit a written report at the end of every assignment.

Helping Haitians Rebuild for the Future

By Kent Allen

ACDI/VOCA

On January 12, 2010, a magnitude 7.0 earthquake hit Haiti. An estimated 3 million people were affected by the quake; the Haitian government reported that approximately 316,000 people had died, 300,000 had been injured, and 1,000,000 made homeless. Additionally, it is estimated that 250,000 homes and 30,000 commercial buildings collapsed or were severely damaged. There was an immediate outpouring of aid for Haiti. But how do you rebuild a nation and help it prepare for the next disaster? Volunteer Kent Allen responded to the call for aid by literally helping Haitians rebuild their lives.

Allen, a 67-year-old from Wyoming with extensive experience in seismic-safe construction, traveled to Haiti for 30 days in October 2010 and trained 40 local trainers and area craftsmen in light construction, seismic- and hurricane-resistant building techniques, and methods for assessing materials used for various types of construction. The four-week, hands-on training was part of a six-month job training program, funded by VOCA and designed by APTECH (Ateliers Pilotes de Technologie, which translates as Pilot Workshops in Technology), a Haitian educational association, to help train workers in new building techniques crucial to this disaster-prone region.

"When I first walked through the gate to APTECH, it didn't take more than a few steps before I had a feeling of overwhelming optimism," Allen says. "I could see the place was doing good things and had the potential to do even greater activities, and I wanted to be at least a small part of it." Allen worked with APTECH, both before and after his trip, to design a Haiti-specific curriculum to help the local technicians and artisans retool their skills so they could build much-needed homes and other buildings that could withstand natural disasters, such as earthquakes and hurricanes. Allen provided the students with specific instruction and then worked with them to put these skills into practice for the community. The result was a newly built classroom for Haitian children.

Moreover, these students, local trainers themselves, now have the skills they need to train other construction workers and artisans in new seismic-safe techniques. "The teachers, like teachers everywhere, were interested in expanding their teaching skills as well as their skills as craftsmen," Allen says. "Truly these teachers were my kind of colleagues." Allen continued, "This project was the kind of situation, as a vocational teacher educator, for which I had been preparing my entire professional life." Allen continues to support APTECH's training efforts by supplying needed reference materials and helping to have the materials translated into Creole. He already is planning his next trip to Haiti in 2011.

Adelante

101 Main Street, Suite B
Seal Beach, CA 90740
(562) 799-9133; Fax: (562) 684-4682
E-mail: info@adelanteabroad.com
Website: www.adelanteabroad.com

Project Type: Archaeology; Community Development;
Economic Development; Education; Natural Conservation
(Land); Orphans; Women's Issues
Mission Statement Excerpt: Adelante does not have a mission
statement.
Year Founded: 1999
Number of Volunteers Last Year: 120
Funding Sources: None
The Work They Do: Adelante provides volunteer and internship
opportunities in locations in Spain and South America.
Volunteers mostly teach English, work with children who
live in poverty, work on environmental conservation proj-
ects or on archeological digs, provide health care, and work
for social or economic development.
Project Location: Adelante's volunteer projects take place in
Oaxaca, Mexico, and San Jose, Costa Rica. Volunteer
accommodations are provided by Adelante, and work sites
can be reached by public transportation. In Mexico, volunteers have their own room within an apartment shared with
other volunteers or locals. In Costa Rica, volunteers stay
with a host family.
Time Line: Adelante's volunteer projects take place year-round,
and all begin on the first Monday of each month.
Volunteers stay for 1 to 12 months in Mexico or 2 to 12
months in Costa Rica; the average volunteer stays for 3
months.
Cost: Adelante's project fee for Mexico ranges from $2,345 to
$5,545 for one to six months; in Costa Rica, it is $3,365 to
$5,775 for two to six months. There is also a $150 applica-

tion fee. Program fees include housing and two or three weeks of intensive Spanish language classes; in Costa Rica, the fees also include meals and laundry services. Volunteers must provide their own international airfare, and Adelante estimates that other living costs, such as local transportation, will cost $300 to $400 per month.

Getting Started: Prospective volunteers can download an application form from Adelante's website or e-mail the organization to request one. Applications are submitted by mail, e-mail, or fax and must be received at least 60 days before the proposed start date. Adelante does require a phone interview of all volunteers. Volunteers receive a predeparture orientation packet, as well as one upon arrival at the language school. Other training is provided on the job.

Needed Skills and Specific Populations: Some Spanish language skills are required for most volunteer experiences other than teaching English in Oaxaca. Volunteers must be at least 18 years old, and senior volunteers are welcome. Adelante may be able to place volunteers with disabilities, depending on the disability, location, and desired position.

African Conservation Trust (ACT)

P.O. Box 310
Link Hills 3652
South Africa
+27 33 342 2844
E-mail: info@projectafrica.com
Website: www.projectafrica.com

Project Type: Archaeology; Community Development; Historic
Preservation; Natural Conservation (Land); Scientific
Research

Mission Statement Excerpt: "The mission of the African
Conservation Trust (ACT) is to provide a means for conservation projects to become self-funding through active participation by the public. This gives ordinary people a chance to
make a positive and real contribution to environmental
conservation by funding and participating in the research
effort as volunteers."

Year Founded: 2000

Number of Volunteers Last Year: 53

Funding Sources: ACT receives funding through the South
African National Lottery and the South African National
Heritage Council

The Work They Do: Most of ACT's programs involve long-term
natural conservation or historic preservation efforts, such as
a hippo project on Lake Malawi and a rock art mapping
project in South Africa. Examples of specific work carried
out by volunteers include radio tracking of various species
of African mammals; sand trapping at holes dug under the
perimeter fence to monitor entry and exit species and
numbers; conducting monthly game counts at water holes
and perhaps walking transects; clearing the fence line of
vegetation and eradicating alien invasive plants on the farm;
exploring the Ukhalhamba-Drakensberg Park in South
Africa for new unrecorded rock art painting and archaeological sites of the indigenous San people; and conducting a
hippo census on Lake Malawi by boat.

Project Location: Projects are carried out in the sub-Saharan countries of South Africa and Malawi. Conditions vary by location. In South Africa, volunteers are based in the mountains at an extensive base camp. The roughest conditions may be found in Malawi, where volunteers camp in expedition conditions. Volunteers usually provide their own camping gear.

Time Line: Volunteers are accepted year-round. Volunteers can commit to as little as a two-week period or as much as a one-year experience; the average stay is about four weeks.

Cost: ACT's program fee is £950 per month, except for the hippo project in Malawi, which is more expensive and which will be priced closer to the project time. The program fee includes pickup from and drop-off at the airport nearest the site, all in-country, project-related transport, accommodations, food, and training. Air transportation to and from the country involved (as well as flights to and from the airport nearest the project site) is not included in the program fee.

Getting Started: Prospective volunteers should contact ACT via e-mail or the organization's website. ACT will provide orientation and training if necessary.

Needed Skills and Specific Populations: In South Africa, the work is very physical and includes working and walking on steep slopes, so volunteers must have hiking or backpacking experience. Volunteers must be at least 18 years old; there is no maximum age limit. ACT cannot accommodate volunteers with disabilities.

African Impact

6 Carlton Close
Professional Village
Noordhoek 7985
Cape Town
South Africa
(800) 606-7185
E-mail: info@africanimpact.com
Website: www.africanimpact.com

Project Type: Community Development; Education;
Medical/Health; Natural Conservation (Land); Orphans;
Rural Development; Youth
Mission Statement Excerpt: "Explore. Inspire. Impact."
Year Founded: 2003
Number of Volunteers Last Year: 1,850
Funding Sources: None outside of volunteer program fees
The Work They Do: African Impact facilitates a wide variety of
volunteer projects with the goal of assisting conservation
initiatives and local communities, while providing a life-
changing experience for international volunteers. African
Impact works hard to build strong relationships with local
authorities and communities. Projects range throughout
southern and eastern Africa and include offerings such as
lion rehabilitation in Zimbabwe, wildlife photography and
conservation education in South Africa, rural preschool and
community development in Mozambique, and coaching
sports in Zambia. Volunteers take on a similarly broad
range of tasks, from assisting in clinics, building orphanages, and teaching in primary schools to doing conservation education, working with lions, and conducting
elephant and leopard research.
Project Location: African Impact operates in southern and
eastern Africa, including Botswana, Kenya, Mozambique,
Namibia, South Africa, Tanzania, Zambia, and Zimbabwe.
While some of its projects involve physical work, such as

walking through the bush, coaching children in soccer, or laying bricks, volunteers are well informed of this before they sign up. For accommodations, volunteers either live at base camps adjacent to the game reserve where the project takes place or in volunteer houses in towns and villages. At all sites, volunteers have a communal area, comfortable bathrooms, and bedrooms that they share with no more than four others.

Time Line: Projects run throughout the year, but most projects do have specific start dates each month. While African Impact is flexible regarding how long volunteers stay, most volunteers work for between two and eight weeks.

Cost: The project fee varies, depending on the specific project, but volunteers generally pay between $2,000 and $3,000 per month. The fee includes accommodations, three meals each day, airport transfers, transport to and from the projects, and a volunteer manual. The program fee does not include flights or travel insurance.

Getting Started: Volunteers must apply online at least three weeks before they wish to depart by completing a detailed questionnaire; no interview is required. African Impact provides volunteers with an orientation, which includes a tour of the surrounding area, an introduction to the local customs and culture, a lesson in the local language, and necessary project-specific training.

Needed Skills and Specific Populations: African Impact does not have any required skills; the only restriction is that, for safety reasons, volunteers with the lion rehabilitation project must be at least five feet tall. Volunteers must be at least 18 years old, but there is no maximum age limit. African Impact enthusiastically works with volunteers with disabilities, and families are welcome as long as all family members meet the minimum age requirement.

AidCamps International

483 Green Lanes
London N13 4BS
United Kingdom
+44 845 652 5412
E-mail: info@aidcamps.org
Website: www.aidcamps.org

Project Type: Community Development; Construction; Education; Medical/Health; Orphans; Rural Development; Youth

Mission Statement Excerpt: "Providing development aid and support to local communities, primarily but not exclusively in developing countries, for the furtherance of the relief of poverty, the advancement of education and health care, and other purposes beneficial to the community."

Year Founded: 2002

Number of Volunteers Last Year: Usually 80 to 100

Funding Sources: Individuals

The Work They Do: AidCamps builds facilities for its community and NGO partners in order to benefit disadvantaged people, with a particular focus on children. Group projects include construction of schools, orphanages, and resource centers, while individual volunteers take part in community-focused projects that might include teaching, conservation work, field research, or other opportunities. Individual volunteer placements are based on the volunteer's skills and interests, as well as the community's needs.

Project Location: AidCamps places volunteers in Cameroon, India, Nepal, and Sri Lanka. All volunteers reside in AidCamps' accommodations in or near the community; conditions vary by country and are usually fairly simple, but AidCamps makes every attempt to make volunteers as comfortable as possible given the local environment. Individual volunteers may choose to stay with a host family.

Time Line: Group volunteer projects have fixed start and end dates and usually last three weeks. Individual volunteers are welcomed throughout the year for a minimum of two weeks and a maximum as allowed by visa constraints. Most independent volunteers participate for between three weeks and three months.

Cost: Group volunteer projects have a per-person registration fee of £250 and a minimum donation of £750, which covers most of the volunteer's in-country costs. Individual volunteers have a £95 registration fee and a minimum donation of £500 for up to five weeks and then £50 per week for every week thereafter, though this does not cover any of the in-country costs.

Getting Started: Volunteers may access application materials on AidCamps' website. The group volunteer programs are first-come, first-served, so prospective volunteers should apply well before their intended departure date. In addition, AidCamps requires criminal record checks for certain placements; for US citizens, this means obtaining a record check from the FBI, which can take five to six months. Otherwise, individual volunteers should apply at least three months before they would like to depart. Volunteers need to complete a phone interview.

Needed Skills and Specific Populations: Volunteers with groups simply need good health, enthusiasm, and cultural sensitivity. Individual volunteers will need skills that match their unique placement. The minimum age for volunteers is 18, unless a family is volunteering together, in which case there is no minimum age. AidCamps does not have a maximum age limit, and works quite a bit with senior volunteers. In general, the situation at AidCamps' work locations are not suitable for volunteers with disabilities.

AIDE Abroad—Association of International Development and Exchange

1221 South Mopac Expressway, Suite 100
Austin, TX 78746
(512) 457-8062 or (866) 6ABROAD; Fax: (413) 460-3502
E-mail: volunteer@aideabroad.org
Website: www.aideabroad.org

Project Type: Community Development; Education;
Medical/Health; Natural Conservation (Land); Orphans;
Trail Building/Maintenance; Youth

Mission Statement Excerpt: "AIDE Abroad will be a catalyst for
change in the world by building bridges between individuals
from diverse cultures."

Year Founded: 2007 (though it grew out of a previous organization, Alliance Abroad Group, which was founded in 1992)

Number of Volunteers Last Year: 400

Funding Sources: None; AIDE Abroad is self-funded

The Work They Do: AIDE Abroad offers a variety of volunteer
projects tailored to the wishes of the individual volunteer or
group. Volunteers can teach English, assist at a sustainable
living center, work on an organic farm, protect sea turtle
habitats, help at an orphanage, assist in hospitals, health
clinics, or pharmacies, work in an animal rehabilitation
center, aid community development initiatives, or contribute
to many other projects.

Project Location: Volunteers are placed in Argentina, Costa
Rica, Ecuador, Guatemala, Peru, and South Africa. Accommodations and meals vary by project site, but in most cases
volunteers are provided a homestay and food.

Time Line: Volunteers are accepted year-round for a minimum
of one week and a maximum of 12 months.

Cost: Program fees range from $950 to $3,500. Fees include
predeparture and postarrival orientations, volunteer placement, airport transfer in the host country, accommodations,
all meals, and travel medical insurance. Volunteers must pay
for their own airfare.

Getting Started: Prospective volunteers should download an application from the AIDE Abroad website, complete it, and send it to AIDE Abroad by postal mail, fax, or e-mail. A phone interview is required. Orientation is provided both before departure and after arrival; on-site training is offered for some programs.

Needed Skills and Specific Populations: Volunteers must be at least 18 years old, and senior volunteers are welcomed. Most volunteer sites cannot accommodate volunteers with disabilities. For some programs, it is necessary to have a basic to intermediate level of Spanish, a bachelor's degree, experience working with children, good physical and mental health, and/or a criminal background check. Volunteers from outside the United States are welcomed as long as a visa for the host country can be obtained.

American Hiking Society

1422 Fenwick Lane
Silver Spring, MD 20910
(301) 565-6704; Fax: (301) 565-6714
E-mail: volunteer@americanhiking.org
Website: www.americanhiking.org

Project Type: Natural Conservation (Land); Trail
Building/Maintenance

Mission Statement Excerpt: "As the national voice for America's
hikers, American Hiking Society promotes and protects foot
trails and the hiking experience."

Year Founded: 1976

Number of Volunteers Last Year: 650

Funding Sources: Government, private, and corporate donors as
well as individual and group memberships

The Work They Do: The American Hiking Society offers a
series of weeklong trail building, maintenance, and restoration projects on America's public lands. Each crew consists
of 6 to 15 volunteers, accompanied by an experienced crew
leader.

Project Location: The American Hiking Society has volunteer
projects in more than 30 states and the US Virgin Islands.
Projects are rated from "easy" to "very strenuous" based on
the type of work needed, accommodations, or amount of
hiking required. Lodging is normally a tent site in either a
campground or a backcountry location. Participants must
provide their own tents, sleeping bags, pads, and all
personal gear. A limited number of projects each year do
feature cabin accommodations, the spots for which fill up
quickly. Tools and supervision are provided by the host
agency or organization.

Time Line: American Hiking Society's volunteer projects are
available from mid-January through mid-December. Projects
offered are 4, 7, or 10 days in length, with the majority
being one week.

Cost: A volunteer's first trip with the American Hiking Society costs $275, which includes a one-year membership in the organization. Each subsequent trip in the calendar year is $175. Food and lodging is provided on all trips, but volunteers must pay their own travel expenses. Participation fees are due at the time of registration.

Getting Started: Prospective volunteers can download a volunteer schedule from the American Hiking Society website, or they can call the number above to request a printed version of the schedule. Registration forms are available on the website and can be completed online, by fax, or by calling the American Hiking Society. Volunteers must register in advance, and since there are a maximum number of volunteers allowed on each trip, early registration is encouraged. Interviews are not required for prospective volunteers. The host of each project provides on-site training.

Needed Skills and Specific Populations: Previous trail-building experience is not necessary, but volunteers do need to be in good physical condition. The American Hiking Society offers "family-friendly" projects, open to families with children between the ages of 14 and 18. The American Hiking Society does not have a maximum age for volunteers; all projects are rated on a scale from "easy" to "very strenuous," giving volunteers the opportunity to select projects that best suit their abilities. For most trips, volunteers must be US citizens or have a J-1 Visa to participate.

American Jewish World Service (AJWS)

45 West 36th Street, 11th floor
New York, NY 10018
(800) 889-7146; Fax: (212) 792-2930
E-mail: volunteer@ajws.org
Website: www.ajws.org

Project Type: Community Development; Economic
Development; Education; Human Rights; Social Justice;
Women's Issues; Youth

Mission Statement Excerpt: "Through grants to grassroots
organizations, volunteer service, advocacy and education,
AJWS fosters civil society, sustainable development, and
human rights for all people, while promoting the values and
responsibilities of global citizenship within the Jewish
community."

Year Founded: 1985

Number of Volunteers Last Year: 560

Funding Sources: Private donors, foundations

The Work They Do: AJWS offers a number of programs,
including seven-week summer projects (Volunteer Summer)
for young adults; weeklong programs (Alternative Breaks)
to college students; the World Partners Fellowship for recent
college graduates and young professionals; and Volunteer
Corps for people ranging from young professionals to
retirees. Alternative Break and Volunteer Summer participants work primarily on building or agricultural projects,
while World Partners and Volunteer Corps participants
work in classroom settings or in the offices of nongovernmental organizations supported by AJWS.

Project Location: Depending on the program, participants can
volunteer in Uganda, Ghana, South Africa, Senegal,
Guatemala, Nicaragua, Honduras, El Salvador, Peru,
Mexico, the Dominican Republic, India, Thailand, and
Cambodia. Work sites include fields and construction sites
as well as classrooms and offices. With assistance from

AJWS, Volunteer Corps participants make their own living arrangements; Volunteer Summer and Alternative Break volunteers stay in compound-like quarters, while World Partner participants live in apartments with other members of their group.

Time Line: AJWS's Volunteer Summer lasts for seven weeks; Alternative Breaks last for one week to 10 days; World Partners Fellowship lasts for 10 months; Volunteer Corps placements range in length from two months to one year, with the average being three to four months.

Cost: Because of the range of programs, AJWS has a number of different program fees. The program fee for Alternative Breaks is $550 per participant. Program fees cover all food and lodging while in the field, tools and supplies for the group's work project, basic staff costs, and financial support for the host organization in their primary work. The program fee for Volunteer Summer is $4,000 for college students and $5,500 for high school students, which includes round-trip airfare to New York for orientation, international transportation, housing and meals while in the field, and international medical assistance. Acceptance to Volunteer Summer is need-blind, and financial aid and scholarships are available. AJWS supplies each World Partners Fellow with a modest stipend, lowest reasonable round-trip airfare, and living accommodations. Fellows are expected to raise a minimum of $1,000 to support AJWS. There is no program fee to participate in AJWS Volunteer Corps. AJWS pays for volunteers' airfare and provides emergency evacuation assistance. Volunteers are financially responsible for health insurance and in-country cost-of-living, including housing, food, and local transportation. These costs vary greatly based on location of service.

Getting Started: AJWS programs require a written application, and many also require a phone or in-person interview. Applications are available online at the AJWS website. AJWS provides training and orientation for all of its programs; orientations for Alternative Breaks, Volunteer

Summer, and Volunteer Corps are conducted in the United States before departure, while the orientation for World Partners Fellowships takes place in the country of service. Orientations provide skills training in the volunteer experience and cross-cultural communication, and, when necessary, language training. All AJWS programs allow participants to discuss and learn more about the intersection of Judaism, international development, and social justice.

Needed Skills and Specific Populations: While Volunteer Summer, World Partners, and Alternative Breaks do not require specific skills, Volunteer Corps members are paired with organizations based on their professional skill set. AJWS Volunteer Summer is open to high school and college-age students (ages 16 to 24); Alternative Breaks are open to college students; World Partners Fellowship is open to recent college graduates and young professionals. Participants in the above programs must be Jewish. For Volunteer Corps, there is no minimum age to participate, but volunteers should have at least several years of professional experience; senior volunteers are welcome. Participants in Volunteer Corps must be Jewish or part of an interfaith couple. Volunteers with disabilities are welcomed, though all volunteers must be able to manage the challenges of living in an economically developing country for an extended period of time. AJWS does not currently have volunteer opportunities for families.

AmeriSpan

1334 Walnut Street, 6th floor
Philadelphia, PA 19107
(800) 879-6640 or (215) 751-1100; Fax: (215) 751-1986
E-mail: info@amerispan.com
Website: www.amerispan.com

Project Type: Community Development; Education;
  Medical/Health; Natural Conservation (Land); Trail
  Building/Maintenance; Women's Issues
Mission Statement Excerpt: "AmeriSpan . . . aims to facilitate
  second-language acquisition combined with temporary
  volunteer opportunities throughout Latin America, Europe,
  Africa and Asia."
Year Founded: 1993
Number of Volunteers Last Year: More than 300
Funding Sources: None; self-funded
The Work They Do: AmeriSpan represents more than 165
  different host organizations in Latin America, Europe,
  Africa, and Asia. Most of these organizations are small,
  local, nonprofit initiatives, but some, such as the Red Cross
  and Habitat for Humanity, are worldwide organizations.
  Others, particularly those that host internship opportunities,
  are for-profit organizations. Volunteer work varies depending on the host organizations, but it can range from highly
  professional projects to caring for orphans, and from
  teaching English to trail maintenance. Customized
  internship and volunteer placements are available.
Project Location: AmeriSpan offers volunteer sites throughout
  Latin America, Europe, Africa, and Asia. The work site is
  most often a direct reflection of the type of volunteer work
  and the economic development of the host country. For
  example, volunteers at an underfunded orphanage in Bolivia
  should expect extremely basic living and work conditions
  and little supervision, due to a lack of staffing. Conversely, a
  volunteer at a marketing firm in Berlin will find work

conditions similar to those in the United States. Volunteers stay with host families during the initial language part of the program, which lasts for two to six weeks, and then stay in lodging just for volunteers, with shared rooms (two people per room) and shared kitchen facilities, during the volunteer experience.

Time Line: Volunteers are accepted year-round. Volunteers must commit to a four-week volunteer experience plus, in most cases, one week or more of the language training program. The average volunteer stays for an eight-week volunteer stint, comprised of four weeks of classes followed by four weeks of volunteering. There is no limit to how long one may volunteer with AmeriSpan.

Cost: Program fees range from $500 to more than $5,000, depending on location, project, and length of the volunteer experience. Fees include language instruction, lodging, full or partial board, and travel insurance. Volunteers must provide for their own airfare, in-country transportation, and meals while at the volunteer placement. AmeriSpan makes direct donations to host organizations, including more than $250,000 worth of medical supplies reaching needy communities in Latin America in a single year.

Getting Started: AmeriSpan's application process includes an application, essay, resume, two reference letters, and a telephone interview. AmeriSpan's partner organizations conduct an in-country volunteer meeting before the work starts, covering details of the organization, the volunteers' duties, and cultural issues. If the placement is close to the language school, the volunteer coordinator will visit the placement with the volunteer before he or she starts work. The training a volunteer receives at the placement varies by organization.

Needed Skills and Specific Populations: Some host organizations require proficiency in the local language; some require education or experience related to the volunteer placement. Most host organizations will accept volunteers who are at least 18 years old, but some have a minimum age of 21 or

23; Amerispan also operates summer-only volunteer programs for teenagers, which have extra supervision. Senior volunteers are welcomed by AmeriSpan. AmeriSpan has had several families volunteer through them; these are accepted on a case-by-case basis and only if parents accompany youth volunteers. Volunteers with disabilities are welcomed, but prospective volunteers should contact AmeriSpan before applying, as not all countries and projects can make accommodations for them.

Volunteering in Bolivia

By Staff Blogger

AmeriSpan

Even though there was no school the first week of my volunteer placement in Hogar Mallorca (an orphanage in Bolivia), the orphans sat and did homework for an hour after I arrived. Their time is very scheduled, with shower time, time to wash your clothes by hand, homework time (that's when I arrived!), and then recess. Even though their days are structured, the boys are allowed to leave if they have a job, such as selling things on the street or washing dishes in a restaurant. There are about 80 boys total here. I'm probably setting myself up for failure by even trying to learn all of their names!

Once the homework hour was up, they popped out of their seats and were excited to ask me my name and to say "Good morning. How are you?" in English. They can't quite figure out my name (Allison), so I've just started introducing myself as Alecia. Close enough. When the boys ask where I'm from and I say the USA, these are their questions:

- Do you know Shakira?
- Do you know Michael Jackson? (I got that one twice.)
- Do you know Harvard University?
- Do you know George Washington?
- Do you speak English?
- Do you speak Japanese?
- Do you speak French?

These boys are very curious and bright. They are especially interested in learning more English. One boy wrote a lot of words on a sheet of paper and then asked me to write the word in English and to say it for him so he could write down how it sounded. He had a lot of trouble with "the." After listening to me say it over and over, he wrote that it sounded like "dfa." I was impressed that the boys seemed to be about at the level in math that I would expect from American kids, which I guess isn't that surprising; I just wasn't expecting it. For example, an older boy was doing fractions over fractions, and a younger boy was doing multiplication with 5 digits times 3 digits. As I said, these boys are bright!

After question and answer time, we had recess together. The boys played marbles, a game with special cards (similar to the Pokemon card game in the States), Uno, and volleyball. For volleyball, they don't have a net, so they just stand in a circle, and if you miss the ball or hit it somewhere that others can't reach, you're out of the circle. I played Uno and volleyball with the boys. One advantage that I have is that I'm taller than everyone here, which is definitely an asset in volleyball.

As for my Spanish, it's getting a real workout. When the boys are talking to me, I understand maybe three-quarters of what they say, which is pretty good. When they're talking to each other, I understand maybe one-quarter. Oh well. I'm sure to improve. I'm really liking it here and am looking forward to my next three weeks.

Amigos de las Américas (AMIGOS)

5618 Star Lane
Houston, TX 77057
(800) 231-7796; Fax: (713) 782-9267
E-mail: info@amigoslink.org
Website: www.amigoslink.org

Project Type: Community Development; Education;
Medical/Health; Rural Development; Youth
Mission Statement Excerpt: "Amigos de las Américas builds
partnerships to empower young leaders, advance community development, and strengthen multicultural
understanding in the Americas."
Year Founded: 1965
Number of Volunteers Last Year: 785
Funding Sources: Support from corporations and foundations
The Work They Do: AMIGOS provides students (typically aged
16 to 20) an opportunity to experience hands-on, cross-
cultural understanding and leadership by volunteering in
teams of two or three as public health, education, and
community development workers in rural communities or
semi-urban neighborhoods. Collaborating with local sponsoring agencies and community members, volunteers help
identify local resources, then implement community
improvement projects in their host community's schools,
health clinics, or residences. Programs include, but are not
limited to, sanitation and development, environmental
education, family nutrition, health education, school
renovations, home improvement, youth group formation
and collaboration, leadership development, and other
community-based initiatives. Examples of past volunteer
projects include teaching nutrition classes, forming local
women's groups, and facilitating creative expression workshops for youth. Since its inception, more than 20,000
AMIGOS volunteers have lived and worked in 15 Latin
American and Caribbean countries.

Project Location: Amigos de las Américas currently offers 13 summer projects located in nine countries: Costa Rica, the Dominican Republic, Ecuador, Honduras, Mexico, Nicaragua, Panama, Paraguay, and Peru. Volunteers live with host families along with one or two other AMIGOS volunteers. In many of the rural communities, electricity (and sometimes running water) is not available. Many of the communities are located in mountainous regions that require hiking and walking.

Time Line: Exact dates vary by year, but almost all projects take place during the summer and are six to eight weeks in length.

Cost: The fee for volunteers participating through AMIGOS's International Office is $4,600, which includes international airfare from Houston or Miami, insurance, training, all room and board, and in-country transportation.

Getting Started: Prospective volunteers can either download an application from the website or contact AMIGOS by phone or e-mail to request one. The application deadline is April 3. Volunteer training includes Latin American history and cultural awareness, health and safety, first aid, positive development approaches, human relations, leadership, management, and presentation skills. Volunteers who live in one of the 28 cities where AMIGOS has a chapter will undergo in-person training over an eight-month period. Volunteers outside of these cities receive their training by correspondence.

Needed Skills and Specific Populations: Volunteers must have taken at least two years of high school Spanish or have an equivalent skill level. Volunteers must be at least 16 years old and have completed their sophomore year of high school. Every effort will be made to successfully place volunteers with disabilities, but those volunteers may be hindered by the conditions in Latin America.

Amity Institute

3065 Rosecrans Place, Suite 104
San Diego, CA 92110
(619) 222-7000; Fax: (619) 222-7016
E-mail: mail@amity.org
Website: www.amity.org

Project Type: Education; Youth

Mission Statement Excerpt: "Building international friendship and cultural understanding through teaching exchange."

Year Founded: 1962

Number of Volunteers Last Year: Over 50

Funding Sources: Private donors

The Work They Do: Amity focuses mainly on teaching English abroad in primary and secondary schools, including the teaching of teachers. Amity volunteers teach or introduce English and share about their own culture. Qualified volunteers may also conduct seminars and workshops for teachers who are nonnative English speakers.

Project Location: Amity's projects take place in Europe and South America, mostly in school settings. Volunteers live with local hosts, who usually provide all meals, though some volunteers help contribute to the cost of food.

Time Line: Volunteer projects take place during the host country's school year, which varies by location. Volunteer terms of service last from 3 to 12 months.

Cost: The program fee for an Amity placement is $500; volunteers are then responsible for their travel expenses and, where applicable, the cost of food. Accommodations are provided by the host community.

Getting Started: Prospective volunteers should contact Amity via e-mail and request an application. Amity does not have fixed deadlines but instead fills opportunities as they become available. Volunteers must have a phone interview before placement. Volunteers receive orientation materials from Amity and in-country training from the host partners as needed.

Needed Skills and Specific Populations: English as a Second Language certificates are preferred but not required; volunteers must be able to adjust to a different culture and adapt to different living conditions. Volunteers on Amity's projects in Germany must be able to prove their proficiency in German; the level of required German varies by project. Volunteers must be 20 years old and physically fit. Amity does not place families or volunteers with disabilities.

Amizade Global Service-Learning

4 Smithfield Street, 7th floor
Pittsburgh, PA 15222
(412) 586-4986; Fax (757) 257-8358
E-mail: volunteer@amizade.org
Website: www.amizade.org

Project Type: Community Development; Education; Historic Preservation; Human Rights; Rural Development; Women's Issues; Youth

Mission Statement Excerpt: "Amizade empowers individuals and communities through worldwide service and learning."

Year Founded: 1994

Number of Volunteers Last Year: 500

Funding Sources: Grants and donations

The Work They Do: Amizade carries out a number of projects in the areas of community empowerment, education, the environment, health care, housing, infrastructure, building of peaceful relationships, and creation of responsible individuals. Current projects open to volunteers include constructing school classrooms and working with physically challenged youth in Bolivia; working with street children in Brazil; volunteering with a community organization in rural Jamaica; supporting women's rights in Tanzania; participating in historic preservation activities at concentration camps in Poland; constructing a library and volunteering in health clinics in rural Ghana; working with organizations that are addressing social, religious, and political divisions in Northern Ireland; tutoring elementary school children at the Navajo Nation in Arizona; and feeding the hungry and homeless in Washington, DC.

Project Location: Amizade carries out projects in Santarém, Brazil; Cochabamba, Bolivia; Petersfield, Jamaica; Belfast and Ballycastle, Northern Ireland; Berlin, Germany; Auschwitz-Birkenau, Poland; Karagwe, Tanzania; Jukwa, Ghana; Puerto Morelos, Mexico; the Navajo Nation,

Arizona; and Washington, DC. Given the huge differences among these places, the work sites and accommodations vary, from the heart of Belfast to a coastal village in Mexico; from the Navajo reservation to a Tanzanian village; and more. At all sites, however, Amizade provides lodging and meals. Lodging varies by site and ranges from home-stays to dorms to hotels. Meals incorporate locally available food and are cooked and served by local Amizade staff.

Time Line: Opportunities exist year-round. Projects run for a minimum of one week and a maximum of six months; the average volunteer stint is approximately three weeks.

Cost: Program fees range from about $850 for a single program week to $12,500 for an entire semester. These fees cover lodging, meals, educational activities, recreational activities, and, in most cases, local transportation. Fees for the courses include university tuition and the course instruction. Partici-pants are responsible for transportation to the work site, immunizations, passport and visa fees, and departure taxes.

Getting Started: Prospective volunteers can either download an application and other documents from Amizade's website or call the office for information; interviews are not required. Once in-country, volunteers receive an orientation from local site directors, which typically includes information on local safety and security, intercultural communication specific to that site, and local history and geography.

Needed Skills and Specific Populations: No specific skills are required, and Amizade does not have any citizenship requirements. Volunteers must be at least 16 years old to work on their own; a parent or guardian must accompany volunteers aged 12 to 15. Senior volunteers are welcomed at all sites. Volunteers with disabilities are encouraged and welcomed to participate in Amizade's programs, though some community conditions are better suited to volunteers with disabilities than others.

On Becoming a Global Citizen

By Matt Clements

Amizade Global Service-Learning

The first time I ever traveled outside the United States was with Amizade. In the summer of 2007, I participated in a service-learning program to Santarem, Brazil. We worked with locals on the construction of a community center. In addition to the physical work, we spent that month learning about international development and Brazilian culture. This amazing month changed my outlook on life forever. My eyes were opened to a larger world and I was challenged to better understand and appreciate the opportunities I have been given.

That initial program prompted me to reevaluate my life. My time in Brazil changed my perspective and my interests. As a result, I charted a new course for myself and developed career goals related to community development in Latin America. To further these new goals, I pursued more travel with Amizade, this time to the city of Cochabamba in Bolivia, and not just once but twice! These international experiences solidified the desire that was awakened within me to become a global citizen and to better understand myself as a global citizen.

In summary, Amizade has changed my life and allowed me to have a more complete understanding of both who I am and what I want to do in the future.

AMPED Abroad (Adventure Minded People Exploring Diversity Abroad)

P.O. Box 24865
Fort Worth, TX 76124
(214) 736-7654; Fax: (214) 276-7727
E-mail: info@ampedabroad.com
Website: www.ampedabroad.com

Project Type: Community Development; Education;
Medical/Health; Natural Conservation (Land); Natural
Conservation (Sea); Orphans; Youth

Mission Statement Excerpt: AMPED Abroad "provides once in
a lifetime journeys abroad that are designed to stimulate
cultural learning, awareness, and understanding for individuals, families, and organizations alike."

Year Founded: 2008

Number of Volunteers Last Year: 6

Funding Sources: None

The Work They Do: AMPED Abroad offers a wide range of
social service projects that involve work in areas regarding
children and at-risk youth, youth sports, health care and
medicine (including public health and dentistry), HIV/AIDS,
conservation, teaching English, the elderly, community
development, and construction. Volunteers may take on a
range of tasks, including helping children in orphanages
with their homework, assisting with patient intake at clinics,
constructing trails, and tagging and tracking animals.

Project Location: AMPED Abroad offers projects in Latin
America and Africa; specific sites range from major cities to
rural communities, with some projects, such as sea turtle
conservation, in very rustic environments. Accommodations
vary by host destination and project, but might include a
stay with a host family, a guest house, or cabins.

Time Line: Projects generally take place throughout the year,
with start dates on the first and third Monday of each
month, though alternative start dates can be arranged by

request. Volunteers may commit to at least one week on some projects, but are generally encouraged to stay at least two weeks and can stay up to 12 months. The average volunteer stay is four to six weeks. Volunteer placements up to or over 12 months may be possible, though volunteers are responsible for their own visa arrangements in these cases.

Cost: AMPED Abroad has a $250 nonrefundable application fee. Although the program fees vary by country and length of stay, they start at around $500 and can range up to over $2,500. Program fees generally include meals, accommodations, and pickup at the airport, but do not include airfare. Free Spanish lessons are available for some destinations in Latin America.

Getting Started: Prospective volunteers may apply online via AMPED Abroad's website. Applications should be submitted at least two months in advance of the desired start date; applications submitted with less time than this may be subject to an expedited application fee, and those submitted with less than two weeks' lead time will not be considered. AMPED Abroad may conduct phone interviews but does not usually do so. Volunteers receive an orientation upon their arrival in-country.

Needed Skills and Specific Populations: While specific skills may be helpful at some project sites, they are generally not required except on medical placements, which require that volunteers be medical students or licensed practitioners. Most projects require that volunteers be at least 18 years old, though there are exceptions to that rule at some sites. Volunteers over 60 are welcome but must provide a signed letter of consent on official letterhead from their primary care physician. Volunteers with disabilities will be evaluated on a case-by-case basis to ensure that AMPED Abroad can provide reasonable accommodations. Families are welcome to participate with AMPED Abroad, as long as children are of school age.

Appalachian Trail Conservancy (ATC)

P.O. Box 224
Blacksburg, VA 24063
(540) 953-3571; Fax: (540) 524-4376
E-mail: crews@appalachiantrail.org
Website: www.appalachiantrail.org/crews

Project Type: Historic Preservation; Natural Conservation
(Land)

Mission Statement Excerpt: "The Appalachian Trail
Conservancy's mission is to preserve and manage the
Appalachian Trail—ensuring that its vast natural beauty and
priceless cultural heritage can be shared and enjoyed today,
tomorrow, and for centuries to come."

Year Founded: 1925

Number of Volunteers Last Year: Over 6,000

Funding Sources: Government and private donors; the USDA
Forest Service and the National Park Service cosponsor the
ATC volunteer trail crews

The Work They Do: The Appalachian National Scenic Trail is
the longest continuously marked footpath in the world and
America's first national scenic trail. It follows the crest of
the Appalachian Mountains for more than 2,100 miles
along ridges and through rural farm valleys and rugged high
country. ATC trail-maintaining clubs are assigned a section
or sections of the Appalachian Trail to maintain. Clubs are
assisted by the ATC volunteer trail crews to complete large-
scale projects. ATC organizes and supports the volunteer
efforts to maintain and build the Appalachian Trail. Trail
work is hard, physical labor. Volunteer work assignments
include new trail construction, rock work, log work, shelter
construction, and other physically demanding tasks. Trail
crews of 6 to 10 volunteers work under the supervision of
skilled leaders. Trail construction involves working with
hand tools, and getting dirty is guaranteed. The crews work
eight-hour days, rain or shine, hot or cold, regardless of
black flies, mosquitoes, and other insects.

Project Location: Volunteers can work anywhere along the length of the Appalachian Trail. Crew base camps are located in northern Maine, central Vermont, Pennsylvania, southwestern Virginia, and the Great Smoky Mountains in Tennessee. Volunteer crew members may backpack into a backcountry campsite and set up a primitive tent camp near the project site. Crews may also work from car camps or developed campgrounds. During the course of the crew season, the weather can vary from sweaty summertime heat to freezing, winter-like cold.

Time Line: The six crews are active from May through October; check the ATC website for exact dates. Prospective participants in any of these crews' programs may volunteer for one to six weeks; the average volunteer stint is 5 to 10 days.

Cost: There is no program fee, though volunteers are responsible for their own transportation to and from their base camp. Once volunteers reach the base camp, most expenses are covered, including shelter, food, transportation to and from work projects, tools, safety equipment, and group camping gear (as available). Crew members need to bring work clothing, sturdy boots, and their own basic camping gear.

Getting Started: Prospective volunteers can go to the ATC website to find additional information on ATC trail crews, learn how to apply, and download a registration form. Crew chiefs informally interview applicants by phone before their volunteer stint begins. Volunteers receive training in "leave no trace" camping techniques and trail crew safety the evening before their project starts. All skills training is provided in the field during the course of the project.

Needed Skills and Specific Populations: Good health, willingness to cooperate, community spirit, and enthusiasm are more important than previous trail experience. Participants should be comfortable living and working in a primitive outdoor setting. Volunteers must be at least 18 years old; senior volunteers are "welcome and encouraged!" ATC is working on developing more programs and work crews for families with children under the age of 18. ATC also welcomes international volunteers who obtain a J-1 Visa on their own, but it cannot assist them in obtaining entry to the United States. All are welcome to participate in the Appalachian Trail Conservancy's crew program, including volunteers with disabilities. Trail crews do hard physical labor, however, so potential volunteers should contact the crew coordinator if they have concerns about participating.

ARCHELON, the Sea Turtle Protection Society of Greece

57 Solomou Street
GR 104 32 Athens
Greece
+30 21 0 523 1342
E-mail: volunteers@archelon.gr
Website: www.archelon.gr/index_eng.php

Project Type: Natural Conservation (Sea)

Mission Statement Excerpt: ARCHELON "protect[s] the sea turtles in Greece through monitoring and research, developing and implementing management plans, raising public awareness and rehabilitating sick and injured turtles."

Year Founded: 1983

Number of Volunteers Last Year: 400

Funding Sources: Government, faith-based, and private sources

The Work They Do: ARCHELON helps to protect Greece's three major turtle nesting areas, which cover about 60 miles of shoreline. They accomplish this mission by protecting more than 2,500 nests from human and animal threats, tagging turtles for monitoring purposes, treating injured and sick turtles (more than 50 per year, on average), teaching more than 18,000 students in environmental education programs, and maintaining a public education campaign that reaches tens of thousands of visitors. Volunteers assist with nest management and habitat protection by conducting morning and night surveys via beach patrols and excavations, and they also provide protection to turtles and their nests. Volunteers can also help with the public awareness campaign by staffing information stations and presenting slide shows. There are also opportunities to assist with the daily treatment of injured sea turtles.

Project Location: Volunteers work at one of the three turtle nesting areas, located in Zakynthos, Peloponnesus, and

Volunteer Johannes joyfully releases a healthy young sea turtle back into the Saronic Gulf just off the coast of Athens. The turtle was rehabilitated at the Rescue Centre in Glyfada, Greece. *Photo courtesy of Athina Tsekoura/ARCHELON, the Sea Turtle Protection Society of Greece*

Crete, or at the Sea Turtle Rescue Center in Athens. In Zakynthos, where the first national marine park for sea turtles in the Mediterranean was established in 1999, volunteers assist in protecting the nesting beaches. In Peloponnesus, volunteers protect nests from foxes and other mammals, help with sand dune restoration and the maintenance of nature trails, and assist in the newly established Nature Information Centres. On the island of Crete, volunteers help manage nesting areas. Volunteers stay free, in campsites that are restricted to ARCHELON volunteers, with very basic outdoor sanitary and cooking facilities that feature cold-water showers, gas stoves, and refrigerators. The exceptions to this are the Rethymno and Koroni projects; in these locations, volunteers stay in public campgrounds and therefore must pay to stay in the campgrounds (this cost is folded into the project fee for these projects). Volunteers must provide their own camping gear, including a tent and a sleeping bag, as well as their own food to cook.

Time Line: Volunteers are welcomed year-round at the Sea Turtle Rescue Center. At the other three sites, volunteers are accepted between May and October. Volunteers must commit to a minimum of four weeks.

Cost: ARCHELON's program fees range from €200 to €300 for four weeks, depending on the time of year. The program fee does not include international travel costs or room and board expenses, the latter of which ARCHELON estimates will cost about €15 per day.

Getting Started: Contact the organization via e-mail, phone, or its website. ARCHELON provides training upon arrival, as well as direct supervision during the first week.

Needed Skills and Specific Populations: The only needed skill is the ability to communicate in both spoken and written English. Volunteers must be between the ages of 18 and 65 and speak English. Volunteers with disabilities will find it difficult at best to work with ARCHELON, given the nature of the work and the basic sanitary facilities at the camp.

ArtCorps

240 County Road
Ipswich, MA 01938
(978) 998-7996; Fax: (978) 356-3250
E-mail: info@artcorp.org
Website: www.artcorp.org

Project Type: Community Development; Education;
Medical/Health; Natural Conservation (Land); Natural
Conservation (Sea); Social Justice; Women's Issues; Youth

Mission Statement Excerpt: "To advance social change
initiatives by promoting art and culture as powerful tools to
generate cooperative and sustainable work between development organizations and the communities they serve."

Year Founded: 2006 (pilot program started in 1999)

Number of Volunteers Last Year: 10

Funding Sources: ArtCorps has seed funding from the New
England Biolabs Foundation and receives additional support
from other foundations, corporate sponsors, and individual
donors

The Work They Do: ArtCorps artists use murals, theater,
stories, puppetry, and other creative facilitation techniques
to educate and inspire people to participate actively in
improving the environmental, health, and social conditions
in their communities. Every ArtCorps artist works directly
with a local development organization that is an expert in
its field, training both community members and organization staff in ArtCorps's "Art for Social Action"
methodology. ArtCorps artists come from a variety of backgrounds, including theater, painting, film, and music.

Project Location: ArtCorps volunteers work in communities
across Guatemala, El Salvador, and Honduras. The climate
varies—from the heat of El Salvador and the Honduran rain
forest to the chilly mountains in Guatemala's altiplano—as
do the communities and living conditions. Host organizations provide each volunteer with basic accommodations

that include a bed, shelves, table, and chair. Most volunteers live in rural communities, but a few live in more urban environments; most have electricity, but a few do not. Some communities have strong Mayan cultures, and others are predominately Ladino. Recent placements include Totonicapan, Guatemala; Salamá, Guatemala; Antigua, Guatemala; Sumpango, Guatemala; Purulhá, Guatemala; La Libertad, El Salvador; and Yoro, Honduras.

Time Line: ArtCorps accepts volunteers for a minimum of 11-month placements. Volunteer assignments begin annually in January.

Cost: ArtCorps and the international host organization provide room and board, a stipend for project expenses, a small personal stipend, medical insurance, training, a mid-year retreat, Internet access (where available), and local transportation. Volunteers are expected to pay for their transportation to the field, bring approximately $1,500 in personal funds to supplement their food and communications, and travel outside of the country every 90 days to renew their visas as required by local immigration law.

Getting Started: ArtCorps has a brief initial screening application available on its website that must be submitted in order to receive the full written application. Volunteers who meet the basic eligibility requirements will be asked to complete a full written application and provide a resume and samples of their art pieces or performances no later than May each year. Finalists will be interviewed by telephone and must provide contact information for three references. All applicants receive notice of the final decision on their application by August. In January, ArtCorps provides a one-week training for all artists, typically in Guatemala. Topics covered include popular education, culture, documentation, and security. ArtCorps artists also have the opportunity to apply their training with a short field practicum. This initial training is supplemented with field support and training opportunities during the year.

Needed Skills and Specific Populations: ArtCorps volunteers must be professional artists, fluent in Spanish, passionate about social or environmental issues, and mature, and they must have community arts experience. ArtCorps has found that its best volunteers are enthusiastic, adaptable, creative, organized, assertive, and flexible team players. ArtCorps prefers candidates with substantial work experience; there is no maximum age limit. Volunteers may be of any nationality but will be responsible for handling their own visa needs. Volunteers must obtain a doctor's signature indicating they are healthy enough to meet the demands of living in a rural community in a developing country; volunteers with disabilities should contact the office to discuss their specific needs. Spouses are welcome to travel with the artists as long as they are able to cover all expenses.

Asociación Centro de Estudios de Español Pop Wuj ("Pop Wuj")

1a Calle 17-72 Zona 1
Quetzaltenango
Guatemala
+502 7761 8286
E-mail: info@pop-wuj.org
Website: www.pop-wuj.org

Project Type: Community Development; Construction; Education; Medical/Health; Natural Conservation (Land); Rural Development

Mission Statement Excerpt: "Teach Spanish as a second language and . . . alleviate poverty and bring opportunities of development to some rural communities in Highlands Guatemala."

Year Founded: 1992

Number of Volunteers Last Year: 550

Funding Sources: Foundations, individuals, former students and teachers

The Work They Do: Pop Wuj creates sustainable, community-organized projects that include a greenhouse, reforestation projects, a day care center, a health care clinic, a brick-stove building project, a scholarship program, and fundraising. Volunteers assist in the administration and daily operation of all of these programs. Pop Wuj also offers an intensive Spanish language course that volunteers can take either before or during the volunteer experience.

Project Location: Pop Wuj's projects are located in the city of Quetzaltenango (the Pop Wuj Medical Clinic) and in rural, highland Guatemala, outside of the city. Volunteers live in the city with Guatemalan host families and travel daily to the community projects. Volunteers also have the option of arranging their own lodging if they prefer not to live with a host family.

Time Line: Volunteers can start at any time, but Pop Wuj requests that they begin on the first Monday of the month when possible. Pop Wuj also asks that volunteers commit to at least three months, but accepts volunteers for any length of time.

Cost: There is no cost to volunteer with Pop Wuj. Volunteers can choose to add language instruction and homestay for $185 to $300 per week, depending on the time of year. Pop Wuj does not cover transportation to the volunteer sites on a daily basis or airfare to Guatemala.

Getting Started: Prospective volunteers should contact Pop Wuj to discuss a time line, the skills the volunteer has, and any dietary needs. Volunteers who wish to add the optional language instruction also need to submit an application, complete with a registration fee, at least two weeks in advance. Experienced volunteers provide orientation and training to new volunteers.

Needed Skills and Specific Populations: While volunteers with agricultural and construction skills are always needed, Pop Wuj welcomes all volunteers. There is no minimum or maximum age for volunteers. Volunteers with disabilities are welcome, though many rural communities are not well-equipped to serve special needs. Families are welcomed and can be housed together or separately, if the family members wish a full language-immersion experience.

Atlas Corps

1133 19th Street NW, 9th floor
Washington, DC 20036-3612
(202) 736-5714
E-mail: apply@atlascorps.org
Website: www.atlascorps.org

Project Type: Community Development; Economic
Development; Education; Human Rights; Social Justice;
Women's Issues; Youth

Mission Statement Excerpt: "To address critical social issues,
Atlas Corps develops leaders, strengthens organizations, and
promotes innovation through an overseas fellowship of
skilled professionals."

Year Founded: 2006

Number of Volunteers Last Year: 31

Funding Sources: Foundations, private donors, and host organizations

The Work They Do: The Atlas Corps Fellowship is a full-time
volunteer fellowship that places young professionals in
office environments outside of their home country. The
volunteer fellows serve at host organizations that are
focused on issues that complement the volunteer's expertise.
For example, an expert in conflict resolution from Uganda
can serve at the US Peace Corps, developing their volunteer
training program, or a grant writer from the United States
may serve at a grant-making organization in Colombia.

Project Location: Atlas Corps volunteer fellows primarily serve
in New York City and Washington, DC, with some opportunities in other US cities, as well as in Bogota, Colombia.
Volunteer fellows are primarily placed in the offices of host
organizations, though some positions also include field work.
Atlas Corps assists volunteers in finding affordable, safe
shared housing that is accessible to public transportation.

Time Line: Volunteer fellows begin their service in March or
August each year and commit to 12 to 18 months of service.

Cost: Volunteer fellows in the US have their travel and insurance covered, and receive a stipend. Volunteer fellows in Colombia receive insurance and pay for their international travel and a $1,000 deposit.

Getting Started: Prospective Atlas Corps volunteer fellows should complete an online application before the annual deadlines in March and November. Applicants will complete an interview via Skype. Atlas Corps provides each volunteer with a five-day in-country orientation that covers culture, business, the local area, and safety, along with ongoing training throughout the term of service.

Needed Skills and Specific Populations: Atlas Corps volunteers must have, at a minimum, a bachelor's degree and 2 to 10 years of professional experience and be fluent in English. The maximum age for volunteers is 35. Volunteers with disabilities are welcome to apply, but not all host organizations will be able to accommodate all disabilities. International applicants are welcome, but, as stated above, Atlas Corps volunteer fellows may not serve in their home country. Atlas Corps does not provide support (neither visa nor financial) to family members of fellows.

Australian Tropical Research Foundation (ATRF)

PMB 5
Cape Tribulation QLD 4873
Australia
+61 7 4098 0063
E-mail: austrop@austrop.org.au
Website: www.austrop.org.au

Project Type: Natural Conservation (Land); Scientific Research;
Social Justice

Mission Statement Excerpt: "To conduct and facilitate research
into terrestrial and aquatic ecosystems in Australia and else-
where; to research human impact on the Australian tropics
and develop and promote sound management practices for
the tropics."

Year Founded: 1988

Number of Volunteers Last Year: 61

Funding Sources: Specific project-based funding for research,
plus some private donations for station operation; some
government support for reforestation

The Work They Do: Previous and current ATRF research projects include the development of techniques for assisted regeneration of rain forests; the development of appropriate
technology (particularly energy conservation and renewable
energy—especially solar) for living in the wet tropics; research
on the productivity, phenology, and pollination of cluster figs,
on the ecology of flying foxes (fruit bats) and their relatives,
on the conservation biology of flying foxes (particularly on
the development of nonlethal deterrent systems), and on weed
control techniques; and the chemical analysis of plant and
insect materials. Volunteers assist in many research and
station activities, including radio-tracking bats, counting figs,
stomping grass for forest regeneration, constructing buildings,
digging holes for tree planting, controlling weeds, and
running the Bat House (ATRF's visitor's center). The ATRF is
part of Al Gore's Climate Project.

Project Location: The station is located in the Daintree tropical
lowlands. Considered the "jewel" of the Australian Wet
Tropics World Heritage Area, the lowlands are sandwiched
between the coastal fringe and the coastal mountain range.
The area features a wide variety of habitats, from coastal
reefs to tropical rain forest, though it claims to be "one of
the most benign tropical rain forest environments anywhere
in the world . . . there are no seriously nasty things here."
The station is based on 25 acres of old revegetated pasture,
less than half a mile from the coast. Accommodations are in
light and airy bunkhouse-style buildings. Breakfast and
lunch are self-catered, whereas dinner is taken as a group.
Food tends to be plentiful, which has led to the site's
tongue-in-cheek nickname, "the Cape Tribulation Cooking
Camp."

Time Line: Volunteers are accepted year-round. Volunteers must
stay at least two weeks; the maximum length of stay is open
for negotiation. The record length of stay is about one year.

Cost: The program fee for volunteers is $35 per day, which
covers all food and accommodations. Volunteers who stay
for more than one month may be able to negotiate a lower
fee. The program fee does not include transportation to
Australia or to the Station from Cairns. Volunteers have
very few on-site expenses, since there are few places there to
spend money. Volunteers are required to pay a 10 percent
deposit in advance; the acceptance e-mail sent to volunteers
by the station includes information on how to pay this.

Getting Started: Prospective volunteers should contact the
station by e-mail and inquire about potential dates. No
formal orientation or training is offered; the station will
provide these as needed.

Needed Skills and Specific Populations: It is preferred that
volunteers be at least 21 years old, but there is no maximum
age limit. The station is not wheelchair accessible; prospective volunteers with other physical disabilities will probably
be able to be accommodated, though they must discuss this
with the organization well in advance of their planned trip.
Families are welcome to volunteer at ATRF.

AVIVA

P.O. Box 60573
Table View 7439
South Africa
+27 21 557 4312; Fax: +27 86 634 2063
E-mail: info@aviva-sa.com
Website: www.aviva-sa.com

Project Type: Community Development; Education; Natural
Conservation (Land); Natural Conservation (Sea); Orphans;
Youth

Mission Statement Excerpt: "AVIVA offers international volunteers the opportunity to make a vital contribution to
Communities and Endangered Wildlife while enjoying a life
changing, hands on volunteering experience in South
Africa."

Year Founded: 2001

Number of Volunteers Last Year: 370

Funding Sources: None

The Work They Do: Volunteers can choose from over a dozen
wildlife, conservation, and community-based projects.
Examples of these projects include helping to rehabilitate
endangered African penguins, monitoring African wildlife,
contributing to shark conservation, preparing meals at a
school, working with orphans by assisting with child development, baby feeding, homework, nursing, food collection,
and a variety of other tasks.

Project Location: Many of AVIVA's projects are situated in and
around Cape Town, South Africa. Accommodations and
self-service breakfasts are provided for all volunteers staying
at the AVIVA House in Cape Town. All meals are provided
for volunteers who participate at the Wild Coast Schools,
Zeekoevlei, Endangered Wildlife Monitoring, African Wild
Life, Tamboti, and Wild Coast Horses projects.

Time Line: Projects are available year-round, though not all
projects are available at all times of year. Most projects have

set start dates which are updated regularly on AVIVA's website. The minimum period for volunteer projects varies from one to six weeks, with longer stays possible. Visas are required for those who wish to stay longer than 90 days; AVIVA can assist with the application process. Volunteers normally stay an average of eight weeks, though volunteers have stayed for periods ranging from one week to 10 months.

Cost: Program fees range from $520 to more than $2,500, depending on the length of the stay. Some programs' fees include all meals, as well as any required domestic flights. Volunteers who stay on for a second project or more receive reduced program fees for these subsequent projects. All program fees include airport transfers, orientation, accommodations, some or all meals, and transportation to the volunteer site. Most projects based in Cape Town include a variety of guided tours. For volunteers joining projects farther afield, an optional Cape Town week can be added to their stay, with these tours included. Volunteers must provide their own airfare to Cape Town.

Getting Started: Prospective volunteers can apply via the online application form found on the AVIVA website. Each volunteer receives a thorough welcome brief from a member of the AVIVA team, and orientation activities are included with most projects to introduce volunteers to Cape Town's cultural and natural attractions. When volunteers join a project, they are given relevant training and supervision.

Needed Skills and Specific Populations: No special skills are needed, though volunteers should be able to speak English reasonably well. Volunteers should indicate any previous experience or qualifications on their application form. Volunteers must be at least 16 years old, and all projects are open to senior volunteers. People with disabilities are welcome to apply, though the nature of the disability may dictate whether or not a project is suitable for them. Due to the nature of the work and the location of many projects, facilities for disabled people may be limited or nonexistent.

Bike and Build

6109 Ridge Avenue, Building 2
Philadelphia, PA 19128
(267) 331-8488; Fax: (661) 752-9806
E-mail: applications@bikeandbuild.org
Website: www.bikeandbuild.org

Project Type: Community Development
Mission Statement Excerpt: "Through service-oriented cycling
trips, Bike and Build benefits affordable housing and
empowers young adults for a lifetime of service and civic
engagement."
Year Founded: 2002
Number of Volunteers Last Year: 270
Funding Sources: Foundations, private individuals, matching
donations, and corporations
The Work They Do: Each year Bike and Build runs eight cross-
country bicycle trips and one shorter regional ride, designed
to provide young adults with a chance to combine sport,
adventure, personal exploration, and growth with advocacy
and action on affordable housing issues. Bike and Build
aims to instill a sense of empowerment among its participants by offering them the opportunity to accomplish big
things and tackle big problems. Volunteers learn about and
advocate for affordable housing during their trip. During
cross-country rides, 10 days are spent on construction,
usually in collaboration with established groups such as
Habitat for Humanity or Rebuilding Together.
Project Location: Bike and Build trips are, by their very nature,
in transit across the United States. Conditions are
challenging; daily cycling mileage starts low and gradually
increases to an average of 75 miles per day, though some
days it will exceed 100 miles. Riders should expect to ride
each day, regardless of the weather; however, they do not
ride in conditions hazardous to their safety and well-being.
Riders usually stay on the floors of churches or local rec

Bike and Build volunteers on the road, living the dream of interweaving two of their loves into one grand adventure: biking and volunteering all across the country. *Photo courtesy of Bike and Build, Inc.*

centers or with affordable housing chapters, and occasionally in tents.

Time Line: Bike and Build rides take place in the summer, between mid-May and late August. Each trip averages about three months.

Cost: Volunteers must raise a minimum of $4,500. At the end of the year, Bike and Build distributes these funds (totaling almost a half million dollars last year) through donations and grants to affordable housing organizations that work with young adults or student groups. Bike and Build's volunteers review and evaluate the proposals and vote on which organizations to fund. Bike and Build provides volunteers with a bike (which they may keep at the conclusion of the trip), food, sports drinks, and accommodations.

Getting Started: Applications are available online each year in the fall; there is a $200 application fee. Trips fill quickly, so while there is no application deadline, prospective volunteers are encouraged to submit their applications as early as possible. Each Bike and Build trip begins with an orientation session.

Needed Skills and Specific Populations: Volunteers must commit to completing 500 miles of training before the start of their trip and must volunteer with an affordable housing organization before starting their trip. Volunteers must also be passionate about affordable housing. Volunteers must be between the ages of 18 and 25 (Bike and Build also hires trip leaders, who may be up to 28 years old). Volunteers with disabilities are accepted on a case-by-case basis. International volunteers are accepted, but they must make their own visa arrangements. Due to the age requirements, Bike and Build does not accept families of volunteers, though siblings have biked together before.

Biosphere Expeditions

P.O. Box 917750
Longwood, FL 32791
(800) 407-5761; Fax: (800) 407-5766
E-mail: northamerica@biosphere-expeditions.org
Website: www.biosphere-expeditions.org

Project Type: Natural Conservation (Land); Natural Conservation (Sea); Scientific Research

Mission Statement Excerpt: "Biosphere Expeditions promotes sustainable conservation and preservation of the planet's wildlife by forging alliances between scientists and the public. Our goal is to make, through our expedition work, an active contribution toward a sustainable biosphere where each part can thrive and exist. At Biosphere Expeditions we believe in empowering ordinary people by placing them at the centre of scientific study and by actively involving them out in the field where there is conservation work to be done."

Year Founded: 1999

Number of Volunteers Last Year: 400

Funding Sources: Biosphere Expeditions receives governmental and nongovernmental grants for their environmental and conservation work, and accepts corporate sponsorships only from sources they consider to be ethical

The Work They Do: Biosphere Expeditions allows members of the public to have meaningful, hands-on engagement with conservation tasks by partnering them with scientists in the field. Volunteers are involved with all aspects of scientific field research. Examples of current projects include snow leopard research in the Altai; leopard and cheetah conservation in Namibia; a biodiversity study in the Peruvian Amazon; a jaguar project in Brazil's Atlantic Forest; whale, dolphin, and turtle research in the Azores; wolf and lynx research in Slovakia; and coral reef conservation in the Caribbean, Middle East, and the Maldives. All data collected during each volunteer vacation are published in a report that includes a review of the expedition and its conservation research. The report is sent to all volunteers within a few months of the end of the expedition, and any suitable material will be published in scientific journals or other publications to make sure as many people as possible know about and benefit from the research performed. Volunteers' names will appear in the acknowledgments of all scientific papers. Volunteers will be sent copies of any publications arising out of their expeditions.

Project Location: Projects can take place anywhere in the world and are constantly changing along with the scientific research being conducted. Biosphere Expeditions does not believe adverse conditions need to be a part of this scientific research; instead, it strongly believes that volunteers need to be well fed and comfortable in order to become proficient research assistants. Accommodations are always locally owned and vary from very comfortable resorts or live-aboard yachts to lodge research centers to tent base camps in a mountain valley. Lodging and food is provided by Biosphere Expeditions.

Time Line: Project dates vary from year to year. The shortest project is one day; the longest is several months. Most volunteers join for one or two weeks.

Cost: Program fees range from $100 to $3,000, which does not include airfare. Once the expedition starts, all reasonable expenses (excluding personal items and souvenirs) are included in the program fee. Biosphere Expeditions guarantees that, on average, two-thirds of the program fee benefits the project directly and locally, while the rest goes toward administrative overhead, research, and the establishment of new expeditions. Each project's expedition report (mentioned above) includes details on how the project's program fees were spent to support the research project.

Getting Started: Prospective volunteers should start by thoroughly reading the information found on the website listed above and by selecting an expedition. Spots on expeditions are reserved with a $600 deposit, which can be sent electronically. Interviews are not a part of the sign-up process. Training is completed as part of the expedition.

Needed Skills and Specific Populations: Biosphere Expeditions works hard to allow many people to take a meaningful part in scientific research. There is no minimum or maximum age limit, and the organization proudly notes that its oldest volunteer to date was 82 years old. Families and people with physical or medical challenges or disabilities are welcome to volunteer with Biosphere Expeditions and are encouraged to contact the organization to discuss their needs.

On the Prowl for Snow Leopards

Interview with Katie Bunting

Biosphere Expeditions

Katie Bunting is a 34-year-old teacher from Bromley, London, who freely admits that she's been bitten by the expedition bug. Not just once, but three times (so far). The motivation to participate in an expedition initially came from her desire to do something different with her holiday. She doesn't want to just go sightseeing or lie on a beach. The opportunity to challenge herself and to learn new skills were two reasons to go on an expedition.

Through her volunteer work on wildlife conservation projects, giving something back to nature has become a lifestyle. Thus far she has participated in the following expeditions:

- Studying bears and wolves in Slovakia
- Observing parrots and macaws in the Peruvian Amazon
- Tracking the Arabian leopard in Oman

Katie explains, "Gaining confidence in identifying animal tracks, and starting to overcome my fear of narrow ledges, was very rewarding. In Peru, waking up each morning to the sounds of the rain forest and seeing animals such as a giant anteater, sloth, tapir, and armadillo was just amazing." Katie states that her most recent trip, on which she was walking the roof of the world, where a snow leopard had walked, was "an experience of a lifetime."

People on expeditions come from all over the world and from all walks of life. No specific skills are required as all training is provided. For Katie, the experience of meeting like-minded people from a variety of countries and working alongside local and knowledgeable people was invaluable.

"I have incredible memories of the expeditions, and I have learned so much about the environment, wildlife, and societies in remote locations. Being involved has opened my eyes to the importance of conservation. I want to do my bit to protect our planet's wildlife," Katie says.

Bob Marshall Wilderness Foundation (BMWF)

P.O. Box 190688
Hungry Horse, MT 59919
(406) 387-3808; Fax: (406) 387-3889
E-mail: trails@bmwf.org
Website: www.bmwf.org

Project Type: Community Development; Education; Natural
Conservation (Land); Trail Building/Maintenance; Youth

Mission Statement Excerpt: "The Bob Marshall Wilderness
Foundation assists in maintaining and restoring the trail
system of the Bob Marshall Wilderness Complex with
national organizations, youth groups and individual volunteers. We foster wilderness stewardship skills and education
through volunteer opportunities in Montana's premier
wilderness area and surrounding wild lands."

Year Founded: 1997

Number of Volunteers Last Year: 400

Funding Sources: Government, foundations, private donors

The Work They Do: Working with four different National
Forests in Montana's Bob Marshall Wilderness Complex,
the BMWF identifies trail system improvements and then
creates educational, challenging, environmentally minded,
and scenic trail service projects in "the Bob." Most of the
projects are focused on trail maintenance and weed eradica-
tion, but the BMWF also offers campsite restoration, river-
based float projects, and seed collection projects. The
offered projects vary in difficulty, so prospective volunteers
should review the descriptions on the BMWF website.

Project Location: Many of the BMWF's projects are located in
Montana's wilderness backcountry and focused around a
base camp near a creek or river. Work areas may be located
up to three miles from base camp, providing a hike to the
project each morning. Base camps are essentially a group
tent site, complete with a kitchen area and primitive latrine
or outhouse; most of the time there is running water nearby,

such as a creek or river. The BMWF will transport food, tools, and group camping gear into camp, but asks volunteers to carry their personal gear to the work site. Occasionally, projects are based out of Forest Service cabins with cooking facilities available, and crews tent-camp around the cabin. Every project is accompanied by a Wilderness Crew Leader who is certified in backcountry medicine and emergencies and has a breadth of technical trail knowledge and camping experience.

Time Line: The field season begins in June and ends in late September. While projects go on throughout the summer, each has definite start and end dates, which are usually posted on the BMWF's website the previous January. The projects range in length from daylong weekend projects to weeklong backpacking trips.

Cost: Overnight projects require a $50 deposit, which is refundable at the end of the project. The BMWF provides all food and prides itself on creative backcountry meals. Volunteers need to bring all necessary personal gear for overnight projects, but the BMWF will provide all tools, group cooking supplies, safety gear, and supervision.

Getting Started: Volunteer registration paperwork is available on the BMWF website or can be mailed to prospective volunteers; interviews are not required. Once volunteers register for a project, they are sent a detailed project description, which includes a packing list, directions to the trailhead, and very specific information about the project. Crew leaders provide training on trail maintenance, tool usage, and safety concerns.

Needed Skills and Specific Populations: For many of the projects, no prior experience is necessary; volunteers just need to come motivated to work, be prepared to have fun, and be ready to make the project a success. Trail maintenance and campsite restoration requires physical labor which involves lifting, bending, and possibly carrying or moving heavy objects, such as rocks or logs. Volunteers signing up for extended trips are expected to be experienced backpackers and will need to provide their own gear and share in camp chore responsibilities. Volunteers under 18 are encouraged to participate if they are up to the challenge, but they will need an accompanying adult on the project. The BMWF welcomes volunteers of all ages and nationalities, as long as their energy, interest, and experience make them a good fit. They proudly note that "our oldest volunteer to date was 89 years old and cleared trail with the best of 'em!" Volunteers with disabilities that would require an adjustment on the part of the crew or crew leader to adapt to the backcountry should contact the Bob Marshall Wilderness Foundation to explore possibilities or to modify a project based on the volunteer's needs. Families, clubs, groups, and organizations that have between four and eight people may ask the BMWF for a custom-made project.

BTCV

Sedum House
Mallard Way
Potteric Carr
Doncaster DN4 8DB
United Kingdom
+44 1302 388883; Fax: +44 1302 311531
E-mail: information@btcv.org.uk
Website: www.btcv.org.uk

Project Type: Community Development; Natural Conservation
(Land); Trail Building/Maintenance
Mission Statement: "To create a more sustainable future by
inspiring people and improving places."
Year Founded: 1959
Number of Volunteers Last Year: 300,000
Funding Sources: Government and private sources, including
lottery revenue
The Work They Do: BTCV is a huge organization that offers
many, many kinds of volunteer opportunities around the
world, including opportunities in Bulgaria, Iceland,
Slovakia, Cameroon, Portugal, Italy, Germany, the United
States, and the United Kingdom. Many of the projects are
conducted outdoors and are conservation oriented, but
many others deal with aspects of community or rural development. Examples of past projects include trailblazing in
the woods in New York, olive picking in Italy, enhancing
the biodiversity potential of woodlands in England's Peak
District, and beachsweeping in Cornwall and Devon in the
United Kingdom. There are over 2,000 UK-based volunteer
options, some of which are just a day long.
Project Location: Seventy-five percent of BTCV's volunteers
work within the United Kingdom; the remaining 25 percent
are spread across the world at partner organizations. Work
sites and conditions vary widely, depending on the

placement. Food and lodging are covered by the program fee, but the exact arrangements depend on the work site.

Time Line: Placements are available year-round. Day projects tend to run from 10:00 AM to 4:30 PM, with a break for lunch. Other BTCV Holiday programs run for a minimum of two days and a maximum of four weeks, with an average of one week for UK programs and two weeks for non-UK programs.

Cost: In the past, program fees have run the gamut from free (for nonresidential programs in the United Kingdom) to £300 per week in the United Kingdom and £625 for two weeks in Italy. Program fees for projects in the United Kingdom may also cover some local transportation costs or leisure activities. For nonresidential programs, transportation costs to the volunteer site are the responsibility of the volunteer. Most of the fees go toward administration expenses, although some community-based non-UK organizations do benefit financially from the program fees.

Getting Started: The entire process is web based, from the selection of a program to registration to payment of the program fee. Go to the website listed above and click "Holidays." Prospective volunteers may also contact a BTCV office in the United Kingdom to ask about opportunities. Training is provided on-site, and BTCV does not require an interview. Applications must be submitted to a program at least six weeks before it begins.

Needed Skills and Specific Populations: Volunteers must speak English well enough to understand and follow instructions and safety information. The minimum age to participate is 16 for some of the UK holidays and 18 for the international holidays. There is no maximum age limit, although BTCV cannot offer insurance to those over 81 years old. Volunteers with disabilities are welcomed, but they should discuss their needs with BTCV to find a suitable opportunity. Families with children under the age of 18 who reside in the United Kingdom may be able to volunteer with BTCV at a local project.

Buffalo Tours

94 Ma May Street
Hoan Kiem District, Hanoi
Vietnam
+84 4 3828 0702; Fax: +84 4 3826 9370
E-mail: volunteer@buffalotours.com
Website: www.educationaltravelasia.com

Project Type: Community Development; Construction; Economic Development; Education; Orphans; Rural Development; Youth

Mission Statement Excerpt: "Buffalo Tours believes Responsible Tourism is one of the most effective tools for poverty alleviation, peace, environmental conservation and sustainable development, besides being an ethical obligation in an affluent world, where the divide between poor and rich seems to have increased in recent years."

Year Founded: 1994

Number of Volunteers Last Year: 750

Funding Sources: None

The Work They Do: Buffalo Tours' projects focus on poverty alleviation, primarily by improving community infrastructure, education, medical treatment, and access to water. Volunteers assist in this mission by doing light construction work, digging and carrying supplies, teaching English, and organizing events and fun activities for village communities and children.

Project Location: Buffalo Tours operates in Vietnam, Cambodia, Thailand, and Laos. Most of their projects take place in poor, rural communities, so volunteers should expect basic conditions and amenities. The volunteer activities also often draw a lot of community interest, so volunteers should be open to taking part in daily life. Volunteers should expect varying conditions, from cool and dry in the winter to hot and humid in the summer. Accommodations range from five-star hotels to village homestays, depending on the project location and the budget or comfort level of volunteers.

Time Line: Buffalo Tours arranges individual volunteer experiences throughout the year, ranging in length from a half-day to three months. Some organizations prefer that volunteers commit to a month or more.

Cost: Program fee ranges from $900 to $1,500 per month, depending on the level of accommodations the volunteer requests. The program fee includes accommodations and airport transfers but does not include meals or international airfare.

Getting Started: Prospective volunteers should send an e-mail to Buffalo Tours with information on their desired volunteer trip. Volunteers who wish to work with children must first complete a child-protection policy agreement and a background check. All volunteers are provided with a country-specific cultural and language orientation, as well as an introduction to the project. Buffalo Tours also provides guidelines on responsible travel, outlining standards of behavior that are expected of volunteers; these guidelines are designed to help volunteers successfully complete their experience in a way that is positive for all involved and to ensure the ongoing success of Buffalo Tours projects.

Needed Skills and Specific Populations: No specific skills are required, and Buffalo Tours does not have any minimum or maximum age requirements for volunteers. Buffalo Tours will "make every effort" to accommodate volunteers with disabilities. They also encourage family volunteers and provide family-specific volunteer opportunities.

BUNAC

P.O. Box 430
Southbury, CT 06488
(800) GO-BUNAC or (203) 264-0901; Fax: (203) 264-0251
E-mail: info@bunacusa.org
Website: www.bunac.org

Project Type: Community Development; Education;
Medical/Health; Natural Conservation (Land); Orphans;
Trail Building/Maintenance; Women's Issues

Mission Statement Excerpt: "BUNAC aims to provide the best
possible opportunities in work and travel programmes
around the world."

Year Founded: 1962

Number of Volunteers Last Year: 500

Funding Sources: None

The Work They Do: BUNAC volunteers work with existing
locally run, community-based projects. Volunteers typically
work in the areas of education, HIV/AIDS awareness, and
women's empowerment, or on environmental or conservation projects. For example, volunteer teachers in Cambodia
might assist a local teacher, eventually taking on classes of
their own, preparing lesson plans and grading student work.
The projects are based in grassroots community projects,
schools, and colleges, all with the goal of developing education for less privileged children and adults.

Project Location: BUNAC operates projects in the United
States, Peru, Ghana, South Africa, India, Cambodia, and
China. Projects generally take place in rural areas and are
carried out in collaboration with local host organizations.
Volunteers are housed with a host family or at a communal
volunteer house.

Time Line: Projects begin monthly and vary in duration from a
minimum of 18 days to a maximum of six months. BUNAC
encourages volunteers to commit to two months or more
when possible.

Cost: While program fees vary depending on destination and project duration, prices range from £950 for an eight-week program in Cambodia to £2,095 for a six-month English teaching program in China. The program fee includes accommodations and all meals during the volunteer project, but does not include airfare to the country of service.

Getting Started: Prospective volunteers should complete an application on BUNAC's website at least 10 weeks before their intended departure date. Applicants must complete a phone interview with BUNAC, which also serves as the volunteer's orientation. Once at the site, BUNAC's host organizations provide an orientation, which lasts from one to five days. These orientations cover topics such as health, safety, culture, customs, language, cooking, and travel arrangements.

Needed Skills and Specific Populations: BUNAC strives to match prospective volunteers with appropriate placements, so no specific skills are required. Volunteers must be at least 18 years old, but there is no maximum age. Volunteers with disabilities should contact BUNAC to discuss what accommodations they may need; the organization will strive to provide them with an appropriate opportunity. Families with dependent children under the age of 18 cannot volunteer with BUNAC.

Camp AmeriKids

88 Hamilton Avenue
Stamford, CT 06902
(203) 658-9671; Fax: (203) 658-9615
E-mail: info@campamerikids.org
Website: www.campamerikids.org

Project Type: Medical/Health; Youth

Mission Statement Excerpt: "To enhance the lives of youth in the New York Tri-State Area who are infected with or affected by HIV/AIDS by providing a traditional summer camp experience, year-round skill building and a supported transition into adulthood."

Year Founded: 1995

Number of Volunteers Last Year: 168

Funding Sources: Private funding through foundations, corporations, and individuals

The Work They Do: Each summer, Camp AmeriKids serves 250 inner-city children living with HIV/AIDS. Campers aged 7 to 15 attend one of two seven-day sessions held in late July and early August. Under the guidance of counselors and program staff, campers participate in swimming, boating, dance, drama, arts and crafts, sports, and nature activities. Volunteers serve as camp counselors on a 24-hour-a-day basis during the camp sessions. Counselors participate fully in all of the camp activities so that campers are encouraged and motivated to learn new things and have a memorable camp experience. Camp AmeriKids also recruits and utilizes psychosocial and medical volunteers.

Project Location: Camp AmeriKids is located in Warwick, New York, about 50 miles from Manhattan. Situated on a beautiful lake, the facility features a large sports field, creative workshop spaces, two swimming pools, and cabins in which the campers and volunteer staff reside. All meals are served family style in the dining hall.

Time Line: Camp AmeriKids operates in late July and early August. Volunteers commit to eight full days, including one and a half days of training and orientation prior to the arrival of the campers. Volunteers can apply to participate in one or both camp sessions.

Cost: There is no program fee to participate in Camp AmeriKids, and accommodations and food are provided for all volunteers. Volunteers must pay for their own travel costs to and from the camp site.

Getting Started: Prospective volunteers should visit the Camp AmeriKids website or call its office at the number listed above for an application. All applicants must complete a phone interview and agree to a background check before being accepted as volunteers. Information is provided to all volunteers regarding camp policies, HIV education, and child behavior and development.

Needed Skills and Specific Populations: Volunteers are not required to have any specific previous experience but must be responsible, caring, and committed, and have enthusiasm, high energy, and a willingness to make a positive difference in the lives of campers. Volunteers must be at least 18 years old; there is no maximum age limit. Camp AmeriKids welcomes volunteers from all backgrounds and nations and with varying physical abilities, although the camp is not entirely wheelchair accessible. All efforts are made to include and accommodate everyone who is part of the Camp AmeriKids community.

Caretta Research Project (CRP)

P.O. Box 9841
Savannah, GA 31412
(912) 447-8655
E-mail: WassawCRP@aol.com
Website: www.carettaresearchproject.org

Project Type: Natural Conservation (Sea); Scientific Research

Mission Statement Excerpt: "The Caretta Research Project is a highly interactive educational research project that trains participants in the disciplines of fieldwork as they gather data on threatened nesting loggerhead sea turtles on Wassaw National Wildlife Refuge, Georgia."

Year Founded: 1973

Number of Volunteers Last Year: 86

Funding Sources: Private donors and grants

The Work They Do: CRP is a research, education, and conservation project that protects the threatened loggerhead turtles that nest on Wassaw Island. Volunteers help patrol the beaches each night, looking for nesting turtles. When nests are located, the turtles are tagged and the nests are protected. Scientific data is also collected for collaborative projects with other organizations.

Project Location: The project is located in the Wassaw National Wildlife Refuge, an island off the coast of Georgia. The work site and available accommodations are basic and rustic, and there is no electricity or hot water.

Time Line: The research project runs from mid-May through early September. Volunteers must commit to at least one week of work, Saturday to Saturday. Volunteers may stay for as many weeks as they wish.

Cost: The program fee is $750. The fee includes food, lodging, and transportation to and from the island on Saturdays. Volunteers should not incur any costs once on the island. Volunteers are responsible for their own transportation to and from Landings Harbor Marina, near Savannah. One hundred percent of the program fee is used to offset the cost of this program.

Getting Started: To ensure that volunteers can work on the dates they desire, they should check the website for available dates and call to make a reservation. After a reservation has been confirmed by phone, volunteers should print the application from the website, complete it, and send it in with a check. CRP requires that prospective volunteers complete a phone interview. Training is provided once volunteers arrive on Wassaw Island.

Needed Skills and Specific Populations: Volunteers should be physically fit, as this volunteer position requires a lot of walking. Flexibility and a sense of humor are also important, as volunteers must cheerfully share living quarters (both with other humans and with a lot of bugs!) in the summer heat and humidity of the American South without much privacy. Volunteers must be at least 15 years old; children aged 13 and over who are accompanied by their parents are also allowed. Senior volunteers are welcomed as long as they are in good physical condition. Prospective volunteers with disabilities should call first to discuss their specific needs, as Wassaw is a remote island with no medical facilities. CRP does not have any citizenship requirements for its volunteers.

Caribbean Volunteer Expeditions (CVE)

P.O. Box 388
Corning, NY 14830
(607) 962-7846; Fax: (607) 936-1153
E-mail: ahershcve@aol.com
Website: www.cvexp.org

Project Type: Archaeology; Construction; Historic Preservation

Mission Statement: "CVE provides an opportunity for volunteers from the US who are interested in historic preservation to spend time in the Caribbean learning local history and architecture, while contributing to preservation."

Year Founded: 1990

Number of Volunteers Last Year: Approximately 40

Funding Sources: None; entirely self-funded

The Work They Do: CVE carries out historic preservation projects, such as building surveys, reports, and cemetery inventories, as well as actual construction on historic projects. Volunteers help by recording buildings through photography and drawings, filling out forms, painting, and performing carpentry work.

Project Location: Projects are located throughout the Caribbean. Most are in towns, but some are in more rural locations. Volunteers usually stay in cabins, hotels, or guesthouses.

Time Line: Projects go on throughout the year, usually for a week at a time.

Cost: Program fees range from $500 to $1,500 for one week. These fees do not include airfare, but they do include lodging and food, which are arranged by CVE, as well as local transportation.

Getting Started: Prospective volunteers should call or e-mail CVE and request an application form. In-country training is provided to volunteers.

Needed Skills and Specific Populations: On some CVE projects, it is helpful to have volunteers with architecture, computer, or drafting skills. Volunteers under 18 must be accompanied by a parent or guardian; families have volunteered with CVE in the past. Senior citizens are welcome to apply, and CVE occasionally partners with Road Scholar (formerly Elderhostel). CVE cannot accommodate volunteers with disabilities.

Casa de Viajes HOY

Rio Mexapa 130
Colonia Hacienda Tetela
62160 Cuernavaca, MOR
Mexico
(777) 176-7868 (in Mexico)
E-mail: hoycommunity@gmail.com
Website: www.wix.com/casahoy/home_casa

Project Type: Community Development; Education; Natural Conservation (Land); Orphans; Youth

Mission Statement Excerpt: "Casa HOY's mission is to foster positive development in underprivileged communities and personal growth in traveler-volunteers through 'give-and-get travel.' Give-and-get-travel offers the best of both worlds: A socially-aware traveler can share knowledge, energy and skills with members of the community through volunteer work at local projects while learning about the people and culture from the inside out."

Year Founded: 2001 (as US nonprofit); 2010 (as Mexican sister company)

Number of Volunteers Last Year: 50

Funding Sources: None

The Work They Do: Casa HOY focuses on the cultural inter-actions between volunteers and the people of the host country, with the goal of increasing awareness of daily life in Mexico. They offer community-service projects, such as pitching in at an assortment of local projects that serve children and adults with different needs, as well as issue-specific group trips, including talks, visits, and interaction with activists working on a range of social issues, such as ecology, human rights, and LGBT equality. Casa HOY also offers group experiences working on community projects for employees of socially responsible businesses.

Project Location: Casa HOY's work is carried out in Cuernavaca, Mexico, or in nearby communities in the state of Morelos. If volunteer work is carried out in Cuernavaca, volunteers stay at Casa HOY, with hostel-style accommodations, hot water, a kitchen, and Wi-Fi access. If volunteer work is based outside the city, volunteers usually stay in very rustic locations, such as on the floor of a family's house or in the local community center, sleeping in sleeping bags.

Time Line: Casa HOY offers weeklong volunteer opportunities, beginning on predetermined Sundays throughout the year. Volunteers must stay for a minimum of one week and are encouraged to stay for two weeks. Groups that wish to volunteer with Casa HOY outside of the preset schedule should contact Casa HOY to see if this is possible.

Cost: Casa HOY's program fee for groups (a minimum of four people) is $600 per person per week, but drops to $550 for groups of six or more. The program fee includes accommodations, breakfast, a daily main meal, daily local transportation, specific talks, and a guided cultural excursion. Volunteers are responsible for their round-trip airfare to Mexico City, airport transfers, and meals not mentioned above.

Getting Started: Prospective volunteers should e-mail Casa HOY at least six weeks before the desired volunteer week. Casa HOY does not require interviews. An hour-long orientation is given on the first day, which covers rules, expectations, a guided tour of downtown Cuernavaca, recommendations for eating and socializing, and a plan for the week.

Needed Skills and Specific Populations: Casa HOY does not require any special skills other than an open mind, an interest in getting to know the host culture, and a willingness to try to communicate in Spanish; a basic knowledge of Spanish is recommended but not required. Volunteers must be at least 18 years old. Minors must be accompanied by a parent or legal guardian. There is no maximum age, though some seniors may not want to participate in certain volunteer activities because of the physical demands of the work. Casa HOY is unable, at this time, to accommodate volunteers with disabilities.

Catalina Island Conservancy

P.O. Box 2739
Avalon, CA 90704
(310) 510-2595; Fax: (310) 510-2594
E-mail: visvol@catalinaconservancy.org
Website: www.catalinaconservancy.org

Project Type: Administrative; Construction; Historic Preservation; Natural Conservation (Land); Scientific Research; Trail Building/Maintenance

Mission Statement: "The mission of the Catalina Island Conservancy is to be a responsible steward of its lands through a balance of conservation, education, and recreation."

Year Founded: 1972

Number of Volunteers Last Year: 588

Funding Sources: Private donors, public grants

The Work They Do: The Catalina Island Conservancy protects and restores the environment on Catalina, promoting and modeling ecologically sustainable communities to create a healthier future for the island. Volunteers commit to a five-night, six-day experience in which they may clean beaches, conduct trail maintenance with a trail manager on the Trans-Catalina Trail, or work in a native plant nursery and help remove invasive plants. Volunteers also have opportunities for structured relaxation, including two nights "on the town" in Avalon, California, and bonfires on two other nights.

Project Location: All work is done on Catalina Island, California, a 76-square-mile island with valleys, coves, and 2,000 peaks. Most projects are conducted outside in beautiful, remote areas of the island with vistas, and they may require short hikes. Shade is not always available, but temperatures tend to be mild. Work usually entails a mixture of moderate to strenuous activities. Volunteers may either camp on Catalina Island or stay in private rentals, which include a range of accommodations from cottages to ocean-view villas.

Time Line: Volunteers are accepted during specific weeks of the month for six-day projects. See the Catalina Island Conservancy website for details.

Cost: The program fee is $1,795 per person, which includes roundtrip boat fare from the Port of Long Beach, on-island transportation, all meals, and a $30 food and entertainment voucher to use in Avalon. Noncamping accommodations are an additional $175 to $500 per person per night.

Getting Started: Prospective volunteers should call or e-mail the Catalina Island Conservancy office. No in-person interviews are required. On-site orientations are held in Avalon, California; they include an overview of the program, training for specific tasks to be accomplished, and instructions for safely handling tools.

Needed Skills and Specific Populations: Volunteers should be in good physical condition and possess a willingness to work, get dirty, and try new things. Volunteers between the ages of 12 and 18 must be accompanied by an adult. Seniors are encouraged to volunteer; some projects may not be accessible to persons with disabilities.

Catholic Medical Mission Board (CMMB)

10 West 17th Street
New York, NY 10011
(800) 678-5659 or (212) 242-7757; Fax: (212) 807-9161
E-mail: info@cmmb.org or asridharan@cmmb.org
Website: www.cmmb.org

Project Type: Medical/Health

Mission Statement Excerpt: "Rooted in the healing ministry of Jesus, Catholic Medical Mission Board (CMMB) works collaboratively to provide quality health care programs and services, without discrimination, to people in need around the world."

Year Founded: 1928

Number of Volunteers Last Year: 68 long-term volunteers and 1,595 short-term volunteers

Funding Sources: Individuals, foundations, corporations, trusts, estates, health and religious-affiliated organizations, and government grants

The Work They Do: CMMB's work focuses on HIV/AIDS, malaria, maternal and child health, and neglected tropical diseases. CMMB's volunteers, as a part of the Medical Volunteer Program, provide direct health care to those in need and build the capacity of local health personnel at health facilities in developing countries around the world.

Project Location: CMMB places volunteers in nearly 30 countries in Africa, Asia, Latin America, and the Caribbean. Most volunteers work in mission hospitals or clinics. Many of these facilities are in rural areas with limited resources, though some are in urban areas. Accommodations and food are provided by the host facilities.

Time Line: CMMB recruits volunteers throughout the year and places accepted volunteers in the fall of each year, following a one-week orientation in New Jersey. While CMMB supports short-term volunteers through partner agencies, the majority of the recruitment is focused on long-term volunteers who make a minimum one-year commitment to serving in the field.

Cost: Volunteers who commit to one year or more receive medevac and hazard insurance, all travel expenses, housing, and a modest monthly stipend. Those volunteering for less than one year receive only insurance coverage. Long-term (one year or more) volunteers are asked to raise some funds prior to their departure.

Getting Started: Prospective volunteers should apply online. Following the completion of the preliminary online application, suitable applicants will be contacted to complete a full application and phone interview.

Needed Skills and Specific Populations: CMMB generally places medical professionals who are licensed in the United States or Canada, including, but not limited to, doctors, surgeons, nurses, physical therapists, occupational therapists, lab technicians, and pharmacists. CMMB also places some non-medical professionals with skills that are in high demand in resource-poor health facilities. CMMB does not require that volunteers be Catholic. Volunteers should be at least 21 years of age. CMMB is open to working with volunteers with disabilities.

Cheyenne River Youth Project (CRYP)

The Main Youth Center and Cokata Wiconi Teen Center
P.O. Box 410
Eagle Butte, SD 57625
(605) 964-8200; Fax: (605) 964-8201
E-mail: info@lakotayouth.org
Website: www.lakotayouth.org

Project Type: Administrative; Community Development; Youth

Mission Statement Excerpt: "The mission of the Cheyenne River Youth Project (CRYP) is to provide the youth of the Cheyenne River reservation access to a vibrant and secure future through a wide variety of culturally sensitive and enduring programs, projects and facilities, ensuring strong, self-sufficient families and communities."

Year Founded: 1988

Number of Volunteers Last Year: 33 long-term volunteers and 200 short-term volunteers

Funding Sources: The Cheyenne River Youth Project receives financial support through grants, private donations, and local fundraising

The Work They Do: CRYP consists of four major components: the Main Youth Center, the Family Services Program, the two-and-a-half-acre Winyan Toka Win ("Leading Lady") Garden, and the Cokata Wiconi Teen Center ("Center of Life"). Volunteers at the Main Youth Center and Cokata Wiconi Teen Center work directly with children aged 4 to 18 and provide support in all aspects of the center's work, such as project fundraising, community activities, and building maintenance. Volunteers are responsible for the implementation of planned activities, the development of recreational activities, arts and crafts, sports activities, and meal and snack preparation.

Project Location: CRYP is located on the 2.8-million-acre Cheyenne River Sioux Tribe Indian Reservation, in north-central South Dakota. Dorm-style accommodations are provided at the center for all volunteers.

Time Line: Volunteers are accepted year-round for commitments of six weeks to two years. The average length of a volunteer's stay is approximately three months.

Cost: Volunteers pay a one-time application fee, which is $200 for domestic volunteers and $250 for international volunteers. Volunteers are provided housing and some meals. Volunteers must travel, at their own expense, to Pierre, South Dakota, by airplane or bus; CRYP provides transportation from Pierre to the reservation upon the volunteer's arrival.

Getting Started: Prospective volunteers can complete an online application via the organization's website. To finalize the application, volunteers must also submit three letters of recommendation, a criminal history background check, and an application fee. Once the application is complete, the CRYP will arrange a telephone interview. New volunteers are given an on-site orientation and must shadow another volunteer for one week before taking on responsibilities.

Needed Skills and Specific Populations: All volunteers must have patience, compassion, energy, dedication, motivation, and commitment. Volunteers who have experience working with children are preferred. Volunteers must be willing to work long hours and view this experience as a full-time job. Volunteers are generally at least 18 years old, but volunteers as young as 16, including those volunteering with their families, will be considered on a case-by-case basis. Senior volunteers and volunteers with disabilities are welcomed, though the position can be physically demanding at times. International volunteers are welcome but must speak English and obtain their own visa.

Child Family Health International (CFHI)

995 Market, Suite 1104
San Francisco, CA 94103
(415) 957-9000; Fax: (415) 840-0486
E-mail: students@cfhi.org
Website: www.cfhi.org

Project Type: Medical/Health

Mission Statement Excerpt: "Child Family Health International (CFHI) is a global family of committed professionals and students who work at the grassroots level to promote the health of the world community."

Year Founded: 1992

Number of Volunteers Last Year: Over 600

Funding Sources: Individual donors and small foundations

The Work They Do: CFHI provides socially responsible global health immersion programs for students of the health sciences and others with a strong interest in global health issues. Participants visit a variety of hospitals and clinics in underserved communities to gain insight into health systems abroad. Typically volunteers have four to six hours per day of clinical rotations, and one to two hours per week are devoted to a weekly meeting with local staff, including medical lectures. Volunteers in Latin America programs engage in Spanish language classes each afternoon, for a total of 30 hours over four weeks. If volunteers are interested, additional service opportunities to volunteer at local orphanages and NGOs are offered through each of CFHI's programs. Evenings and weekends are generally free, and participants often take weekend trips to explore the surrounding area.

Project Location: CFHI offers global health education programs at over 20 different program sites in Bolivia, Ecuador, India, Mexico, and South Africa. Housing is with local homestay families or, where homestay families are not available, in guest houses.

Time Line: All CFHI programs are 4 weeks long, though participants may choose to volunteer for 5, 6, 7, or up to 12 weeks in one location, or they may combine different four-week programs for a comparative experience. Programs run year-round. In most cases, programs begin on the first Saturday of each month.

Cost: Program fees are approximately $2,000 for four weeks—exact costs vary from site to site. Program fees include predeparture orientation materials, two or three meals per day, accommodations in a homestay or a guest house, 20 to 30 hours of Spanish classes in Spanish-speaking programs, weekly medical lectures with CFHI's local medical director, cell phones, emergency insurance, airport transfers, and an in-country orientation. International airfare is not included in the program fee. Evaluations can be provided for those seeking academic credit.

Getting Started: All applications are processed online via CFHI's website; applicants are encouraged to apply at least three months before their desired departure date, although last-minute applications will also be considered. The application consists of short-answer questions, references, and a diagnostic Spanish test for Latin America programs; interviews are not required. An application fee must also be submitted. After acceptance, participants receive predeparture orientation materials. Volunteers also receive debriefing materials to assist them in their return home, and they have access to CFHI alumni opportunities and services.

Needed Skills and Specific Populations: CFHI programs are open to all students of the health sciences, including pre-medical and pre-health students, as well as nursing, public health, and medical anthropology students and students in related fields. Students outside the health sciences fields who have a strong interest in global health issues are also welcome to apply. Many students are able to earn academic credit for participation in a CFHI program. CFHI programs are not open to already qualified, practicing health professionals. Volunteers must be at least 20 years old at the start of their program. Senior volunteers are accepted, but the large majority of CFHI volunteers are in their 20s. Prospective volunteers with disabilities are welcome to apply, but they should consult closely with CFHI's program staff to make sure that the selected site is accessible. CFHI does not typically host volunteers with families.

Children Walking Tall (CWT)

"The Mango House," House No. 148/3
Karaswada
Mapusa 403526
Goa
India
+91 98 22 124802
E-mail: childrenwalkingtall@hotmail.com
Website: www.childrenwalkingtall.com

Project Type: Community Development; Education; Human Rights; Medical/Health; Orphans; Youth

Mission Statement Excerpt: "To give children a childhood worth remembering."

Year Founded: 2004

Number of Volunteers Last Year: 25

Funding Sources: Foundations, individuals, faith-based organizations, schools, and companies

The Work They Do: CWT assists low-income families by providing education and health care for children. CWT operates a drop-in center where children can obtain food, first aid, and formal or informal education. CWT's objective is to add fun and interest to these kids' lives. Volunteers assist in this mission by providing child care, creating resources, implementing projects, helping with medical care, playing games, and distributing clothes and food in local communities.

Project Location: CWT is located near Mapusa, Goa, in India. "The Mango House" is a large, old Portuguese house that has been painted to create a child-friendly environment. Some of the volunteers' work is also done in low-income neighborhoods, which can be hot and dusty. Volunteers are responsible for finding their own accommodations, which are available nearby for a range of prices.

Time Line: While volunteers are welcome throughout the year, most volunteers choose to arrive between October and May.

Volunteers must commit to at least three months of volunteering.

Cost: Volunteers make a £50 deposit, which is returned after the initial three months have passed. There are no other program fees, though volunteers are responsible for all of their own travel and living costs; food and accommodations are not provided by CWT.

Getting Started: CWT has a limited number of volunteer slots available, which are often claimed quickly. Prospective volunteers are encouraged to apply at least three months in advance by contacting CWT through the website above. An informal orientation, which covers child safety, rules, and regulations, is provided to volunteers upon arrival. Volunteers do not have to complete an interview but do need to provide the results of a police background check from their country of origin.

Needed Skills and Specific Populations: While CWT does not require that volunteers have any specific skills, a background in teaching or in Hindi language is very helpful. Volunteers must be at least 18 years old; there is no maximum age, as long as volunteers can cope with the heat of India. CWT would consider having volunteers with disabilities, though there are not currently any special accommodations available; the building is not wheelchair accessible.

CHOICE Humanitarian
(Center for Humanitarian Outreach
and Inter-Cultural Exchange)

7879 South 1520 West, Suite 200
West Jordan, UT 84088
(801) 474-1937; Fax: (801) 474-1919
E-mail: info@choicehumanitarian.org
Website: www.choicehumanitarian.org

Project Type: Agriculture; Community Development; Construction; Economic Development; Education; Medical/Health; Rural Development

Mission Statement Excerpt: "The goal of CHOICE Humanitarian is to empower and mobilize rural villages across the globe. We provide villagers with a community development model that encourages villagers to reach their potential and eradicate their own poverty. We hope to spread this model in a way that is environmentally and socially responsible, always keeping sustainability at the core of everything we do."

Year Founded: 1982

Number of Volunteers Last Year: 300

Funding Sources: Foundation support and individual donors

The Work They Do: CHOICE Humanitarian works with motivated villages to alleviate and, hopefully, to eventually end poverty. They accomplish this by providing organizational and leadership skills to villagers in the developing world. On a CHOICE expedition, volunteers work side-by-side with villagers on grassroots projects such as building schools, greenhouses, water systems, and community health posts. Volunteers can choose how physically demanding they want their experience to be, as CHOICE offers both strenuous and nonphysical opportunities. CHOICE measures success not in physical structures but in cultural understanding and global awareness; they believe in building people, not just projects.

Project Location: CHOICE works in Mexico, Guatemala, Bolivia, Kenya, and Nepal. Work sites are generally outside and range from very cold to very hot. Volunteers are usually housed in camp-like settings in schools or community centers and are required to bring a sleeping bag and foam pad. Outside of the village, volunteers usually stay in hotels.

Time Line: CHOICE sends expeditions of volunteers at set times throughout the year. Standard expeditions last for eight days and generally run from Saturday to Saturday.

Cost: CHOICE expedition fees range from $1,995 to $2,195 and cover lodging, local transportation, meals, leadership, and related project costs and materials. Discounts are extended to student groups and families. Volunteers are responsible for their own international airfare.

Getting Started: Applications can be downloaded from the CHOICE website. There are no application deadlines; applications are accepted until a trip is full. Interviews are not required but are encouraged, as CHOICE likes to get to know their volunteers before the trip begins. CHOICE usually has two orientation meetings about one month before the trip, which can be completed in person in Utah or over the phone. These orientations cover general topics such as cultural awareness and norms, as well as more specific topics such as effective packing.

Needed Skills and Specific Populations: No specific skills are needed to volunteer with CHOICE, though volunteers should be open-minded and "willing to challenge their perceptions of where they are in the global community." CHOICE does not have any minimum age and encourages families to volunteer together, but requests that children under the age of 13 be particularly well behaved. Senior volunteers are welcome to apply, though they might want to talk with CHOICE to ensure that they meet general health requirements. Volunteers with disabilities are welcome to volunteer with CHOICE and should contact the office to determine which volunteer trip can best accommodate their needs.

Christian Peacemaker Teams (CPT)

P.O. Box 6508
Chicago, IL 60680
(773) 376-0550; Fax: (773) 376-0549
E-mail: delegations@cpt.org
Website: www.cpt.org

Project Type: Human Rights; Political Action; Social Justice

Mission Statement Excerpt: "Christian Peacemaker Teams (CPT) offers an organized, nonviolent alternative to war and other forms of lethal intergroup conflict. CPT provides organizational support to persons committed to faith-based nonviolent alternatives in situations where lethal conflict is an immediate reality or is supported by public policy."

Year Founded: 1988

Number of Volunteers Last Year: 111

Funding Sources: Donations from church congregations and individuals, including a small percentage from church denominations; small grants from private, church, or human rights–oriented foundations; CPT is an initiative of the Historic Peace Churches (Mennonites, Church of the Brethren, and Quakers) with support and membership from a range of Catholic and Protestant denominations

The Work They Do: CPT focuses on violence deterrence, human rights observation and documentation, accompaniment of vulnerable individuals or groups in conflict areas, and nonviolent public actions. Volunteers meet with local peacemakers and populations affected by violent conflict, engage in human rights documentation, and participate in nonviolent direct action. Volunteers also commit to sharing their experiences with a wider audience upon return to their home communities. CPT also has opportunities for full- and part-time longer-term volunteers who are part of the Peacemaker Corps and who commit to a three-year term. Those serving full-time receive a needs-based stipend. Participation on a short-term delegation is the first step to joining the longer-term Peacemaker Corps.

Project Location: As of this writing, volunteers work in Palestine, Iraq, Colombia, and in native communities in Canada, but this list changes as human rights situations change around the world. Volunteer teams stay in modest accommodations in the city, such as apartments or modest hotels or hostels with shared rooms, and they may travel to the countryside, where accommodations are similar to camping. Volunteers are housed together with at least two people (often more) per room. Depending on the location, volunteers may be required to walk over rough terrain, scramble over muddy riverbanks, or endure extreme heat or cold. Two meals per day are provided.

Time Line: The schedule changes yearly, but there are volunteer opportunities available throughout the year, though not always in every location. In general, locations accept volunteer teams four to six times per year for periods of one to two weeks.

Cost: Program fees run from about $500 to about $3,000, depending on project location. Cost includes international airfare (except for US or Canadian projects), two meals each day, modest accommodations, and in-country travel.

Getting Started: Prospective volunteers should fill out an application for a "Short Term Delegation." These applications can be downloaded from the CPT website and are also available from the Chicago office. CPT does not require any special training or an interview prior to delegation participation. They do provide printed orientation materials, including background readings and logistical information before departure.

Needed Skills and Specific Populations: Volunteers should have experience or an interest in working for human rights and cross-cultural understanding, a commitment to nonviolence, and a willingness to participate in nonviolent public witness, team worship, and reflection. CPT does not require that volunteers identify as Christian. The minimum age to volunteer with CPT is 18; many participants have been in their 70s, and a few have been 80 years old and older. However, a degree of physical stamina, such as the ability to walk two

A new Palestinian friend pours tea for a delegation of visitors while his son and a volunteer look on. This team was visiting the South Hebron Hills in the West Bank. *Photo courtesy of Christian Peacemaker Teams*

or three miles over rough terrain, is required. CPT may not be able to accommodate persons with certain kinds of disabilities; for example, limited transportation options in the West Bank might preclude the acceptance of a volunteer who uses a wheelchair for that program.

CNFA

1828 L Street NW, Suite 710
Washington, DC 20036
(888) 872-2632 or (202) 296-3920; Fax: (202) 296-3948
E-mail: info@cnfa.org
Website: www.cnfa.org

Project Type: Agriculture; Economic Development;
Professional/Technical Assistance; Rural Development
Mission Statement Excerpt: "CNFA is dedicated to stimulating
economic growth around the world by nurturing entrepreneurship, private enterprise and market linkages."
Year Founded: 1985
Number of Volunteers Last Year: 228
Funding Sources: USAID
The Work They Do: CNFA specializes in engaging private
companies of all sizes in partnerships to expand economic
activity and increase incomes. Through its volunteer
program, CNFA helps people build a free market–based food
and agricultural system. Since 1993, more than 1,200 volunteers have participated in this program. In order to achieve
the greatest impact, CNFA sends multiple volunteers to long-
term projects, with each volunteer assignment building upon
previous ones. CNFA's long-term projects seek to develop
private farmer associations, cooperatives, private agribusinesses, women's and young farmer groups, and other
organizations that can help people increase their incomes.
Volunteers provide help to a wide variety of groups,
including dairy processors and producers, beef cattle farmers,
mushroom producers, honey producers, fruit growers, and
greenhouse producers. The majority of volunteer hosts are
democratically structured farmers' associations and cooperatives or small-scale agribusinesses. Typical assignments focus
on strengthening associations, developing marketing skills
and business planning, and developing financial management
skills. Occasionally, CNFA will field a volunteer to train in

crop production or processing for an individual farmer or agribusiness enterprise.

Project Location: American volunteers travel to 15 countries in three regions (Europe, the Caucasus, and Central Asia; southern Africa; and East Africa) to share their knowledge. Volunteer site locations vary from rural villages to capital cities. In cities, volunteers are provided with an apartment, and they have full access to bathing and cooking facilities and restaurants, as well as to laundry and cleaning services. In villages, each volunteer stays with a host family or in a rented apartment. Although lodging conditions are modest, every effort is made to provide comfort during the volunteer's stay. The host family, if there is one, also provides meals.

Time Line: Volunteers are accepted throughout the year, for periods of 16 to 19 days. The average volunteer assignment is 18 days, and assignments rarely last more than 21 days in-country.

Cost: There is no program fee; all costs for volunteers are covered by CNFA.

Getting Started: Potential volunteers may submit an application and resume online, which is followed by an interview by phone or e-mail. Other than a predeparture briefing, volunteers receive no training, since selected volunteers already have highly established professional experience and are experts in their respective agriculture or agribusiness field.

Needed Skills and Specific Populations: CNFA seeks experienced volunteers from a variety of specialties: farmers and ranchers, cooperative specialists, food processing professionals, agribusiness executives, extension agents, agricultural organization leaders, and others. Superior technical expertise and the ability to effectively share their knowledge is the main volunteer requirement. A certain amount of predeparture and postassignment work is required. All potential volunteers must pass a routine medical examination to be eligible. Volunteers with disabilities are welcomed, but no special accommodations may be made. CNFA volunteers must be US citizens or green card holders. Volunteers with CNFA may not bring family members with them.

The Colorado Trail Foundation (CTF)

710 10th Street, #210
Golden, CO 80401
(303) 384-3729
E-mail: ctf@coloradotrail.org
Website: www.coloradotrail.org

Project Type: Natural Conservation (Land); Trail
   Building/Maintenance
Mission Statement Excerpt: "The mission of the Colorado Trail
   Foundation is to provide and to maintain, through volun-
   tary and public involvement . . . a linear, nonmotorized,
   sustainable recreation trail between Denver and Durango,
   Colorado."
Year Founded: 1974
Number of Volunteers Last Year: 531
Funding Sources: Primarily private donors
The Work They Do: CTF maintains the 486-mile, high-altitude,
   nonmotorized trail between Denver and Durango,
   Colorado. Volunteers rehabilitate sections of eroded trail,
   build bridges, create waterbars to divert water off the trail,
   install culverts, and reroute sections of the trail.
Project Location: Volunteers work in National Forests along the
   spectacular Colorado Trail and camp in tents, which volunteers must provide. Campsites are reached by conventional
   vehicle, a four-wheel-drive vehicle, or backpacking. Elevations range from 6,000 to 12,500 feet. A description of each
   camp and work site is given with the crew registration
   materials. CTF provides the food for each volunteer crew.
Time Line: Volunteers are accepted in the months of June, July,
   and August. Volunteers work weekends, from Friday
   evening through Sunday afternoon, or for a full week,
   Saturday through Saturday.
Cost: Weekend crew members pay $30, and weeklong crew
   members pay $60. Volunteers who join the CTF for
   multiple crews in one summer pay full price for the most

expensive crew and half price for every other crew. Obviously, for this low price, transportation costs to Colorado are not included in the program fee. All fees are nonrefundable.

Getting Started: Prospective volunteers can download a registration form and waiver from CTF's website; these are also available by calling or e-mailing the office listed above. CTF does not require interviews as a part of the registration process. Trail crew leaders conduct a crew orientation session, a trail-building session, and a tool safety session on the first day.

Needed Skills and Specific Populations: Volunteers must be at least 16 years old; there is no maximum age limit, and previous trail work experience is not required. Due to the remote and rugged nature of their work, CTF cannot accommodate volunteers with disabilities. Families are welcome to volunteer with CTF, but all members must meet the minimum age requirement.

Common Hope

P.O. Box 14298
St. Paul, MN 55114
(651) 917-0917; Fax: (651) 917-7458
E-mail: visionteams@commonhope.org
Website: www.commonhope.org

Project Type: Community Development; Economic
Development; Education; Human Rights; Medical/Health;
Women's Issues; Youth

Mission Statement Excerpt: "Common Hope promotes hope
and opportunity in Guatemala, partnering with children,
families, and communities who want to participate in a
process of development to improve their lives through
education, health care, and housing."

Year Founded: 1986

Number of Volunteers Last Year: Over 250

Funding Sources: Private individuals, foundations, faith-based
organizations, and occasional corporate support

The Work They Do: Common Hope focuses on providing
access to education for those who cannot afford it and on
improving educational resources and effectiveness in
Guatemala. They seek to help teachers implement more
interactive, engaging curricula and offer individualized
support for students who may be at risk for dropping out.
They also provide integrated services in the areas of health
care, housing, and family development. Volunteers may
assist in tutoring sessions or in a preschool, or share arts
and crafts with youth groups. Other volunteer opportunities
include visiting families with a social worker, attending
informational talks with staff members, and constructing
homes for families.

Project Location: Common Hope operates in 17 villages in the
Antigua Valley of Guatemala. Volunteers stay at Common
Hope's project site in dormitory-style accommodations, five
minutes from the city of Antigua. Volunteers also have the
option of booking their own accommodations in Antigua.

Time Line: Common Hope sends two teams each month throughout the year. Teams go for eight days and consist of 10 to 12 people. Teams are filled on a first-come, first-served basis, require a team leader, and generally consist of people who know one another. Volunteers who wish to stay longer or travel independently can sign up for a short-term volunteer program; these volunteers generally stay for two to six weeks, though some may stay for three months.

Cost: Each individual in the team pays a program fee of $800, and the team commits to paying an additional $4,000 as a "fundraising commitment" to Common Hope's programs. The program fee includes food, accommodations, and transportation to and from the airport, but does not include international airfare to Guatemala.

Getting Started: Usually one volunteer decides to lead a team, contacts Common Hope to reserve a time slot on the organization's calendar, and then recruits other team members to join him or her. Individual volunteers can also be placed into teams that are currently recruiting participants. Interviews are not required. Common Hope provides two orientation sessions, which usually last two hours each, either in person in Minnesota or remotely.

Needed Skills and Specific Populations: No specific skills are required, though Spanish language skills are a plus. Volunteers who are 14 to 18 years old must be accompanied by an adult who is 21 or older; there is no maximum age to volunteer with Common Hope. Common Hope can accommodate volunteers with disabilities. Families frequently volunteer with Common Hope, especially if children are high school age or older.

Concordia International Volunteers

19 North Street
Portslade BN41 1DH
United Kingdom
+44 1273 422218; Fax +44 1273 421182
E-mail: info@concordia-iye.org.uk
Website: www.concordiavolunteers.org.uk

Project Type: Agriculture; Archaeology; Construction; Education; Historic Preservation; Natural Conservation (Land); Youth

Mission Statement Excerpt: "Concordia is a charity committed to international volunteering as a means to promoting intercultural understanding and peace."

Year Founded: 1943

Number of Volunteers Last Year: 200

Funding Sources: None

The Work They Do: Concordia offers short-term volunteer projects in the areas of conservation, restoration, archaeology, construction, the arts, social work, and education.

Project Location: Concordia operates in over 60 countries in Europe, North America, the Middle East, Latin America, Africa, and Asia. Accommodations vary by site, but are usually basic, such as tents, town halls, schools, gymnasiums, youth hostels, or occasionally homestays. Volunteers are expected to bring and use a sleeping bag and to share their living space with other volunteers.

Time Line: Volunteer projects are available throughout the year for two to four weeks.

Cost: Volunteers pay a program fee of £180 to Concordia and an additional project fee of £80 to £150 to the host organization on-site if the project takes place in Latin America, Asia, or Africa. Volunteers are also responsible for their travel costs, visas, and insurance.

Getting Started: Applications may be completed on Concordia's website. Volunteers going to Africa, Asia, and Latin

America must attend compulsory weekend training in Brighton, United Kingdom, for an additional £40.

Needed Skills and Specific Populations: Volunteers must be at least 18 years old for most projects, though some projects allow volunteers as young as 16 to participate. Concordia does not have a maximum age limit. Volunteers with disabilities should contact Concordia, which will do its best to help identify a suitable project. All volunteers must be resident in the United Kingdom in order to apply, regardless of citizenship. Some projects are designated as family friendly.

Coral Cay Conservation (CCC)

Elizabeth House
39 York Road
London SE1 7NJ
United Kingdom
+44 20 7620 1411; Fax: +44 20 7921 0469
E-mail: info@coralcay.org
Website: www.coralcay.org

Project Type: Natural Conservation (Land); Natural Conservation (Sea); Scientific Research

Mission Statement Excerpt: "Using the best science we will support the preservation of coral reefs and through learning and education support the dependent communities, in the most cost-effective means possible."

Year Founded: 1985

Number of Volunteers Last Year: More than 400

Funding Sources: No outside sources

The Work They Do: CCC carries out tropical forest and coral reef conservation projects. Volunteers help collect scientific data, which is then used to form sustainable management recommendations.

Project Location: CCC volunteers work on marine expeditions in remote, tropical environments in the Philippines and Cambodia, and on CCC's newest project in Kenya's largest closed-canopy forest. CCC provides basic accommodations, which are similar to those of a basic hostel, with numerous bunk beds in a large bedroom and shared bath facilities.

Time Line: Projects run year-round and have monthly start dates, with a two-week minimum stay required. If volunteers have never dived, CCC recommends a four-week minimum stay in order to complete the Skills Development Programme, contribute to the research, and get the most out of the experience.

Cost: Marine expeditions vary, depending on whether the individual has, at a minimum, a PADI open water certification. Dive Trainee prices start at £925 for two weeks, whereas dive-trained individuals pay £825 for the same period. CCC also offers discounts for returning volunteers and groups of seven or more people. The program fee for forest expeditions in Kenya is £565 for two weeks. Program fees include accommodations, food, and training. The costs of flights, insurance, and some equipment are not included.

Getting Started: Prospective volunteers should see CCC's website or contact the office to request more information. If required, scuba training can be provided on-site.

Needed Skills and Specific Populations: Volunteers do not need to have scientific or scuba training before volunteering. Volunteers must be at least 16 years old; there is no maximum age limit. Families are welcome to volunteer, but all members of the family must meet the minimum age requirement. CCC accepts volunteers from around the world. Volunteers with disabilities should contact CCC's office to discuss their particular situation.

Cross-Cultural Solutions (CCS)

2 Clinton Place
New Rochelle, NY 10801
(800) 380-4777 or (914) 632-0022; Fax: (914) 632-8494
E-mail: info@crossculturalsolutions.org
Website: www.crossculturalsolutions.org

Project Type: Community Development; Education;
Medical/Health; Orphans; People with Disabilities; Women's
Issues; Youth

Mission Statement Excerpt: "Our mission is to operate volunteer programs around the world in partnership with sustainable community initiatives, bringing people together to work side-by-side while sharing perspectives and fostering cultural understanding."

Year Founded: 1995

Number of Volunteers Last Year: Over 3,000

Funding Sources: CCS occasionally receives funding from private donors

The Work They Do: CCS operates international programs that offer a wide range of volunteer opportunities. Volunteer placements are based on the needs of the local community and on each individual's skills and interests. Each volunteer is required to fill out a Skills & Interest Survey that helps CCS place the volunteer with a local organization. Specific examples of volunteer positions available with CCS include taking care of children in day care centers and orphanages; teaching conversational English; conducting educational activities for teenagers; working with women's groups; caring for and developing activities for the elderly; observing and assisting with local health professionals; taking care of people with mental and physical disabilities; and taking care of people living with HIV/AIDS. CCS is a recognized leader in the field of international volunteering; CCS has Special Consultative Status with the United Nations and is in partnership with CARE, one of the world's largest international humanitarian organizations. CCS has been profiled in more than 1,000 news outlets.

Project Location: CCS volunteer programs are located in Brazil, China, Costa Rica, Ghana, Guatemala, India, Morocco, Peru, Russia, South Africa, Tanzania, and Thailand. Volunteers work in partnership with sustainable community initiatives in settings such as schools, orphanages, elderly homes, community homes, clinics, and offices. CCS provides a home base for all volunteers in each country, which typically consists of a comfortable house in a residential neighborhood. Clean, modest accommodations with shared rooms are the standard. Accommodations always have basic amenities such as linens and running water, as well as hot water where necessary. As part of the CCS program, staff cooks prepare and serve daily meals and snacks based on the regional cuisine. Staff drivers provide daily and airport transportation.

Time Line: Volunteer programs are offered year-round. Volunteers stay for 1 to 12 weeks, though longer programs may be arranged on an individual basis.

Cost: CCS's program fee starts at $2,923 for two weeks and increases by $376 for each additional week. Included in the program fee are all accommodations, meals, and in-country transportation; cultural and learning activities, including excursions to nearby points of interest and special events; and comprehensive travel medical insurance. International airfare is not included in the program fee. Less than 10 percent of CCS's program fee goes toward administrative expenses.

Getting Started: Prospective volunteers can enroll in a program via CCS's website or by contacting CCS; only the Teen Volunteer Abroad application requires an application and a phone interview. Start dates for volunteer programs are offered year-round, and volunteers typically enroll for programs at least 60 days prior to their chosen start date. Prospective volunteers are encouraged to call CCS to discuss their expectations and to choose the program and site that fits them best. Because CCS participants are from all over the world, there is an in-country orientation that is run by the in-country staff.

Needed Skills and Specific Populations: No specific skills, background, or experience are required to volunteer with CCS, though volunteers must have at least a basic knowledge of the English language. The minimum age for unaccompanied volunteers is 18, and CCS also offers a Teen Volunteer Abroad program with increased supervision and support for 15- to 17-year-olds. The minimum age for a child traveling with a parent or guardian is eight; CCS has worked with hundreds of families at all of their sites. Senior volunteers are warmly welcomed. Volunteers with disabilities are also welcomed, and CCS encourages people with disabilities to enroll. Volunteers from all countries are welcome, provided they can obtain a visa for their country of service.

Cultural Destination Nepal (CDN)

G.P.O. Box 11535
Kathmandu
Nepal
+977 1 437 7623 or +977 1 437 7696;
Fax: +977 1 437 7696
E-mail: cdnnepal@wlink.com.np or
info@volunteernepal.org.np
Website: www.volunteernepal.org.np

Project Type: Community Development; Education;
Medical/Health; People with Disabilities; Rural
Development; Youth

Mission Statement Excerpt: "Cultural Destination Nepal (CDN)
aims to introduce the participant to Nepal's diverse
geographical and cultural environment and to promote
intercultural understanding through experiential learning in
Nepal."

Year Founded: 1996

Number of Volunteers Last Year: 35

Funding Sources: None outside of volunteer fees

The Work They Do: Most volunteers teach English, social
studies, mathematics, science, or environmental studies in
Nepali schools. CDN also provides placements in nonprofit
organizations that work with women's issues, the environment, disabled children, and other areas; however, volunteers in these more specialized fields must be qualified both
through work or previous volunteer experiences and
through their education. Volunteers also have the opportunity to participate in outdoor activities and excursions, as
well as in cultural exchanges. Secondary projects may also
be available at the placement site.

Project Location: All volunteers work in Nepal and India.
During the two-week orientation, volunteers stay with a
host family near CDN's offices; during the volunteer project,
volunteers reside with a host family or in a hostel.

Time Line: Volunteers begin their experience as part of a group in February, April, June, August, or October. Volunteers commit to two- to four-month stints, with the average volunteer staying three to four months.

Cost: The program fee is €650. The fee includes a two-week orientation program (preservice training); lodging with a host family; two meals a day (breakfast and dinner); a cultural orientation tour; cross-cultural orientation; a hiking day trip; lectures on Nepali religion, cultures, political system, history, and gender relations; guided meditation; cultural activities; volunteer placement; a village excursion; a jungle safari; white-water rafting; and in-country transportation. Expenses not included in the program fee are the volunteer's airfare to and from Nepal, insurance, personal expenses, visa fees, and entrance fees to tourist sites visited during training.

Getting Started: Prospective volunteers should contact CDN and request an application form, which must be returned by registered mail along with a resume, four copies of passport-sized photographs, and a nonrefundable application fee of €50. CDN offers what appears to be a very impressive two-week orientation program, which includes a general orientation to Nepali customs, language (taught by professional language teachers), and community interaction skills, all conducted while volunteers stay with host families. The cultural orientation includes discussions about Nepali history and a tour of historic cities within the Kathmandu Valley. Interestingly, it also includes a tour of basic service providers, such as the post office, banks, and health clinics. The orientation also includes a one-day hiking trip outside of Kathmandu and lectures on religion, culture, history, politics, geography, necessary health precautions, women in Nepal, and various other topics that explain the diversity of Nepali life. Volunteers can request specific lectures if they want to learn more about a particular topic during orientation.

Needed Skills and Specific Populations: Volunteers must be at least 18 years old and have a high school diploma, though no other specific skills are required. Senior volunteers are welcomed; the eldest CDN volunteer to date was 65 years old. Volunteers with disabilities are welcomed, but may not be able to participate in all of the planned activities. Couples are welcomed and encouraged to apply.

Growing in Nepal

By Ms. Leez Nicholls

Cultural Destination Nepal (CDN)

Nepal is a beautiful place to be, especially if you are looking for a new challenge. I wanted to grow, to embrace different cultures, and to develop my cross-cultural skills. Teaching elementary school in Nepal allowed me to do these things.

First, I should say that the people of Nepal, whether they are old or young, are just beautiful people, both inside and out. After only three months here, I have so many friends and families that are dear to me. Both of my host families showed and shared their hospitality with me. I was welcomed and felt like I truly had a new home. I am grateful and thankful. Even strangers whom I met while trekking would greet me with big, wide smiles and beautiful wrinkles on their faces that shouldn't be wiped off. They offered help and shared their knowledge and trekking skills. And at school, I admit that I fell in love with all my beautiful, beautiful students. These children do whatever they are asked to do, and I love them all so much.

Concerning communication, I have noticed that language is not a barrier. I mean, people don't use English much, some not at all, but it doesn't matter. Use your body language and your facial expressions. That always helps. In fact, I usually felt like an actress when trying to communicate. Hahaha! There is one Nepali expression I definitely learned, "*dherai dherai dhanyabad*," which translates literally as "very very thank you." You say this phrase when you are sincerely grateful, which I was, a lot of the time!

I was challenged by Nepal and came away from my teaching experience there with better skills at adapting to different environments and cultures. I am also more tolerant and accepting now. I am glad that I followed my heart to Nepal. My whole volunteer experience has given me so many things and I truly hope that I have given something back (especially to the Nepalese children). So, what are you waiting for? Just go and have the experience of a lifetime. Go for it! You'll be looked after and you'll be happy with the outcome. Hey, I did!

Cultural Embrace

7201 Bill Hughes Road
Austin, TX 78745
(512) 469-9089; Fax: (512) 233-5140
E-mail: volunteer@culturalembrace.com
Website: www.culturalembrace.com

Project Type: Community Development; Construction;
Economic Development; Education; Medical/Health;
Orphans; Trail Building/Maintenance

Mission Statement Excerpt: "Our mission is to encourage
people to recognize and appreciate cultural diversity."

Year Founded: 2002

Number of Volunteers Last Year: 250

Funding Sources: None

The Work They Do: Cultural Embrace arranges and tailors
opportunities for individuals and groups to intern, volunteer,
work, teach, take cultural classes, and travel. Volunteers
have the opportunity to take on a wide variety of tasks,
including orphanage assistance, social welfare, community
work, animal and wildlife conservation, teaching, tutoring,
medical work, renovations, environmental work, and administrative assistance. For example, volunteers in Guatemala
can assist youth in a community center; volunteers in Kenya
can work at an orphanage outside of Nairobi; in China,
volunteers can help care for elders; in Australia and New
Zealand, volunteers have the opportunity to help combat
deforestation; and in South Africa, volunteers get to track
and monitor lions, elephants, birds, and other animals.

Project Location: Cultural Embrace's projects take place at
schools, community centers, orphanages, and conservation
centers for beaches and forests in Africa, Asia, Australia,
Europe, and Latin America. Project sites are clean, comfortable, and safe. Some sites are basic and rustic, while others
are quite comfortable. Water and cooked meals for volunteers are typically included, and various dietary restrictions

can be accommodated. Cultural Embrace arranges a private room with a host family or a shared room at a volunteer guest house, either of which is located near the volunteer's project.

Time Line: Projects take place year-round. Volunteers commit to a minimum of one week and a maximum of one year, with the average volunteer staying for one month.

Cost: Fees vary based on destination, project, and duration, but generally start between $1,100 to $1,300 for one week, and increase by $175 to $300 for each additional week. Cultural Embrace's fees typically include the volunteer placement, housing, meals, airport transfers, insurance, and social and cultural activities. Transportation to the volunteer placement is not included in the program fee. One leader of each group will be awarded a no-cost project if that person brings 10 full-paying volunteers on the Cultural Embrace program.

Getting Started: Prospective volunteers should complete an application form on the organization's website. A 20-minute phone interview is required as part of the application and placement process. Cultural Embrace asks volunteers to apply three months in advance in order to be able to properly make arrangements. Most projects include a one-day to weeklong orientation and training, depending on the background, skills, and experience of the volunteers. A predeparture cultural kit is provided to volunteers to assist them in preparing for their project, tasks, and living and volunteering abroad.

Needed Skills and Specific Populations: While past work experience and language skills are preferred and helpful, they are not necessarily required. Volunteers must be at least 18 years old; minors must also either have consent from or travel with a guardian. There is no maximum age, as long as the volunteer is healthy. Volunteers with disabilities are welcome "as long as they will be of service to the project and local community, and not require the project staff's attention, time, and energy." Similarly, families are welcome to volunteer with Cultural Embrace as long as all members can be of service to and help the local community and the project.

Dakshinayan

c/o Mitali Chatterjee
2/1A Mahendra Road
Kolkata 700025
West Bengal
India
+91 98 36 596426
E-mail: dakshinayan@gmail.com or info@dakshinayan.org
Website: www.dakshinayan.org

Project Type: Education; Rural Development; Youth
Mission Statement Excerpt: "Dakshinayan is a volunteer-based organization providing education and health care to tribal and other rural communities in India."
Year Founded: 1992
Number of Volunteers Last Year: 30
Funding Sources: None; Dakshinayan is self-funded
The Work They Do: Dakshinayan offers volunteers the opportunity to teach primary education classes to children in remote villages in India. Volunteers help teach basic English, games, and art. Dakshinayan's objective is to provide people who are concerned about development issues with a unique opportunity to observe and experience the culture of rural India and to study the problems of communities while gaining an in-depth perspective of the myth and reality of poverty in an economically developing nation. Dakshinayan's emphasis is not on work but rather on volunteer participation in ongoing project activities and community life. Therefore, work and activities are not organized especially for the volunteers.
Project Location: Dakshinayan's project is located near Roldih village in the Godda Block of Godda District in Jharkhand, India. Volunteers are placed in relatively remote sites that do not have electricity or running water. Living conditions are basic, and food consists of simple vegetarian meals made from whatever seasonal vegetables are available locally.

Time Line: Volunteers are accepted year-round, but they must apply at least one month before they wish to depart. Volunteers must commit to at least one month of work, and the maximum stay is four months.

Cost: Dakshinayan's program fee is $300 per month, which includes food and accommodations while at the project. Transportation costs to and from the project are not included.

Getting Started: Prospective volunteers should request, complete, and return a questionnaire by e-mail, which will then be screened. No orientation is given nor interview required, though Dakshinayan provides some instructions and informal conversations before departure.

Needed Skills and Specific Populations: No special skills or certifications are required, as most volunteers teach basic English or mathematics to small children. A volunteer who cannot teach either subject may teach the children about the volunteer's own culture. Volunteers must be 18 to 30 years old. Dakshinayan cannot accommodate volunteers with disabilities or families, though couples may volunteer together. Volunteers must be very culturally sensitive, as they are placed in rural villages that have had little exposure to other cultures.

Earthwatch

114 Western Avenue
Boston, MA 02134
(800) 776-0188; Fax: (978) 461-2332
E-mail: info@earthwatch.org
Website: www.earthwatch.org

Project Type: Archaeology; Community Development; Historic
Preservation; Natural Conservation (Land); Natural Conservation (Sea); Scientific Research
Mission Statement Excerpt: "Earthwatch inspires connections
between people and the environment. We offer life-
enhancing experiences on genuine scientific research projects
by giving people unique opportunities to develop their own
skills and knowledge, while contributing to crucial environmental research projects in some of the most remote and
threatened places on Earth."
Year Founded: 1971
Number of Volunteers Last Year: 4,000
Funding Sources: Grants, foundations, individual memberships,
donations, and corporate partnerships
The Work They Do: Earthwatch expeditions provide short-term
volunteer opportunities to directly assist qualified and
respected scientists in their field research and to work on
critical and current issues. Research topics span a wide
range of scientific study and include climate change, coastal
oceans, ecology, zoology, archaeology, and cultural impacts.
The range of tasks on Earthwatch expeditions is enormous,
from using dental picks to coax free a dinosaur bone to
freeing a bird from a mist net or tracking Pacific grey
whales from a kayak. Other examples of volunteer activities
include monitoring populations of fish on a coral reef,
recording the behavior of brown hyenas and whales and
dolphins, developing education and outreach materials for
use in school and communities where there is conflict
between human populations and wildlife, and utilizing

scientific instruments (from a gravity meter to a satellite tracking system to a pair of tweezers and a magnifying glass). Other volunteers might whisk the dust off of a bowl that was last seen by a Roman soldier in the first century A.D. or dig up bones of dinosaurs from the late Triassic Period. In addition to individual opportunities, teams are often available for teens, families, and groups.

Project Location: Volunteer projects are carried out in 31 countries around the world, from the United States to Thailand to Brazil. Much of Earthwatch's work takes place in wildlife reserves, at important historical sites, and in national parks. In some cases, volunteers work in areas that are inaccessible to tourists, in pristine regions that only researchers are allowed to enter. Accommodations vary widely and might take the form of hammocks, dorm rooms, country inns, formal hotels, or condos. Food ranges from spaghetti cooked over a fire to four-course meals in a safari camp. Earthwatch's online project descriptions provide specific details for each trip.

Time Line: Projects are offered year-round, though each project takes place in a specific time frame. Most projects are 10 to 14 days long, but there are also one-week, three-week, and weekend opportunities available. The shortest projects take place over a weekend, and the longest projects run for 16 days.

Cost: Program fees range from $350 to $5,195, the average being about $2,700. The program fee includes accommodations and food, travel during the expedition, and any permits that are needed. Only 16 percent of the program fees go to administrative overhead costs; the remainder goes toward paying for the volunteer's expenses and for the scientific research project. Volunteers must provide their own airfare to the work site and pay for other personal expenses.

Getting Started: Prospective volunteers can sign up for an expedition online, over the phone, or through the mail. Interviews are not required of prospective volunteers. Volunteers receive an expedition briefing that includes all of

A string of volunteers work together with a very long net to conduct a fish survey in the Bahamas. The data they collect will help scientists develop restoration plans to improve the quality of the near-shore fish habitat. *Photo courtesy of Dale Curtis*

the necessary program details. In the field, volunteers are given one or more training sessions that cover all needed skills with the exception of scuba certification, which is required by one or more projects. Some projects require volunteers to have extensive backpacking and camping experience before their arrival.

Needed Skills and Specific Populations: Other than family teams, which provide options for children and their guardians, all projects have a minimum age requirement of either 16 or 18. Senior volunteers are encouraged to work with Earthwatch. Volunteers with disabilities are welcomed, provided that the type and level of disability can be accommodated by the specific project. Expeditions that require a high level of fitness or scuba certification are clearly identified in their online descriptions. Earthwatch also operates expeditions that are specifically geared toward families, which are clearly labeled on their website; family teams have a minimum age of 10 years old.

Eco-Centre Caput Insulae–Beli (ECCIB), Research and Educational Centre for the Protection of Nature

Beli 4

51559 Beli

Croatia

+385 51 840 525

E-mail: caput.insulae@ri.t-com.hr

Website: www.supovi.hr/english/index.php

Project Type: Archaeology; Natural Conservation (Land); Rural Development; Scientific Research

Mission Statement Excerpt: "Protect and preserve natural diversity and work toward the protection of original values and cultural-historical heritages."

Year Founded: 1993

Number of Volunteers Last Year: 280

Funding Sources: Government and private funding

The Work They Do: ECCIB works to protect Eurasian griffon vultures and the natural and historical heritage of the island of Cres in Croatia. Volunteers help conduct observations of griffon vultures, learn about and maintain historic stone walls, assist with trail maintenance, build labyrinths, maintain the interpretative center, and assist with other jobs as necessary.

Project Location: Volunteers live and work in the village of Beli, to the north of the Adriatic island of Cres, in Croatia. The village dates back to 4,000 B.C.E., and 2,000 years ago it was a Roman settlement. Volunteers stay in dormitories that have shower and kitchen facilities, with a chef who provides meals.

Time Line: Volunteers are accepted from March through October. Volunteers must stay for at least 10 days, and the maximum volunteer stint is six months. The average volunteer stays for three or four weeks.

Cost: Volunteers pay for 10-day terms: one term is €250, two terms are €480, and three terms are €720. The program fee

A volunteer in the large outdoor bird-cage holds one of the Eurasian griffon vultures so that it can be weighed. These griffons can get up to 22 pounds! The rescue center monitors the injured birds before releasing them back into nature on the island of Cres, one of the islands of Croatia. *Photo courtesy of Eco-Centre Caput Insulae–Beli*

includes transportation between Cres and Beli, accommodations, three meals each day, training, and insurance.

Getting Started: Prospective volunteers may access an application form on ECCIB's website. Applications should be sent in at least one month before travel, preferably more for the summer months. Prospective volunteers should closely read ECCIB's website and volunteer contract, as this must be signed on the first day. Also on the first day, volunteers are given an introductory lecture that includes information on the Eurasian griffon vulture and the surrounding area. For the first few days, volunteers accompany a coordinator or an ecocenter staff member to learn more about the work done at the center. Later during their stay, volunteers take a daylong hike along the ecotrails in the area and have the opportunity to explore the island of Cres.

Needed Skills and Specific Populations: Volunteers must be at least 18 years old, speak English or Croatian, and be in good physical condition. Senior citizens are welcome to volunteer with ECCIB, as are volunteers with disabilities and families.

El Porvenir

P.O. Box 125247
San Francisco, CA 94117
(720) 237-9486; Fax: (303) 861-1480
E-mail: info@elporvenir.org
Website: www.elporvenir.org

Project Type: Community Development; Construction; Rural
Development

Mission Statement: "El Porvenir partners with poor communities in Nicaragua to improve their quality of life through
sustainable development of drinking water, sanitation, and
reforestation projects, and health education."

Year Founded: 1990

Number of Volunteers Last Year: 118

Funding Sources: Foundations and faith-based sources

The Work They Do: El Porvenir works with villagers to build
wells, latrines, communal wash facilities for bathing and
washing clothes, fuel-saving stoves, and community tree
nurseries. Water and sanitation projects may include
building a communal washing facility near the village well,
which will relieve women of the burden of carrying water
long distances to wash clothes; rehabilitating a well to
ensure that the community has access to safe drinking
water; or building latrines to prevent the spread of disease
and to protect the water source. Reforestation projects
include clearing brush areas, planting seedlings, fencing
areas, and building smoke-free, fuel-saving family cookstoves. Villagers who are assisted by this project live in
adobe or brick homes with dirt floors, and they rarely have
electricity. The conditions are poor, but the villagers are
committed to improving their lives and they welcome the
volunteers to their communities. Volunteers work alongside
villagers mixing cement, laying bricks, cutting and tying
wire, sifting sand, and filling bags for planting trees. The
tasks range from easy to difficult, and the volunteers decide

which tasks they will perform. All of El Porvenir's projects are initiated, built, and maintained by the villagers, and El Porvenir purchases its materials in Nicaragua, supporting locally owned businesses whenever possible.

Project Location: Projects are carried out in central Nicaragua in the small villages near the towns of El Sauce, Camoapa, San Lorenzo, Terrabona, Ciudad Dario, and Wiwili. Volunteers stay in modest hotels in nearby towns and travel daily via four-wheel-drive trucks to the work sites in small villages. Most meals are eaten in restaurants, though some are eaten in the host communities.

Time Line: Trips are offered throughout the year, usually in January, February, March, June, July, August, September, and November, and they are one to two weeks in length.

Cost: A two-week trip with El Porvenir costs $1,135, plus airfare. The program fee includes food, lodging, all in-country transportation, two bilingual guides, travel and health insurance, and activity fees. Volunteers are responsible for their own transportation to and from Nicaragua. Out of the program fee, $200 goes directly to the project being constructed.

Getting Started: Prospective volunteers should contact El Porvenir via e-mail or phone to request an information form. An orientation and a brief history of Nicaragua are provided to volunteers upon arrival.

Needed Skills and Specific Populations: A parent must accompany volunteers who are younger than 18. Volunteers with disabilities are welcomed as long as they can climb in and out of a four-wheel-drive truck, climb steps, and live comfortably in a tropical climate. Refrigeration is available for medications. Volunteers from outside the United States should check Nicaragua's visa regulations before applying.

Engineering Ministries International (EMI)

130 East Kiowa Street, Suite 200
Colorado Springs, CO 80903
(719) 633-2078; Fax: (719) 633-2970
E-mail: info@emiusa.org
Website: www.emiworld.org

Project Type: Community Development; Construction; Professional/Technical Assistance; Rural Development

Mission Statement Excerpt: "EMI's vision is to mobilize design professionals to minister to the less fortunate in developing nations—we proclaim the Gospel of Jesus as we help others change their world—through the development of hospitals, schools, orphanages, bridges, water supplies, electricity and more."

Year Founded: 1982

Number of Volunteers Last Year: 200

Funding Sources: Individual donors and faith-based organizations

The Work They Do: EMI primarily works in two ways: designing relief projects that mitigate physical and spiritual poverty, such as hospitals, schools, orphanages, bridges, and water supplies; and by serving Christian missionaries by providing free design services for infrastructure that enables them to serve the poor and preach the Gospel with greater effectiveness and impact. EMI volunteers use their specific technical skills in pursuit of these goals.

Project Location: EMI has completed over 900 projects in over 85 economically developing countries around the world. Projects have been located in Africa, Asia, Central America, South America, Europe, the Middle East, and the South Pacific. EMI volunteers serve in both urban and rural placements, and usually work in conjunction with local missionary teams who provide guidance and support, including accommodations. Work site and housing conditions range greatly depending on the region of the world and on how much development work has already occurred on-site.

Time Line: EMI carries out projects throughout the year, usually for two weeks at a time, though occasionally there are longer trips, which can be up to a year in length.

Cost: EMI's program fee is $650, which covers accommodations, in-country travel, and meals. Volunteers must pay for their own airfare. EMI estimates that most volunteers pay between $1,200 and $3,000 total for their volunteer vacation.

Getting Started: Prospective volunteers can read about planned trips on EMI's website, which are available seasonally in the winter, spring, and fall. Applications are available on the website, and project leaders interview all applicants in advance of the trip. Training is included as a part of the volunteer experience.

Needed Skills and Specific Populations: Volunteers must have a technical skill that matches the need of the planned trip; examples of these skills include, but are not limited to, architecture, civil engineering, structural engineering, surveying, and electrical engineering. Because of this, almost all of EMI's volunteers have at least a college degree. Senior volunteers are encouraged to participate in EMI's trips, and volunteers with disabilities may also be able to participate on a case-by-case basis. EMI is a Christian organization, but accepts both Christian and non-Christian volunteers. EMI volunteers are sometimes joined by a spouse or partner, but trips are not designed for entire families.

Experiential Learning International (ELI)

1557 Ogden Street, Suite 5
Denver, CO 80218
(303) 321-8278; Fax: (303) 857-5445
E-mail: info@eliabroad.org
Website: www.eliabroad.org

Project Type: Community Development; Education;
Medical/Health; Orphans; Social Justice; Women's Issues;
Youth

Mission Statement Excerpt: "ELI facilitates flexible international learning programs for independent travelers by partnering with local organizations to give participants the opportunity to experience and contribute to sustainable ongoing local projects throughout the world."

Year Founded: 2001

Number of Volunteers Last Year: 600

Funding Sources: Foundations and private donors

The Work They Do: Volunteers work on a wide range of projects, helping with everything from teaching English to digging wells.

Project Location: ELI currently operates projects in Argentina, Brazil, Chile, Mexico, Peru, Ecuador, Nicaragua, Costa Rica, Guatemala, France, Italy, Germany, Poland, Ghana, Kenya, Tanzania, Uganda, South Africa, India, Nepal, Thailand, Vietnam, China, and the Philippines. In most countries, the program fee includes accommodations in a guesthouse, volunteer house, host family, or on-site. In countries where accommodations are not included, ELI can assist the participant in acquiring suitable housing.

Time Line: ELI offers projects throughout the year. Most projects require a minimum commitment of two weeks and will accept volunteers for up to six months. The average volunteer stay is around six to eight weeks.

Cost: Prices vary by project and duration. An eight-week volunteer placement, for example, ranges from $695 to $2,525.

The program fee includes airport pickup and, in most cases, food and accommodations.

Getting Started: Prospective volunteers can apply online and pay a $100 or $200 application fee, depending on the country; this fee is refunded if ELI cannot place the volunteer in a desired position. In general, volunteers should apply three to four months before their desired date of travel. Applicants for programs in Ireland and China must complete a phone interview. Volunteers receive printed materials and telephone support before departure. After arrival, volunteers receive an orientation and city tour. Some placements also offer cultural and tourist activities.

Needed Skills and Specific Populations: Volunteers must be open-minded and willing to fully engage with the host culture. For some placements, such as those in medical fields, volunteers must have training commensurate with the work being done. Most programs in Latin America require that volunteers have some level of Spanish language proficiency; in all other countries, volunteers must be fluent English speakers. ELI volunteers must be at least 18 years old; there is no maximum age to volunteer, and ELI has hosted volunteers up to the age of 75 in the past. ELI "highly encourages" families of volunteers, though children under the age of 18 must be accompanied by a parent or guardian and will only be allowed in a limited number of countries. ELI welcomes volunteers with disabilities, who should talk with ELI staff before applying to ensure a successful placement.

Farm Sanctuary

P.O. Box 150
Watkins Glen, NY 14891
(607) 583-2225; Fax: (607) 583-2041
E-mail: intern@farmsanctuary.org
Website: www.farmsanctuary.org

Project Type: Administrative; Agriculture; Political Action; Social Justice

Mission Statement Excerpt: "Farm Sanctuary works to end cruelty to farm animals and promotes compassionate living through rescue, education and advocacy."

Year Founded: 1986

Number of Volunteers Last Year: 100

Funding Sources: Individual donors and corporate grants

The Work They Do: Farm Sanctuary volunteer interns help take care of and feed hundreds of rescued animals and run the organization's two shelters. Their Volunteer Internship Program provides a way for volunteers to get closely involved in the work of a national animal advocacy organization. Interns live at the shelters and get daily hands-on experience with animals. Interns also get the unique experience of living and working with other like-minded people. The program is designed to be educational and offers many educational opportunities on a variety of topics of the interns' choosing. Interns visit a working stockyard to see what it is like. They also have the option of working directly with the animals at the shelters or working in other departments (campaigns, development, communications, education, or administration).

Project Location: Farm Sanctuary owns two farms: a 175-acre shelter in upstate New York, near Ithaca, and a 300-acre shelter in northern California, 30 miles west of Chico. These farms house more than 1,000 rescued cows, pigs, chickens, turkeys, sheep, goats, rabbits, donkeys, ducks, and geese. On-site housing is offered to all Farm Sanctuary volunteers;

Volunteers crowd around to pet and admire Kirsty, a former resident of the Farm Sanctuary who is now healthy and living on a good farm. *Photo courtesy of Farm Sanctuary*

accommodations include shared bedrooms, bathrooms, and kitchen facilities.

Time Line: Farm Sanctuary internships are available year-round. Positions are filled on an ongoing basis as applications are received; summer months are the most popular for volunteers, so prospective summer volunteers are well advised to apply early. Volunteer positions begin on the first day of every month. Volunteers must commit to at least one month of service. All volunteers work a full-time, 40-hour-per-week schedule. The shelters are open seven days a week, so volunteer schedules generally include weekends and holidays.

Cost: There is no program fee to volunteer with Farm Sanctuary, and housing is provided at no charge; however, there is a $150 deposit that is refundable upon completion of the internship. Volunteers must provide their own transportation to the work site and are responsible for buying and preparing their own food. Weekly trips to the grocery store are provided for volunteers without vehicles.

Getting Started: Prospective volunteers can complete an online application, available at Farm Sanctuary's website, or can call the phone number listed above to request an internship application. Applicants are asked to submit two letters of recommendation on their behalf and need to complete a phone interview. Volunteers receive an orientation on their first day, which covers expectations, an overview of the program, farm and house rules, and protocols. Further specific training is given to each volunteer in their individual department.

Needed Skills and Specific Populations: Unaccompanied volunteers must be at least 18 years old, while volunteers between the ages of 12 and 17 must be joined by a parent or guardian; senior volunteers are welcomed. All volunteers must have a strong commitment to Farm Sanctuary's goals and a personal commitment to veganism. Interns live a vegan lifestyle for the duration of the internship, which includes diet (no meat, dairy products, eggs, honey, or other animal by-products), personal care items (cruelty-free and no animal by-products), and clothing (no leather, fur, silk, wool, etc.). Volunteers with disabilities are welcome, but some tasks require specific physical skills; Farm Sanctuary will make efforts to arrange for volunteer opportunities that best suit the volunteers' needs. There are no citizenship requirements to volunteer with Farm Sanctuary.

Flying Doctors of America (FDOA)

P.O. Box 923563
Norcross, GA 30010
(770) 558-3300; Fax: (678) 496-4610
E-mail: fdoamerica@aol.com
Website: www.fdoamerica.org

Project Type: Medical/Health

Mission Statement Excerpt: "Flying Doctors of America brings together physicians, dentists, nurses, chiropractors, other health professionals and nonmedical support volunteers to care for people who otherwise would never receive professional medical care."

Year Founded: 1990

Number of Volunteers Last Year: 160

Funding Sources: None

The Work They Do: FDOA provides medical and dental care to areas around the world that lack access to basic medical facilities. They operate under the "Mother Teresa Principle," focusing on serving the poorest of the poor.

Project Location: FDOA operates projects around the world, but has a focus on Asia and Latin America. They have three levels of trips: comfortable, challenging, and arduous, and each trip is clearly marked as one of these three on their website. "Arduous" trips generally include sleeping in tents and a level of physical exertion to reach the project site.

Time Line: FDOA typically operates 9 to 12 trips each year. Complete itineraries are available on their website, with contact information for the trip leader.

Cost: Program fees cover the cost of the trip; each trip has a different cost, but most are around $2,000 for a one-week volunteer trip.

Getting Started: Prospective volunteers should contact the team leader directly for a given trip; contact information is available by trip on FDOA's website. While some documents and waivers are required of trip participants, there is no formal application process. Team leaders do contact each applicant before departure to ascertain qualifications. Most training is done on-site.

Needed Skills and Specific Populations: FDOA provides opportunities for certified health professionals as well as nonmedical support volunteers; each team usually has around 14 to 16 members, of which two or three will be nonmedical support staff. Medical volunteers must be licensed to practice in the United States or Canada. Volunteers may be as young as 16 if accompanied by a parent, or 18 if unaccompanied. Senior citizens are encouraged to volunteer with FDOA; those over 105 need a letter from their primary care physician. FDOA does not exclude volunteers with disabilities, but not all trips can accommodate all disabilities.

Foundation for Sustainable Development (FSD)

517 Potrero Avenue, Suite B
San Francisco, CA 94110
(415) 283-4873
E-mail: info@fsdinternational.org
Website: www.fsdinternational.org

Project Type: Agriculture; Community Development; Economic
Development; Education; Human Rights; Women's Issues;
Youth

Mission Statement Excerpt: "Our mission is to overcome the
effects of poverty by empowering underserved communities
and their citizens to be agents of their own sustainable
change."

Year Founded: 1995

Number of Volunteers Last Year: 250

Funding Sources: Private donors and grants

The Work They Do: FSD offers three programs: the Intern
Abroad program for students and young professionals
entails a 9- to 52-week placement in the field with a
community-based partner organization; Service Learning
Trips (SLTs) are available for students and professionals
seeking a 1- or 2-week program; Pro Corps Volunteering is
designed for seasoned professionals and retirees looking to
spend 4 to 52 weeks working alongside a community-based
partner. Specific project work depends on how the participant's skill set aligns with the most pressing needs on the
ground. Examples of volunteer projects include engaging
youth in a sustainable waste management system in Bolivia,
teaching an embroidery training class in India, and creating
a simple rainwater catchment system in Kenya.

Project Location: FSD works with community-based partner
organizations in Argentina, Bolivia, India, Kenya, Nicaragua, and Uganda. Both rural and urban placements are
available. Living conditions may be basic, but almost all
sites have running water and electricity. Program partici-

pants stay with local host families for the duration of their program.

Time Line: Volunteer and intern opportunities are available year-round. FSD's website has complete, up-to-date information on program start dates.

Cost: Program fees vary by country, but they range from about $1,000 to $5,000. The program fees cover all in-country expenses including room, board, transportation, training materials, language lessons (except in Latin America), communications, a host organization grant or a service project grant, a group leader, translation, logistical support, health insurance and emergency evacuation coverage, orientation and debriefing sessions, and program support. It does not include airfare to and from the country of service.

Getting Started: Prospective participants can apply online through FSD's website; applications are accepted on a rolling basis. FSD requires that all applicants complete an extensive phone interview with the local site team before final placement decisions are made. FSD provides an information packet prior to departure, as well as a one-week, in-country orientation and training program.

Needed Skills and Specific Populations: Volunteers should have a demonstrated interest in international development and must be committed to working full-time in collaboration with their host organization in order to leave behind a meaningful and relevant contribution to the community. Spanish is required for volunteering with the Latin American internship program. Volunteers must be at least 18 years old; senior citizens are welcomed. FSD is able to accommodate some volunteers with disabilities, but not families.

Friends of the Great Baikal Trail (FGBT)

2150 Allston Way, Suite 460
Berkeley, CA 94704
(510) 717-1805; Fax: (510) 859-9091
E-mail: baikal@earthsland.org
Website: www.greatbaikaltrail.org

Project Type: Community Development; Economic Development; Historic Preservation; Natural Conservation (Land); Natural Conservation (Sea); Trail Building/Maintenance

Mission Statement Excerpt: "Our organization is designed to promote sustainable economies in eastern Russia, first and foremost by encouraging the development of ecotourism in the region."

Year Founded: 1991

Number of Volunteers Last Year: 750

Funding Sources: Government and private sources

The Work They Do: FGBT helps to recruit and organize teams of international volunteers to work on any of dozens of trail-building projects that occur each spring and summer in the parks and nature reserves around Lake Baikal, the largest and deepest lake in the world. International volunteers work alongside local people to build the Great Baikal Trail as a way to promote low-impact tourism to the region. In some instances, volunteers help with design, interpretation (both language and natural interpretation), and other, less manual aspects of the FGBT's work. However, most of the work involves digging, leveling, and the construction of campsites and other wooden structures along the trail. Half of the members of volunteer groups are Russians from local towns and cities, and half are non-Russian citizens.

Project Location: Volunteers work at one of 20 to 25 work sites along the shores of Lake Baikal in Russia. Most work sites are within one or more of the national parks around the lake. Several of the project areas run into the nearby mountain ranges that surround Baikal. Most work sites are located in wilderness areas and are often not easy to access by roads or other public transport, although most are accessible by boat. Accommodations are almost always in tents, which are provided by FGBT. Food, which is also provided by FGBT, is prepared at campsites. Most trail-building sites are located within walking distance of the lake, where volunteers can swim and hang out on the shore. The national parks approve each work site, along with the trails themselves, to make sure that the environmental impact is minimal.

Time Line: Projects run from June to September, and each lasts for two weeks. Each year there are also several programs in winter and spring, often involving language-learning. Volunteers can work on two consecutive projects in the summer, and volunteers with extensive trail-building experience may sign up for more than that.

Cost: Volunteers pay a program fee of $500 for two weeks, which covers all of the on-site program costs, including food and lodging in tents, language interpretation, and training. Volunteers are responsible for their travel to Irkutsk via Moscow (which involves traveling by either air or train), as well as to the project site. Volunteers may elect to pay an additional $100 for help in getting to the project site from Irkutsk. Volunteers are also responsible for covering all Russian travel visa fees.

Getting Started: Prospective volunteers should send an e-mail to the address listed above, or they may visit the Great Baikal Trail website to find an application and a list of project dates and locations. Interviews are not required before volunteering. Orientation and training take place on the first full day of each project and include cultural pointers. Training in the proper and safe use of tools is also given on the first day, with "reminder training" given daily. Prospective volunteers should be aware that passport holders from some nations, particularly African ones, may have problems obtaining visas to enter Russia.

Needed Skills and Specific Populations: No trail-building or Russian language skills are required, though the FGBT encourages people who possess these skills to apply. Volunteers must be in good health and have both a sense of adventure and a willingness to work physically. Volunteers must be at least 18 years old (though exceptions to this rule can be made for volunteers traveling as part of a school group led by teachers or parents). Senior volunteers who are physically inclined to manual work and wilderness living are also heartily welcomed. Volunteers with disabilities may be able to volunteer with FGBT in the future, once a fully accessible portion of the Great Baikal Trail is completed. Each year there is at least one special Great Baikal Trail project for families with children, both from abroad and locally. In addition, the FGBT welcomes families on other projects, with the prior consent of the crew leaders and the parks where they will be working.

Frontier

50–52 Rivington Street
London EC2A 3QP
United Kingdom
+44 20 7613 2422; Fax: +44 20 7613 2992
E-mail: info@frontier.ac.uk
Website: www.frontier.ac.uk

Project Type: Education; Natural Conservation (Land); Natural Conservation (Sea); Scientific Research

Mission Statement Excerpt: "Frontier's mission is to conserve the world's most endangered wildlife and threatened habitats and to build sustainable livelihoods for marginalized communities in the world's poorest countries. To create solutions that are apolitical, forward-thinking, community-driven, and innovative, and which take into consideration the long-term needs of impoverished communities."

Year Founded: 1989

Number of Volunteers Last Year: Over 1,000

Funding Sources: Government and private donors

The Work They Do: Frontier works in conjunction with counterpart organizations and government departments to carry out biodiversity, habitat, and socioeconomic surveys in areas of great value to conservation, but in which there are communities that suffer through a range of problems, such as environmental conflict, acute poverty, and deprivation. Volunteers are responsible for the collection and processing of field data, reconnaissance trips to assess possible new survey sites, participating in remote satellite camps, equipment maintenance, and ensuring a well-run base camp. Frontier also has a smaller number of teaching opportunities abroad. In general, Frontier's programs fall into the general categories of conservation, education, diving, animal welfare, ethical adventures (which combine volunteering and traveling), and language (combining language acquisition with volunteering).

A volunteer gently pets a cheetah in a wildlife sanctuary just outside of Cape Town, South Africa. Due to population growth and a decrease in natural habitat, many cheetahs are now orphaned or injured, at which point they can no longer survive in nature and are removed to a wildlife sanctuary for care. *Photo courtesy of Frontier*

Project Location: Frontier currently operates almost 270 projects in more than 50 countries. Lodging is provided in communal hostels or huts; food is cooked by the group and mostly consists of the local staple, such as rice or noodles, supplemented with fresh fruit, vegetables, bread, meat, fish, herbs, and spices.

Time Line: Frontier's projects run throughout the year. Volunteers can join projects for a length of time ranging from 9 days to 20 weeks.

Cost: Program fees begin at £350 for nine days and go up to £3,395 for 20 weeks. The program fees include an orientation session in the United Kingdom, accommodations, transfers, food, and group expedition equipment. Volunteers are responsible for their flights, visas, insurance, and personal equipment.

Getting Started: Prospective volunteers can apply online; all volunteers must complete a short telephone consultation about their project. Within a week of their interviews, applicants will be notified in writing whether their application has been successful. An optional weekend orientation program takes place in the United Kingdom six weeks before departure. Health and safety, scientific, and (as needed) scuba training are provided upon arrival.

Needed Skills and Specific Populations: Frontier volunteers do not need a science or teaching background; above all, Frontier values resilience, resourcefulness, flexibility, and imagination. Volunteers also need to be in good physical shape, be team players, speak fluent English, and be able to use their initiative. Volunteers must be at least 16 years old, and most volunteers are between 16 and 30, though senior volunteers may also participate. Frontier also welcomes volunteers with disabilities.

Fundacion Aldeas de Paz
(Peace Villages Foundation)

Centro Comunitario
Lomas de Piedra Canaima via Sampai
Santa Elena de Uairen 8032
La Gran Sabana, Estado Bolivar
Venezuela
+58 414 870 4895 or +58 289 416 0718
E-mail: info@aldeasdepaz.org
Website: www.aldeasdepaz.org

Project Type: Administrative; Community Development;
Construction; Education; Natural Conservation (Land);
Youth

Mission Statement Excerpt: "We promote a 'Culture of Peace'
through enriching cross-cultural exchange for people of all
races and nationalities and we practice voluntary community service where we provide additional opportunities in
educational, recreational and environmental fields and assist
our beneficiaries to develop their potential and improve
their own lives."

Year Founded: 2001

Number of Volunteers Last Year: 54

Funding Sources: None outside of program fees

The Work They Do: Aldeas de Paz carries out several programs,
including the operation of a mobile school in low-income
neighborhoods; teaching and tutoring; working with youth;
conservation projects; riding for disadvantaged youth;
carpentry and ecological building; and nonprofit management and administration. Volunteers create their own work
schedule.

Project Location: Volunteers work in and around Santa Elena
and remote indigenous villages within "La Gran Sabana"
National Park in Venezuela. Volunteers live in the Aldeas de
Paz guest house, with a host family in the village, or on the
foundation's campground.

Time Line: Volunteers are accepted year-round for a minimum of one week and a maximum of one year.

Cost: Program fees vary with the length of stay and level of accommodations. Staying at the foundation's guest house, which includes all meals, ranges from $1,295 for six weeks to $4,950 for a full year. Accommodations at the foundation's campground for six weeks costs $975. The program fee covers transfers from the local bus station, free conversational Spanish classes, and participation in excursions and cultural exchanges. Volunteers must provide their own airfare to Venezuela. A 50 percent deposit is required to secure the volunteer placement.

Getting Started: Prospective volunteers can complete an application form on the Aldeas de Paz website listed above. Volunteers should apply at least one month in advance of their desired arrival date. Volunteers are provided with a complete orientation upon arrival.

Needed Skills and Specific Populations: Individual volunteers, families, and groups are welcome, regardless of age, experience, or background. Volunteers under the age of 18 must have permission from their parents. Volunteers do not have to speak fluent Spanish, as full on-site support and 24-hour back-up from local staff is provided. Volunteers should be enthusiastic, willing to learn, ready for a challenge, and have a desire to take initiative and dedicate a lot of caring and passion to the position. Volunteers with disabilities are welcome, though those with mobility challenges will find that the terrain may be difficult to navigate.

Galapagos ICE: Immerse Connect Evolve

Barrio la Union
Puerto Ayora, Galapagos
Ecuador
+593 5 301 5108
E-mail: epozo@galapagosice.org
Website: www.galapagosice.org

Project Type: Community Development; Education;
Medical/Health; Natural Conservation (Land); Rural Development; Youth

Mission Statement Excerpt: "Galapagos ICE strives to improve
the educational and medical systems in the Galapagos
Islands, and to encourage ecological efforts that recognize
the local population as integral participants in the conservation of this unique natural habitat."

Year Founded: 2005

Number of Volunteers Last Year: 105

Funding Sources: Individual donors and faith-based organizations

The Work They Do: Galapagos ICE helps place volunteers in
the Galapagos Islands in specific opportunities that take
advantage of the volunteer's background and training. Galapagos ICE has placed people from a wide range of professions, including health care professionals, teachers,
eco-architects, yoga instructors, muralists, artists, and
university professors.

Project Location: Galapagos ICE primarily works on Santa
Cruz Island, though they have also had volunteers on
Isabela Island. Most volunteers stay with host families.

Time Line: Volunteers are accepted year-round for one week to
six months.

Cost: Volunteers pay a $50 application fee. Once on-site, volunteers pay $350 for accommodations only or $450 for room
and board combined for the first two weeks. Volunteers
who stay longer than two weeks have the option to instead

pay $500 for accommodations only, or $700 for room and board for up to four weeks. After the first month, every two weeks volunteers pay $220 for accommodations only, or $300 for room and board. Flights to the Galapagos are relatively expensive, but Galapagos ICE arranges to have the park entrance fee waived.

Getting Started: Prospective volunteers should contact Galapagos ICE via e-mail. Completed applications require a resume, two references, and the $50 application fee. All volunteers receive a short orientation upon arrival and further training as needed.

Needed Skills and Specific Populations: The minimum age for volunteers is 18, unless a group of high school students volunteer together; there is no maximum age for volunteers. Galapagos ICE welcomes volunteers with disabilities and families, though both of these populations should organize their trip well ahead of their arrival.

Gibbon Conservation Center (GCC)

P.O. Box 800249
Santa Clarita, CA 91380
(661) 296-2737; Fax: (661) 296-1237
E-mail: gibboncenter@earthlink.net
Website: www.gibboncenter.org

Project Type: Education; Natural Conservation (Land); Scientific Research

Mission Statement Excerpt: "The mission of the Gibbon Conservation Center is to prevent the extinction of this small Asian ape and to advance its study, propagation, and conservation by establishing secure captive gene pools in case attempts to preserve species or subspecies in the wild fail. We educate the public, assist zoos and rescue centers in better captive care, encourage noninvasive behavioral studies, and support ongoing field conservation projects."

Year Founded: 1976

Number of Volunteers Last Year: Approximately 180, including 17 live-in volunteers (most of the rest were in groups)

Funding Sources: Private donors and grants from foundations

The Work They Do: GCC is one of the few facilities in the world devoted exclusively to gibbons, an increasingly rare ape; it boasts the largest collections of gibbons in the Western Hemisphere, housing five of the seventeen living species. GCC houses nearly 40 gibbons, which are the rarest apes in the Western Hemisphere. Among the center's gibbons are 5 of the 18 living species. GCC specializes in nonintrusive behavioral studies on gibbons that are conducted by students, scientists, and volunteers working at the center, and it also has one of the largest gibbon libraries in the world. Volunteers have three work options. Primate keepers provide direct care of the gibbons, including feeding, cleaning, and changing water. This role may also include administering medication, doing behavioral observations, maintenance work, and assisting with administrative duties. Most resident volunteers are primate keepers, and they work from approximately 7 AM to 5 PM, five days per week. Center assistants may do maintenance work, take behavioral observations, clean, and help with administrative tasks; they also keep a minimum distance of six feet from all enclosures. Clerical assistants help with administrative tasks and may do behavioral observations.

Project Location: All volunteers work at the GCC site, which is located about one hour north of Los Angeles. GCC is on five acres in a rural canyon area on the outskirts of a medium-sized city and is in a semidesert area. Weather conditions can be extreme, reaching from a high of 105°F in summer months to a low of 35°F at night in the winter. GCC provides lodging to resident volunteers in an older, basic travel trailer with free access to bathroom, kitchen, and laundry facilities. Volunteers are responsible for providing their own food and personal items.

Time Line: Volunteers are welcome seven days a week, year-round. Resident volunteers must commit to a minimum of two months; there is no stated maximum stay. Many volunteers stay for several months, with the average being two months. Resident volunteers who have completed at least two months in the past may volunteer again for less than two months.

Cost: Resident GCC volunteer primate keepers are asked to pay a nonrefundable fee of $350 per month for a minimum of two months, which covers their lodging, utilities, and training. Resident volunteers purchase and prepare their own food. Nonresident primate keepers, who are local or arrange their own off-site accommodations, are asked to pay a $150 fee to cover their training and to commit to providing at least 100 hours of service within the first six months after training. Volunteers are responsible for their own transportation to and from the work site, as well as for personal expenses incurred during the volunteer experience. GCC also requires a number of medical exams and inoculations before volunteers may enter the facility. Volunteers must provide evidence of valid health insurance coverage.

Getting Started: Prospective volunteers may download an application from the GCC website or contact the office to receive an application. Applications must include a resume, a cover letter, and two letters of recommendation; GCC does not require interviews of prospective volunteers. A four-day training session is required, covering mandated procedures and GCC's own goals of cleanliness, welfare, breeding, and safety. The training is conducted by an experienced primate caregiver.

Needed Skills and Specific Populations: GCC wants volunteers who are self-motivated and have a love for animals. No smoking is allowed at the center. All volunteers must be at least 21 years old, and resident volunteers must be at least 23 years old. There is no maximum age for volunteers, as long as they are capable of undertaking strenuous work. Volunteers who serve as primate keepers must be physically fit. Volunteers with disabilities will be considered on an individual basis. Families may be able to volunteer with the GCC under specific circumstances, but children must be supervised at all times.

Global Ambassadors for Children (GAFC)

40 Executive Drive, Suite E
Carmel, IN 46032
(317) 814-5318; Fax: (317) 814-2116
E-mail: contact@ambassadorsforchildren.org
Website: www.ambassadorsforchildren.org

Project Type: Construction; Education; Medical/Health;
Orphans; Social Justice; Youth

Mission Statement Excerpt: "Global Ambassadors for Children
is a not-for-profit organization dedicated to serving children
around the world through short-term humanitarian service
trips and sustainable projects."

Year Founded: 1998

Number of Volunteers Last Year: Approximately 500

Funding Sources: Private donors, corporate sponsors, and grants

The Work They Do: Global Ambassadors for Children supports
children in approximately 10 locations around the world by
identifying and supporting sustainable programs. Examples
of these programs include developing small businesses to aid
socioeconomically disadvantaged families in Belize and El
Salvador; building and supporting an orphanage in India;
and supplying and shipping medical equipment to Uganda,
El Salvador, Malawi, and Jordan. Global Ambassadors for
Children also provides a large variety of activities for GAFC
volunteers traveling on short-term humanitarian trips to
implement in orphanages, schools, and communities. These
projects include opportunities such as teaching English as a
second language, supervising sporting and recreational
activities at orphanages, schools, and communities; and
assisting with medical and dental assessments of children.
GAFC has created opportunities for education majors in
colleges and universities to work in Malawi developing
curricula and teaching the fundamentals of reading and
storytelling. GAFC also works with nurses and nurse practitioners to support a medical initiative in Costa Rica that

provides check-ups to the children in the orphanages. Lastly, Global Ambassadors for Children has partnered with architecture firms to build a school in Uganda and to install irrigation systems in Santa Fe, New Mexico.

Project Location: GAFC currently operates humanitarian trips to Costa Rica, Peru, Malawi, Kenya, Uganda, Cambodia, Honduras, New Mexico, and Miami. Housing for most of GAFC's trips is provided in unique guesthouses, boutique hotels, moderate hotels, and eco-lodges. All accommodations have access to water and plumbing.

Time Line: GAFC operates at least one trip almost every month of the year and usually offers more than 30 volunteer programs per year. Trips vary in length from five days to two weeks, with most falling in the 7-to-10-day range. GAFC offers multiple trips and destinations over spring breaks, summer vacation, and at Christmas. GAFC will also customize trips for groups of volunteers with 10 or more people.

Cost: Ground packages including transfers, accommodations, orientation, welcome dinner, farewell dinner, some meals, a tour, and a donation to the volunteer sites start at $1,000 for domestic programs and range to approximately $2,500 for international programs, depending on the length of the trip. Airfare is not included in GAFC's pricing.

Getting Started: Prospective volunteers should contact GAFC via e-mail or phone. GAFC requires a $500 deposit, a volunteer profile, and a completed waiver of liability before the volunteer can officially join a GAFC trip. Interviews are not required of prospective volunteers unless GAFC is developing the trip specifically for the volunteer or group of volunteers. Beginning two months before the trip, GAFC provides both an orientation guide and the services of a trip leader. GAFC also offers an on-site orientation during the first day of the trip, which includes basic information on GAFC; the history, culture, and food of the destination; an overview of the itinerary; and an introduction to the volunteer work and global partners.

Needed Skills and Specific Populations: No specific skills are required, but GAFC always encourages teachers, students, doctors, dentists, carpenters, and other skilled professionals to volunteer. There is no minimum age limit, but volunteers under the age of 18 must be accompanied by an adult. Senior volunteers are welcomed, and GAFC does not have restrictions on citizenship. Volunteers with disabilities are also welcomed, provided that they have someone accompanying them who can provide help as needed. GAFC has been working with families since its inception and strongly encourages family volunteers.

Global Buddies

22701 Burbank Boulevard
Woodland Hills, CA 91367
(310) 651-8948
E-mail: globalbuddies@me.com
Website: www.globalbuddies.net

Project Type: Community Development; Construction; Education; Orphans; Professional/Technical Assistance; Women's Issues; Youth

Mission Statement Excerpt: "Global Buddies' mission is to inspire, educate, and empower people of all ages, from around the world, to become lifelong global citizens and environmental stewards. We do this by offering opportunities for cultural exchange and volunteer service, while nurturing personal connections and authentic exchange between equals."

Year Founded: 2006

Number of Volunteers Last Year: 100

Funding Sources: Private individuals and schools

The Work They Do: Global Buddies partners with host organizations to create custom projects for each trip, based on the needs of the local community at the time. Specific projects in the past have included building a playground in Mfuleni Township, near Cape Town, South Africa; teaching English classes and painting a school in Cambodia; setting up Internet connections for an after-school program and teaching computer skills; and planting a garden for local families.

Project Location: Global Buddies operates projects in South Africa, Uganda, China, and Cambodia. Housing arrangements are made by Global Buddies and vary from trip to trip. Typically, accommodations will include apartments, bed and breakfasts, and hotels; volunteers on longer-term projects stay in local homes. Preference and budget can help determine volunteer housing options.

Time Line: Global Buddies can arrange trips for groups at any time during the year. The average trip is two weeks, but trips of any length can be arranged.

Cost: Global Buddies' program fees vary widely by country and project, from $1,500 up to almost $5,000. The program fee includes accommodations and most meals, but not international airfare.

Getting Started: Prospective volunteers can complete an online application; deadlines vary from year to year and trip to trip. Global Buddies does require an interview prior to departure to ensure that the organization is a good fit for the volunteer. Staff members from Global Buddies will be in touch with volunteers prior to departure and will also supply an in-depth reading list. An in-country orientation is provided on the first day of the program, and additional training is held throughout the trip.

Needed Skills and Specific Populations: Global Buddies was originally founded to provide volunteer experiences to families, which remains their specialty. Global Buddies welcomes volunteers of all ages, though it recommends that volunteers be at least six years old. Youth who are at least 15 years old may volunteer unaccompanied by an adult. Volunteers with disabilities are welcome. Although Global Buddies specializes in family volunteer experiences, they work with many different individuals and groups of volunteers.

Global Citizen Year (GCY)

466 Geary Street, Suite 400
San Francisco, CA 94102
(415) 963-9293
E-mail: info@globalcitizenyear.org
Website: www.globalcitizenyear.org

Project Type: Agriculture; Community Development; Economic
  Development; Education; Medical/Health; Women's Issues;
  Youth
Mission Statement Excerpt: "Global Citizen Year (GCY) seeks
  to re-envision the transition to college in the US as a unique
  opportunity for young Americans to cultivate a global
  education through a year of direct immersion in the developing world."
Year Founded: 2009
Number of Volunteers Last Year: 57, with a commitment to the
  Clinton Global Initiative to engage 1,000 young Americans
  by 2015
Funding Sources: Foundations and private donors
The Work They Do: GCY fellows work in both community and
  organizational placements; while some fellows work directly
  with an established organization, others may be matched
  with a community that offers them opportunities for
  involvement across a wider range of sectors. Fellows have
  worked on a range of topics, from public health to coffee
  cultivation, but regardless of the specific nature of the work,
  GCY seeks to expose emerging young leaders to the global
  challenges they will encounter in their academic and professional careers. As GCY fellows, volunteers may monitor the
  installation of efficient cookstoves, plant and harvest coffee,
  assist in pharmacies and clinics, build and stock a library,
  teach art and dance classes to at-risk youth, or any number
  of other projects in conjunction with GCY's varied local
  partners.

Project Location: GCY currently works in Senegal, Brazil, and Ecuador, with a planned expansion into Asia. Fellows work at a variety of sites: some conduct house visits around a region, and others focus their efforts on a certain town or village. Fellows' placement locations include the Millennium Villages Project location in Senegal, small mountain towns of Ecuador, and beachside cities of Brazil, where they work with urban youth in local community centers. Some fellows perform physical tasks such as lifting sacks of coffee, while others work in laboratories or clinics. Fellows live with carefully screened host families who provide a cultural immersion environment as well as a point of entry into the communities in which they are placed. Although conditions vary greatly across countries, and even communities, fellows can expect water, electricity, a single-gender room, and an on-site latrine or toilet.

Time Line: Volunteers begin preparing for their experience in the summer and then depart in September, returning ten months later in May. All volunteers participate on this time line.

Cost: GCY does not want the ability to pay to be a barrier to participation, so they do not apply a flat fee to all participants. Instead, they work with each family to determine an appropriate program fee; the remaining costs are covered by financial aid. The full program fee is $26,300, but a full financial aid package could cover everything except a $500 deposit. The program fee is all-inclusive, including international airfare.

Getting Started: Applications are available online and are due in November, February, and May, with applications accepted on a rolling basis thereafter. The selection process is rigorous and requires both letters of reference and interviews with the prospective applicant and the applicant's parents. Interviews are done in person whenever possible and over the phone in all other cases. Selected fellows have a two-week training program in the United States, led by experts in business, education, and social entrepreneurship. Once

Madeleine, age 19, tries her hand at sifting peanuts outside her host family's home in Leona, Senegal. *Photo courtesy of Madeleine Balchan*

in-country, they have a month of orientation and complete ongoing training throughout their experience, highlighted by monthly seminars. Finally, they complete a reentry training upon return to help smooth their transition back home and into college.

Needed Skills and Specific Populations: GCY seeks emerging young leaders who demonstrate all or most of the following qualities: resourcefulness, independence, resilience, adaptability, passion, and curiosity. Applicants must be in the bridge year between high school and college; those with disabilities will be accommodated on a case-by-case basis. Fellows must be US citizens or legal permanent residents. Families cannot volunteer with GCY.

Jigeen Jambar: The Women Warriors of Senegal

By Madeleine Balchan

Global Citizen Year (GCY)

Suma yaay (my mom), Ndiy, tried to escape to the field without me, but I was ready: lathered in sunscreen and wearing my capris and bandanna. Even as Ndiy protested I'd be hungry and tired, I hopped on the crowded carriage at 9 AM—a wooden slab laden with 10 women and their large buckets and bowls, all pulled by one horse. Is this a moment when insisting I can get my hands dirty has gotten my mom legitimately mad?

Raking my hands through the sand to find straggling peanuts, I could feel the sun beating on the strip of back above my pants that my shirt exposes when I lean over like this. Note to self: next time wear a longer shirt. I worked on my own, feeling stupid for insisting on coming, and talking to myself: you *will* stay out here until 7 PM with them. You *will not* be hungry. Just because they have a system of working in pairs and you're the odd man out, you *will* show them that you can be helpful: like preparing each pile for the separation process . . . they'll be glad you came. Hopefully . . .

"*Nafi Kia!* [Come over here!]" Fatou Sec, my neighbor, who must be 50 years old, called from across the field. I went as beckoned. She handed me a woven wooden basket with gaps—a peanut sifter—and showed me how to use it. "*Baxna! Yow laay fi.* [Good, you sift here for me.]" The sun was giving me a nice burnt stripe on my back, but I continued sifting for Fatou for an hour and a half. It didn't take long before other people began summoning me to sift for them.

Ndiy told me to rest; the sun was turning my *tubab* (white person) skin *xonk* (red, pronounced "honk"). I told her I'd rest when she did and continued sifting. Everyone began calling me *Jambar*, which means warrior.

Eventually Ndiy let me try *guttehing* (wind winnowing)— slowly dumping the mixture of peanuts and hay. The wind carries away the lighter sticks and empty shells, and after approximately 9,873 times, they're left with only good peanuts. Holding a heavy tub of peanuts way above my head is an acquired skill, and I wasn't doing it quite right. They had me go back to sifting. I looked over at Fatou Sec, who had been doing this work for hours and was still going strong. *Jambar* (warrior). We finally began walking back at 6:30 PM— each woman carrying a heavy tub of peanuts on her head for the entire 30-minute walk.

The next morning, Fatou came over, bragging about me to my father, Djiby: "*Nafi jambar!* [She is a warrior!]" I stopped her and said what I'd been thinking about the women here for weeks but had yet to say aloud. "*Jigeen fi, jambar.* [You women, you are warriors.] You wake up early, sweep sand out of the house, wash the kids, make breakfast, do the laundry, cook lunch, go to the fields, come home, cook dinner, wash the kids, sweep the house, go to bed late, and wake up the next day to do it all over again." "*Waaw, liggeey, liggeey, liggeey rekk!* [Yes, work, work, work only!]" She agreed.

Her next comment couldn't have made me happier. "*Jigeenu Senegal Jambar. Yow jigeenu Senegal. Yow, jambar.* [Yes, Senegalese women are warriors. You're a Senegalese woman. You're a *jambar*.]"

Global Citizens Network (GCN)

129 North 2nd Street, #102
Minneapolis, MN 55401
(612) 436-8270 or (800) 644-9292; Fax (612) 436-8298
E-mail: info@globalcitizens.org
Website: www.globalcitizens.org

Project Type: Community Development; Education; Rural
Development; Social Justice

Mission Statement Excerpt: "In partnership with people of
diverse cultures, GCN promotes cross-cultural understanding and interconnectedness through authentic
immersion experiences."

Year Founded: 1992

Number of Volunteers Last Year: 200

Funding Sources: Individual private donors

The Work They Do: GCN carries out community development
and cultural immersion programs. Participants stay with
local families or at other facilities within the community
while working on site-directed development projects. Examples of volunteer projects include building health clinics,
renovating a youth center, and teaching in a primary school.
Examples of specific volunteer tasks include recording the
stories of elders, roofing housing for refugees, building
retaining walls for school buildings, refurbishing community
centers, and building health clinics.

Project Location: Projects take place in the United States
(Arizona, Minnesota, and Washington) as well as internationally in Canada, Kenya, Tanzania, Nepal, Thailand,
Mexico, Guatemala, Ecuador, Peru, and Brazil. GCN
arranges immersive lodging and other accommodations in
remote, rural communities. Accommodations will vary, but
the team will often be divided in pairs (or more) among
local host families. Housing ranges from bedding provided
by families to sleeping on bed mats in community locales.
Participants experience riding local transportation, taking

Volunteers and members of the Luo people of Odienya, Kenya, take a break from laying brick to build a local health clinic in their community. *Photo courtesy of Global Citizens Network*

bucket showers, and cooking on wood-burning stoves. Some GCN sites are located at high altitude and others are in jungle regions. For volunteer sites in Africa, Latin America, and Asia, trip participants usually bring sleeping bags, bed mats, and mosquito nets.

Time Line: Projects take place throughout the year and last from 10 to 21 days. Participants may arrange for back-to-back volunteer stints for a total of six weeks.

Cost: Costs vary according to the length and location of the project, but they range from $900 for sites in the United States to $2,850 for international programs. Program fees include food and lodging, a donation to the project, training materials, and emergency medical and evacuation insurance (for non-US sites), and in-country transportation. Program fees do not include airfare. A portion of the fees go to cover GCN program costs. Discounts are available for returning volunteers, children, groups, and those who register early.

Getting Started: Prospective volunteers can download an application from GCN's website, or they can call or e-mail to request an application. Predeparture orientation is provided to volunteers by the team leader via e-mail or telephone. During the first evening of the volunteer experience, all teams hold an orientation meeting; daily team meetings are held for the duration of the project.

Needed Skills and Specific Populations: Trip participants must have a willingness to experience and accept a new culture. No specific physical or occupational skills are required. Volunteers must be at least eight years old, and participants under the age of 18 must be accompanied by an adult. Senior citizens are "absolutely!" encouraged to volunteer with GCN. Prospective volunteers with disabilities should confer with GCN before applying to ensure that accommodations will be available. Because of their unusually low minimum age requirement, GCN is particularly family friendly. GCN also has no citizenship requirements for its volunteers.

Finding Myself in Nepal

By Judy Wachs

Global Citizens Network (GCN)

I just returned from a Global Citizens Network trip to Nepal. I was part of a team placed in the Tibetan refugee village of Jampoling to assist in the repair of some roofs damaged by the recent monsoons. Ah, but it was so much more than just construction. What I found a world away from my comfort zone was an appreciation of what is really important in life. I met and interacted with people who had nothing materially, but who functioned with a spirit that I have never seen before. Each and every person, from a three-year-old to a senior citizen who had escorted the Dahli Lama over the mountains to India 30 years previously, had a love of life and an appreciation for peace that was truly magical.

Yes, we did repair a roof. But there was so much more. The interaction with the people, the daily teatime, the sharing of meals. All of it showed me a way of life that was peaceful and loving. We exchanged gifts and stories. We interacted in a way that one could never do on a typical vacation tour. I celebrated my 75th birthday there, and my team and the cooks and the villagers all combined to make it one of the best birthdays I had ever experienced. From the first day we arrived, we were treated royally and reciprocated this treatment.

A closing ceremony was held at the end of our time in the village. It involved 40 pounds of rice pudding, scarves, and speeches. My team truly joined in with the community to do the work, to live, and then to say goodbye and thank you. With tears in our eyes, we drove away on our last day convinced that we had indeed made a difference in their lives, but what they didn't know was that they had also changed ours, and we will never forget.

Global Crossroad

4425 West Airport Freeway, Suite 210
Irving, Texas 75062
(866) 387-7816; Fax: (972) 852-7999
E-mail: info@globalcrossroad.com
Website: www.globalcrossroad.com

Project Type: Education; Medical/Health; Natural Conservation (Land); Natural Conservation (Sea); Orphans; Women's Issues

Mission Statement Excerpt: "Global Crossroad's focus on grassroots projects, cultural immersion, and travel learning opportunities reflects the unique, alternative approach that we have adopted to garner memorable experiences for our volunteers."

Year Founded: 2002

Number of Volunteers Last Year: More than 10,000

Funding Sources: None; Global Crossroad is self-funded

The Work They Do: Global Crossroad offers volunteer placements in a variety of projects. In each host country, Global Crossroad has developed a project working with disadvantaged children and teaching English; additional projects vary depending on the country. Conservation projects range from maintaining trails in national parks to supporting reforestation, from sea turtle conservation on the Pacific coast to an elephant conservation program in Asia. Community development projects include working with local women's groups on microcredit development in India, working on a community organic coffee farm, and even assisting with a variety of projects in a single community pertaining to self-sustainability. Volunteers may help care for children in an orphanage, teaching them English, leading them in games and activities, helping to cook and distribute food at mealtimes, and mentoring the children. Volunteers in health care projects assist a local doctor or nurse in a health clinic or hospital to the extent that their skills and experiences allow.

Project Location: Global Crossroad currently operates in over 17 countries, including Argentina, Cambodia, China, Costa Rica, Ecuador, Ghana, Guatemala, India, Kenya, Nepal, Peru, South Africa, Sri Lanka, Tanzania, and Thailand. Because of the enormous variety of projects and host countries, the work settings vary tremendously. Projects involving children are usually indoor projects and are usually set in an orphanage, children's home, or school. The Costa Rica turtle and Sri Lanka elephant orphanage conservation projects are usually outdoors, and they often involve considerable physical labor. Depending on the exact placement, lodging may be with a host family, at a hostel, or at a "home base" (a Global Crossroad–owned home for volunteers). Most lodging is with host families, especially in Africa and Latin America. Food is included as part of the placements and is usually provided by the host family; volunteers staying at hostels or hotels may eat there or at local restaurants.

Time Line: Projects begin on the first and third Mondays of each month. The minimum volunteer stint is one week, and the maximum is usually 12 weeks (this can sometimes be extended to 24 weeks, depending on the country's visa regulations). The average volunteer works for Global Crossroad for about six weeks.

Cost: Global Crossroad's program fees run from $70 to approximately $2,500, averaging about $1,000. Most program fees include all housing, meals, and comprehensive travel insurance. The program fee does not include airfare to the host country, visa and airport fees, or immunizations.

Getting Started: Prospective volunteers can apply either online through Global Crossroad's website or by completing and submitting an application form (which can be downloaded from the website) and submitting it by mail. Prior to arrival in their chosen countries, volunteers receive a predeparture booklet and placement details. On the first day of their projects, volunteers receive a one-day orientation session that covers safety, health, culture and customs, general information on the country, and an introduction to the project, host family, and living conditions. A one-week language and cultural orientation course is offered as an optional beginning for the volunteer trip.

Needed Skills and Specific Populations: Health care placements require that the volunteer have a health care background, such as being a medical student, nurse, or therapist, or having extensive volunteer experience in a hospital. Teaching positions in China and Thailand require that the applicant be a native English speaker. Volunteers aged 15 and under must be accompanied by a parent or close adult relative; Global Crossroad has hosted a number of families. Volunteers aged 16 and 17 may volunteer unaccompanied but must have a permission letter from their parents. Senior volunteers in good health are welcome to volunteer. Volunteers with disabilities should contact Global Crossroad's office to discuss their specific needs.

Global Humanitarian Expeditions (GHE)

602 South Ogden Street
Denver, CO 80209
(303) 858-8857; Fax: (303) 649-9017
E-mail: kimt@globaldentalrelief.org or
info@globaldentalrelief.org
Website: www.globaldentalrelief.org

Project Type: Community Development; Medical/Health;
Orphans; Youth

Mission Statement Excerpt: "The mission of Global
Humanitarian Expeditions is to recruit and connect volunteers to meaningful experiences with charitable
organizations in the United States and around the world."

Year Founded: 2002

Number of Volunteers Last Year: 170

Funding Sources: Individual donors

The Work They Do: GHE provides education, community
development, and health care services to children in need.
Projects include setting up and running mobile dental clinics
that provide dental care and education to children; building
schools; working with local communities to develop income-
generating programs that help the communities maintain
autonomy and become self-sufficient; and working with
teachers to develop teaching curriculum. Volunteers assist in
these projects by providing dental care as a dentist,
hygienist, or nondental volunteer. Nondental volunteers
manage patient flow in and out of clinics; teach oral hygiene
instruction; keep records; train teachers in reading, writing,
and math education skills; or participate as part of the
community development team by working with local
communities to develop income-generating programs.

Project Location: GHE works in Nepal, India, Vietnam,
Guatemala, and Nicaragua. The work sites vary greatly
from project to project, but most take place in rural village
locations that are within driving distance of larger cities.

163

Dental clinics are set up in school classrooms, as are education and community development projects. GHE's school-building projects are more physically demanding than are their other projects. All lunches are brought in from nearby restaurants that meet GHE health standards. GHE also provides bottled water for volunteers at the project site and in their hotels at night. Accommodations vary depending on location and type of project, but, in general, volunteers stay in two- or three-star hotels. In some cases, especially in Nepal and Nicaragua, volunteers may camp during part or all of their volunteer experience, in which case GHE provides tents, food, showers, bathrooms, and other necessities for volunteers.

Time Line: GHE operates 10 to 12 volunteer projects each year between January and May and between July and November. Projects run for a minimum of seven days and a maximum of one month.

Cost: GHE's program fee for one week of volunteering is $890, which includes most meals, accommodations, and all in-country transportation; volunteers are responsible for their own airfare to the country of service. GHE also offers volunteers the opportunity to follow their week of volunteering with a week of sightseeing, in which case the program fee is approximately $3,800; this fee includes international airfare from Los Angeles or San Francisco. The exception to this is Guatemala, which is just $2,280 for the volunteering-plus-sightseeing option.

Getting Started: Prospective volunteers complete an application packet, available upon request from GHE. The application packet includes information on the volunteer's experiences, skills, and expectations. Volunteers should apply at least six to eight months before their desired departure date. Interviews are not required, but GHE does talk with prospective volunteers by phone before departure. Training and orientation is completed in-country, and volunteers receive a pre-departure packet of information.

Needed Skills and Specific Populations: Medical volunteers must have appropriate licensure; nonmedical volunteers are not required to have any specialized credentials, just flexibility and a willingness to serve the host community. The minimum age is 12 years old, but only one or two children will be accepted on each project; there is no maximum age for volunteers. GHE welcomes volunteers with disabilities, and encourages these volunteers to talk with a staff member to determine which placement might be most appropriate to accommodate their specific needs. Families are welcome to volunteer with GHE, but all family members are expected to volunteer and assist with the project.

Global Potential (GP)

c/o Encuentro 5
33 Harrison Avenue, 5th floor
Boston, MA 02111
(617) 544-7523
E-mail: info@global-potential.org
Website: www.global-potential.org

Project Type: Community Development; Construction; Education; Rural Development; Social Justice; Women's Issues; Youth

Mission Statement Excerpt: "To provide urban youth from low-income communities with the skills and perspective that enable them to effect positive change in their lives, communities, and the global community, through engagement in leadership training, social entrepreneurship, international cultural exchange, and service-learning."

Year Founded: 2007

Number of Volunteers Last Year: 90

Funding Sources: Government grants, foundation support, and private donations

The Work They Do: Global Potential empowers low-income urban youth aged 15 to 23 to create positive change in their lives and communities. For five months, youth participants engage in a social entrepreneurship and leadership training program at their high school, in which they gain skills and knowledge that will prepare them to live and volunteer for six and a half weeks in a rural village in a developing country. During this initial phase and the international experience that follows, GP youth hold discussions, workshops, and youth conferences on gender, racism, migration, human rights, culture, identity, poverty, and sexual and reproductive health and HIV/AIDS, and they learn Spanish and Creole. During their international experience, GP volunteers teach English and literacy, operate day-camp programs, collect census data, build irrigation canals and latrines, paint murals, serve in local health clinics, and help with community cleanup efforts. Youth volunteers also engage in twice-weekly internships with local village leaders, curriculum classes, group reflection, personal reflection, and individual advising sessions; create family biographies and portraits for each of their host families; and conceive and produce documentary films. Upon returning to their home communities, youth engage for the next 10½ months in their selected professional or personal track, which is based on social enterprise, community development and activism, documentary filmmaking, or leadership in the school, and internship within Global Potential.

Project Location: The international volunteer projects take place in Haiti, the Dominican Republic, and Nicaragua; youth volunteers also complete projects in their home communities as a part of their training. While abroad, all accommodations are in homestays with local families with whom GP has an existing relationship and who are selected by local village leadership councils.

Time Line: The international portion of the GP program takes place in the summer, usually in July and August, for six or seven weeks.

Cost: Youth volunteers do not pay a program fee, but are expected to raise $300 each. This covers all expenses associated with the GP experience, including airfare. Volunteer staff pay airfare and homestay costs to subsidize some of the cost for the youth. This has never surpassed $950, and GP works with every volunteer staff member to fundraise and find funds when possible.

Getting Started: Prospective summer staff volunteers should send a resume and cover letter by e-mail to Global Potential by December of the year before they want to volunteer; those who wish to volunteer during the rest of the year should contact Global Potential by June. There are no set deadlines, but spots fill up quickly. Prospective volunteers must interview in person at the GP offices when possible; phone interviews may be arranged as necessary. Extensive

predeparture training takes place at the youth volunteer's
high school or at the GP offices.

Needed Skills and Specific Populations: Youth and other volunteers must have an eagerness to help other communities and to learn from the GP process; Spanish, Creole, or French language skills are a plus. Youth must be between 15 and 23 years old. GP has opportunities for volunteer staff members to conduct training and accompany the students during their international experience; these volunteers must be at least 20 years old. Volunteers with disabilities are welcome, and GP partners with Mobility International USA to make reasonable accommodations. Youth volunteers come from low-income families in inner-city neighborhoods; siblings and cousins are welcome to volunteer together with GP. Most of GP's volunteers come from New York and Boston, though they are open to accepting applications from youth in other cities, as long as training can be arranged.

An Unusual Friendship and a Transformative Trip

By Jessica Bolen

Global Potential (GP)

Jean and Lesly make for an unusual pair of friends. Both are seniors at a public high school in Crown Heights, Brooklyn, yet they come from different backgrounds and possess contrasting demeanors. Jean is originally from Haiti, while Lesly is from Honduras. Jean is a reserved young man who speaks quietly, listens well, and has always wanted to help others. Lesly is a former gang leader who exudes charisma, expressiveness, and passion. Yet their joint involvement in Global Potential, including their volunteer service trips to the Dominican Republic and Nicaragua, helped them to see past their differences and work together for a common purpose: to change the world.

In their efforts to make a change in the world, Jean and Lesly's relationship has also changed. Although there used to be tension and the threat of violence between them, Jean assisted in recruiting Lesly and drawing him away from a life of gangs. Now they work hand in hand to impact the lives of other teenagers in their neighborhood. Rather than feel threatened or marginalized because of their differences, Jean and Lesly now realize that their varying experiences, skills, and personalities promote a diversity of perspectives and a deeper understanding of local and global issues. Through their participation in Global Potential, Jean and Lesly have come to learn that the power of genuine, lasting change does not rest in the hands of a single individual but, rather, in the solidarity of many unique individuals working toward a common cause.

Global Reach Institute (GRI)

P.O. Box 2229
Coeur d'Alene, ID 83816
(888) 727-3224; Fax: (866) 741-8480
E-mail: info@globalreachinstitute.org
Website: www.globalreachinstitute.org

Project Type: Community Development; Economic Development; Education; Medical/Health; Natural Conservation (Land); Orphans; Youth

Mission Statement Excerpt: "The mission of Global Reach Institute (GRI) is to empower and inspire each of us to act on our humanitarian spirit by sharing international friendships, education, and experience through journeys abroad."

Year Founded: 2005

Number of Volunteers Last Year: 1,100

Funding Sources: Foundations and private donors

The Work They Do: GRI partners with a volunteer hosting organization in southern Africa to provide volunteers with opportunities in education, medicine, child care, HIV/AIDS awareness, construction, conservation, photography, coaching, and animal rehabilitation. Volunteers are placed individually with these host organizations in specific positions that can best utilize their talents and abilities for the good of the host community, while also filling the volunteer's needs and wishes. Examples of possible volunteer projects include child care in orphanages, constructing a community library, and feeding baby lions.

Project Location: GRI primarily works in Africa, specifically in South Africa, Botswana, Namibia, Lesotho, Mozambique, Zambia, Tanzania, Uganda, Kenya, Madagascar, Swaziland, Ghana, Malawi, and Zimbabwe. They also have a limited number of placement opportunities in Asia. Volunteer accommodations vary widely by project site, but may include a guesthouse, hotel, dorm room, or thatched-roof hut.

Time Line: Volunteers can commit to projects that last anywhere from one week to six months or longer, depending on their individual needs and wishes. Most volunteers spend between two and three weeks on their project.

Cost: Program fees begin at $800 for short-term programs in the United States and rise from there, depending on program and placement. The program fee includes airport transfers, accommodations, and all meals; it does not include international airfare to the country of service.

Getting Started: Prospective volunteers should contact GRI by e-mail or phone to discuss their interests and how they might match up with the hosting organizations' needs before completing an application. In-country project managers will then match volunteers with projects. Orientation takes place once the volunteer is on-site.

Needed Skills and Specific Populations: Required skills depend on the placement site; some organizations require specific skills, while others do not. Because of this, GRI does not have a stated minimum age, as placement depends more on skill sets than age; senior volunteers are welcome with approval from their doctor. GRI will cooperate with volunteers with disabilities to ensure that they find projects that fit their skill sets and needed accommodations. GRI also encourages volunteer families and will work with them to find one or more appropriate projects to fit their needs.

Global Routes

1 Short Street
Northampton, MA 01060
(413) 585-8895; Fax: (413) 585-8810
E-mail: mail@globalroutes.org
Website: www.globalroutes.org

Project Type: Community Development; Construction; Education; Natural Conservation (Land); Orphans; Rural Development; Youth

Mission Statement Excerpt: "Global Routes . . . [sends] people of all ages throughout the world to participate in community service projects both in groups and individually."

Year Founded: 1986

Number of Volunteers Last Year: 300

Funding Sources: None; Global Routes is self-funded

The Work They Do: Global Routes volunteers participate in projects focused on teaching, community development, construction, work with children, and environmental conservation. Working in groups, volunteers build community centers, schoolhouses, playgrounds, and health clinics in rural communities. Volunteers teach in primary and secondary schools in rural settings. In some instances, they have their own classrooms; in others, they will serve as a tutor or teacher's aide. Volunteers also undertake additional small-scale development projects consistent with their own interests and the needs of the local community. Such projects can include working with women's cooperatives, offering an English class for adults in the evenings, organizing a choir or a day camp, or working on hygiene or sanitation projects.

Project Location: Projects take place in Belize, Cambodia, China, Costa Rica, the Dominican Republic, Ecuador, Ghana, India, Kenya, Nepal, Peru, Tanzania, and Thailand. Accommodations consist of host-family homes or group living situations in rural villages or small towns, and food is provided. Volunteers generally work in school settings that are basic. In some instances, there is only one classroom and no electricity; in other cases, schools are larger, with several classrooms, electricity, and other amenities. Volunteers typically live with a family in a simple home, generally with electricity and indoor plumbing, though this can vary from country to country. Volunteers have their own sleeping area within the home. In some instances, volunteers live in an apartment in a larger town and either commute to their village school or work at a school in the town.

Time Line: High school programs run for 2 to 5 weeks in the summer; gap-year and college programs run for 7 weeks in the summer and 12 weeks in the fall, winter, and spring. Adults are placed throughout the year for varying lengths of time.

Cost: Program fees range from $4,000 to $6,500. All fees include accommodations, food, and all in-country costs other than personal expenses. Volunteers must provide their own airfare. Adults participating via an independent placement pay a $1,400 fee plus $40 per week for food and accommodations.

Getting Started: Applications are available on Global Routes' website, and a phone interview is required for gap-year and older participants. The in-country orientation lasts from 4 to 10 days.

Needed Skills and Specific Populations: Volunteers must be at least 14 years old to participate in high school programs, 17 years old for gap-year/college programs, and a minimum of 18 years old for an independent placement. Volunteers with disabilities cannot be accommodated. Global Routes has organized some individualized family trips in Africa, Asia, and Latin America.

Global Service Corps (GSC)

3543 18th Street, #14
San Francisco, CA 94110
(415) 551-0000; Fax: (415) 861-8969
E-mail: gsc@globalservicecorps.org
Website: www.globalservicecorps.org

Project Type: Agriculture; Community Development; Education;
Medical/Health; Orphans; Professional/Technical Assistance;
Rural Development; Youth

Mission Statement Excerpt: "Global Service Corps' mission is to
design and implement community development programs
that benefit the volunteers and positively impact the communities they serve."

Year Founded: 1992

Number of Volunteers Last Year: 85

Funding Sources: The United States Department of Agriculture
and Canadian Food Grains Bank fund some of the GSC's
rural development projects in Tanzania

The Work They Do: GSC is a nonprofit international volunteer
organization that provides volunteer opportunities for
people to live and work in Cambodia, Thailand, or Tanzania. In Cambodia, volunteers work on HIV/AIDS education and prevention, sustainable agriculture, public health,
and orphanage care programs. In Thailand, volunteers work
on orphanage care, English education, and Buddhist immersion projects. Programs available in Tanzania involve sustainable agriculture, nutrition and hunger relief, public
health, and HIV/AIDS prevention. GSC volunteers assist
with agricultural demonstration plots, help teach sustainable
agriculture methods of farming and other food security
innovations, and provide HIV/AIDS awareness talks and
seminars. GSC also runs an annual Life Skills HIV/AIDS
education and prevention summer youth day camp in
Tanzania and Cambodia.

Project Location: GSC's projects in Cambodia are located in
Phnom Penh and surrounding areas; in Thailand, they are
located in the Singburi and Rajburi Provinces; in Tanzania,
projects are located in Arusha and surrounding rural
villages reaching Maasai and other indigenous cultures.
Volunteers are immersed in the cultures in which they work.
Volunteers stay with local host families in homes that are
"comfortable by Western standards." All meals and project-
related transportation are included in the program fee, and
host families often include their volunteer guests in outings
and activities and teach them about the culture, lifestyles,
and family customs. Each volunteer has his or her own
furnished room, and GSC can arrange for friends or couples
to stay together.

Time Line: Projects are carried out year-round with monthly
start dates in each country. Applications are accepted on a
first-come, first-served basis. Participants must volunteer for
at least two weeks; volunteers have stayed up to six months
previously, though GSC may allow volunteers to stay even
longer than this. The average volunteer stays for several
weeks.

Cost: Program fees begin at $1,480. The program fees include a
cultural orientation and technical training in the first week,
language lessons, airport pickup and project transportation,
accommodations in a hotel, hostel, or homestay, all meals, a
weekend excursion, project administration, and support.
International airfare is not included in the program fee.

Getting Started: To apply, prospective volunteers should submit
an online application through the GSC website and, in the
same online session, upload a resume and personal statement. A completed application form, downloaded from the
online session, should be sent with a $300 deposit (refund-
able upon completion of program). Upon registration for a
project, volunteers receive an orientation manual with information on the country and the program, a reading list, a
packing list, and other health and travel tips. Volunteers

also receive an on-site orientation and technical training, which is conducted by the in-country coordinators and includes language lessons and cultural tips for successful immersion.

Needed Skills and Specific Populations: GSC does not require that volunteers have specific skills, since the organization provides orientation and technical training at the start of the project. Volunteers should, however, have a mature and respectful attitude and a desire to make a difference in the country in which they choose to volunteer. Volunteers must be at least 18 years old, unless they are accompanied by a parent or legal guardian; families are encouraged to apply. Seniors and volunteers with disabilities are also encouraged to apply, as long as they can successfully and safely complete rural trainings and program requirements. Accommodations will be made when possible.

Global Vision International (GVI)

66 Long Wharf, Suite 562
Boston, MA 02110
(888) 653-6028; Fax: (617) 674-2109
E-mail: info@gviworld.com
Website: www.gviusa.com

Project Type: Community Development; Construction; Education; Natural Conservation (Sea); Orphans; Rural Development; Scientific Research

Mission Statement Excerpt: "Global Vision International aims to promote the advancement of sustainable development through the creation of partnerships, promotion of local and global education, opportunities and via direct financial support."

Year Founded: 1998

Number of Volunteers Last Year: Over 3,000

Funding Sources: None

The Work They Do: GVI runs conservation and humanitarian projects, working locally to promote sustainable development through environment research, conservation, and education. Examples of GVI's projects include working with indigenous communities in Central and South America, participating in a rain forest conservation and community development expedition in Ecuador, marine conservation in the Seychelles, teaching Buddhist monks in Laos, and monitoring humpback whale activity in Brazil. Specific tasks might include teaching and lesson planning, building an energy-efficient stove, collecting and collating scientific data, mist netting for birds, survey diving, data collection, or environmental education.

Project Location: GVI operates volunteer projects in over 40 countries worldwide, including Kenya, Seychelles, South Africa, India, Laos, Thailand, Vanuatu, Australia, Costa Rica, Guatemala, Honduras, Mexico, Nicaragua, Greece, Romania, Brazil, Ecuador, and Peru. GVI has a wide range of housing options for volunteers, depending on the placement site, including host families, dormitories, shared apartments, and camping.

Time Line: GVI's projects operate year-round, and most projects have weekly start dates. Volunteers can sign up for projects that last anywhere from one week to one year.

Cost: Short-term, two-week programs begin at around $1,000; fees range up to $4,695 for 10-week expeditions and even higher for longer-term programs, which can last for more than six months. In general, GVI's program fees include all meals and accommodations, as well as airport transfers; international airfare is not included.

Getting Started: Applications are accepted online via GVI's website on a rolling basis, without deadlines. Applicants do not complete an interview but do talk informally with a GVI regional coordinator, who will answer any questions that the volunteer may have. Before departing for their volunteer experience, participants receive a field manual with details on their placement site, as well as safety and predeparture training information.

Needed Skills and Specific Populations: GVI provides training for any required skills. Volunteers must be at least 18 years old; there is no upper limit on volunteer age. Youth who are accompanied by family members may be allowed; family applications are screened on a case-by-case basis. Similarly, applications from volunteers with disabilities will be reviewed individually to ensure suitability and feasibility of placement sites.

Global Volunteer Network (GVN)

P.O. Box 30-968
Lower Hutt 6001
New Zealand
(800) 963-1198
E-mail: info@volunteer.org.nz
Website: www.globalvolunteernetwork.org

Project Type: Agriculture; Community Development; Construction; Education; Medical/Health; Natural Conservation (Land); Orphans; Trail Building/Maintenance

Mission Statement Excerpt: "Our vision is to connect people with communities in need. We do this by supporting the work of local community organizations through the placement of international volunteers."

Year Founded: 2001

Number of Volunteers Last Year: 1,400, contributing to a total of more than 14,500 volunteers

Funding Sources: No outside sources

The Work They Do: GVN offers volunteer opportunities in the areas of teaching, environmental work, wildlife care, orphanages, disabled children, medicine, HIV/AIDS education, and economic sustainability. Working with partner organizations, volunteers may teach in a school in Ghana, help in an orphanage in Vietnam, work with mistreated wildlife in Thailand, or participate in reforestation projects on the Galapagos Islands.

Project Location: GVN runs projects in Cambodia, China, Costa Rica, Ecuador, Ethiopia, Ghana, Guatemala, India, Kenya, Nepal, Panama, Peru, Philippines, Rwanda, South Africa, Thailand, Uganda, the United States, and Vietnam. Volunteers generally live and work in the same conditions as members of the host community.

Time Line: Projects are available throughout the year and range from one week to six months in length. The average volunteer project is about four weeks long.

Kent, an 18-year-old volunteer in Kenya, heads home to his host family after volunteering all day, accompanied by a friendly crowd of orphaned children. *Photo courtesy of Kent McIlraith/Global Volunteer Network*

Cost: All volunteers pay an application fee of $97, which allows them to participate in as many projects as the volunteer wishes for five years. Program fees vary by project, but they average about $1,997 for four weeks. Each program varies, but most program fees cover accommodations, meals, and most in-country costs; volunteers are responsible for airfare, insurance, and visas.

Getting Started: Volunteer application forms are available on GVN's website. Applications are accepted on a rolling basis. Partner organizations provide training and orientation programs; the length and content of this training and orientation varies from program to program. Applicants are not required to complete an interview as a part of the application process.

Needed Skills and Specific Populations: With the exception of medical projects, most programs do not require specialized skills. Families are welcome on a number of GVN's programs. Most projects require volunteers to be at least 18 years old, GVN offers a specialized Youth Tour for 15- to 17-year-olds. Senior volunteers are welcomed but are advised that some project sites are more physically strenuous than others. Prospective volunteers with disabilities will be considered on a case-by-case basis.

Lay Down Your Heart

By Hannah Ford

Global Volunteer Network (GVN)

I stepped through the doorway of Sea View Sculpture Art Centre in Bagamoyo, Tanzania, and was overwhelmed by the sea of smiling faces that greeted me with handshakes and light fist punches. A swirl of foreign names filled my head as I was introduced to each student. They called me *mwalimu*, which is Swahili for teacher. I suggested they just call me Hannah, but the response was a chorus of "oh nooo." Teachers are highly respected within Tanzanian culture. One of the students presented me with the only seat while everyone else gathered in a circle, sitting either on the ground or on logs of wood that would later be carved into works of art. As I looked around at the 15 faces, alive with excitement at the prospect of what I might teach them, I suddenly felt ill-equipped for the task. These were professional artists, their talent and imagination evident all around me. Within this crumbling ruined building, beneath the only remaining section of roof, they displayed their art: brightly painted canvases, detailed wood carvings, cement castings of heads in all shapes and sizes, beaded jewelry, and knitted bags. It dawned on me that for the first time in my life, I was a teacher. What would I teach with the limited materials available? Would I have anything new to teach them? What did they expect from me? It wasn't too long before I discovered my students weren't expecting anything specific from me but were simply grateful I was there. They were ready to absorb whatever knowledge I could impart that might help develop or promote their art, which in turn would sustain their living.

What took place in the following months was, more than anything, a sharing of ideas, cultures, and past learnings. When our first project, a collection of Tibetan-inspired mandala paintings, was displayed in the windows, the pride in the smiling faces of my students filled me with warmth and confirmed why I was there. Occasionally I struggled with the concept of being a *mzungu* (white person) in a country where being white equals wealth. But when I walked through the door of Sea View each day, these feelings evaporated. Here I was not viewed in terms of my skin color, my gender, or my age—I was simply a teacher and a friend.

I filled my days teaching English with my gradually improving Swahili, introducing Australian art, creating papier-mâché masterpieces, hand-drawn business cards, and painted gift cards, and learning from my students. I was always learning. The foundations upon which Sea View was built were so much stronger than the crumbling ruins from which the group works. Together they laid the groundwork of community and, gradually, layer upon layer of shared ideas and inspiration have been added. Each canvas is a window into an individual's view of the world in which they live. Each intricately carved sculpture captures an expression, a gesture, a moment. The open doorway (without a door) leads into a world where artistic expression, in all its forms, is valued. Between the cracked and crumbling walls lives a shared belief in the power of art to convey a story, to educate people about a culture. The finished product is a building that is a work of art in itself. It exists not only in its material nature, or what is left of it, but deep in the hearts of those who are a part of it. The thing that strikes me the most about volunteering is that once you do it, you can never walk away. You're inevitably tied to a place, a people . . . their stories take root somewhere deep within and you never forget. And neither do they. Lay down your heart.

Global Volunteers

375 East Little Canada Road
St. Paul, MN 55117
(800) 487-1074
E-mail: email@globalvolunteers.org
Website: www.globalvolunteers.org

Project Type: Community Development; Economic
Development; Education; Orphans; Rural Development;
Social Justice; Youth

Mission Statement Excerpt: "Global Volunteers engages short-
term volunteers to work on long-term development projects
in the areas of child and maternal education, nutrition,
health, and welfare under the direction of host community
partners worldwide."

Year Founded: 1984

Number of Volunteers Last Year: 2,800

Funding Sources: Global Volunteers receives a small number of
private donations, mostly from individuals

The Work They Do: Global Volunteers supports development
partnerships in more than 100 host communities through
ongoing volunteer assistance, direct project funding, host
community student scholarships, and child sponsorships.
Volunteers work on locally initiated projects, one-on-one
with local people and under the direction of community
leaders. Projects include teaching conversational English and
classroom subjects, caring for at-risk children, supporting
elders, assisting with family support projects, constructing
and repairing community buildings and facilities, working
to develop and promote natural resource conservation,
assisting with health care, conducting youth recreation
programs, and assisting with economic development and
capacity building. Working in cooperation with local
people, past Global Volunteers have built schools in
Tanzania and China; constructed community buildings in
Australian, Costa Rican, and Jamaican villages; built new
homes in Appalachia; assisted with physical therapy for

Ecuadorian and Peruvian children with disabilities; taught English to future leaders of China, eastern Poland, southern Italy, Hungary, Tanzania, Ghana, and Greece; and provided care to vulnerable babies in Romania and Brazil and orphans in Peru and southern India. Volunteers serve on teams of between 10 and 20 individuals and are led by local country managers or trained volunteer team leaders. Full-day work projects are planned by local hosts and in-country staff to comply with US IRS requirements for tax deductibility.

Project Location: Global Volunteers maintains development partnerships in China, the Cook Islands, Costa Rica, Ecuador, Ghana, Greece, Hungary, India, Italy, Jamaica, Mexico, Peru, Poland, Portugal, Romania, St. Lucia, South Africa, Tanzania, the United States, and Vietnam. While specific housing accommodations vary by country, volunteer teams are generally lodged in tourist hotels or guest houses, double occupancy, with single supplements available in many communities. Meals are shared as a team in the host community, with evening meals at area restaurants or prepared by local cooks.

Time Line: More than 170 programs are scheduled annually and are available year-round. The standard service program is 2 or 3 weeks, but 1-week options are available for most programs, and extended stays of up to 24 weeks are available in a few host communities.

Cost: Program fees range from $995 for one week in the continental United States to $3,195 for three weeks in Italy. Each fee includes a direct contribution to long-term development projects and covers the volunteer's meals and accommodations, as well as ground transportation, emergency medical evacuation insurance, and airport transfers. Volunteers must also pay for their airfare to the host country. Only 16 percent of the program fee goes toward administrative overhead. Discounts are available for students, groups, and families.

Getting Started: An online application is available at the Global Volunteers website; prospective volunteers can also call the

Frequent volunteer Kathleen Hubbard-Ismail returns to "her village" of Senchi Ferry, Ghana, several times a year to care for the elders and teach English language skills to the children. *Photo courtesy of Esther Kwarteng*

office to speak with a volunteer coordinator, who can give advice on which programs might be the most suitable. Although they do not have to be interviewed, applicants must provide personal references and complete a health and skills questionnaire, and they should apply 2 to 10 weeks before they wish to depart. Volunteers receive predeparture orientation materials that outline Global Volunteers' procedures and philosophy as well as project and country information and tips for responsible travel. The first few days of each program are devoted to extensive orientation sessions, team-building exercises, and community introductions, as well as to basic language instruction. Optional evening and weekend cultural and educational programs are planned.

Needed Skills and Specific Populations: Global Volunteers has welcomed families since 1984 and has one of the lowest minimum age requirements; it accepts volunteers as young as 6 for some programs and as young as 11 for others. Senior volunteers are encouraged to volunteer with Global Volunteers. Volunteers with minor disabilities may be able to serve with Global Volunteers, depending on project size and logistics; specifics should be discussed with a volunteer coordinator. Volunteers who wish to teach English must be native speakers.

A Volunteer Vacation That Changed My Life

By Kathleen Hubbard-Ismail

Global Volunteers

For the past 15 years, I have spent two weeks of my annual vacation doing volunteer work around the world. I was always afraid go to Africa, based on television programming that portrayed the continent as a warring, dirty, and unfriendly place with brutal poverty, disease, and danger. Finally I decided to go to Africa despite the negative portrait. I went to Ghana. And then I went back, again and again, a total of four times so far. And unlike any other place on earth, the children and the village of Senchi Ferry captured my heart.

Senchi Ferry is a safe, friendly, and joyous village, and the Queen Mother and Chiefs welcomed the volunteers with warmth and ceremony. No one asked for anything, but they offered us their generosity and wisdom. I grew to love and understand this community as we worked side-by-side during oppressively hot days to achieve the common goals that they want for their children. Their dreams are about health and education . . . they want their children to learn. They don't talk about cars or fancy houses. They talk about growing a mind. All the children want is to finish school so they can find a fulfilling job that allows them to help their family and community. I know this. I talked to the children. While there, I had the distinct honor of teaching for three delightful weeks. These beautiful children had no books, no paper, no crayons . . . all they had was a blackboard and a willing teacher. Yet they were eager and bright and hungry for any scrap of knowledge I could pass along to their open and thirsty minds.

This village is a community of harmony. There are Christians and Muslims here who live in peace, with understanding and tolerance. The Christians and Muslims' only difference is their dress; not their beliefs or values. To them, God is one God to be worshipped and glorified in each person's manner of choice. Listen to this wisdom coming from the small, unknown, unmapped village of Senchi Ferry, Ghana! How Washington, DC, Palestine, and Israel could learn from these wise people!

You learn so much on a volunteer vacation. As you can tell, this trip shattered my prejudices. You learn from the community, the country, and its history. You learn from the remarkably intelligent, giving, patient, and open volunteers who join you on your odyssey of sharing and giving in the community you serve. And you learn that you—personally—can truly make a difference.

I think of the news on the television about Africa; I think of the impressions a tour group would have driving through this village on their way to the next tourist site. Sure, they may stop, take a few pictures, and shake a hand or two. They'll even get that sought-after photo of the smiling face of that sweet African child. Their photos and my photos may look quite similar, but will their photos have that subtle touch of love shining through the smiling eyes of that sweet African child? Will they know that child's name, her family, her history, her life? No, they only have a snapshot taken while blowing through the village. When we volunteers, called *Obronies* (white folk), return home, we will have much more. We have sat in conversation with that elderly woman stirring her roiling pot of *fufu* (a local staple food) over an open fire. We have been the recipient of their outrageous laughter when we attempt our morning greeting in the local language Twi of

"*Me ho ye*" (I am doing well) as we stroll through the village on our way to work. We know the eagerness of a child who proudly waves his paper in the air with pride to show us how well he has done. We have sat with the Queen Mother and village Chiefs and learned of their dreams for the community that they so proudly serve. And . . . I have the profound advantage of being received by open, welcoming, and wise arms that hold no grudges but simply want to create a more meaningful future for their kids, that's all.

Ghana. Its history is unmatched. This place called Ghana truly captured my heart and the heart of other volunteers as well, who remain dear friends to this day. I'm committed to returning again and again to contribute what I can to this little corner of the world.

Global Works

2342 Broadway
Boulder, CO 80304
(303) 545-2202; Fax: (303) 545-2425
E-mail: info@globalworkstravel.com
Website: www.globalworkstravel.com

Project Type: Community Development; Construction; Education; Natural Conservation (Land); Natural Conservation (Sea); Rural Development; Trail Building/Maintenance

Mission Statement Excerpt: "Global Works strives to provide young adults with rewarding service, language learning, and adventure travel programs, which foster personal growth and promote social and cultural awareness for the participant and the communities involved."

Year Founded: 1990

Number of Volunteers Last Year: 1,000

Funding Sources: No outside funding sources; Global Works is self-funded

The Work They Do: Global Works is an environmental and community-service travel program for high school students that offers options for language learning and homestays. Examples of past volunteer work include an archaeological dig in France; environmental work in the Gredos Mountains of Spain; water projects in Nicaragua; home construction in Puerto Rico; community construction projects in Costa Rica and in Fiji; work with a reforestation nonprofit in Ecuador; playground construction work for the local schools in Peru; work with a kiwi habitat in New Zealand; work on recycling and conservation projects; assistance at the Panda Reserve, in a soup kitchen, and at the orphanage in China; and work with day care centers in Argentina.

Project Location: Projects are available in Spain, France, Fiji, New Zealand, Australia, Costa Rica, Puerto Rico, Ecuador, Panama, Peru, Argentina, China, and Nicaragua. Groups of volunteers usually stay together in inns, bed and breakfasts, hostels, or eco-lodges. Individual volunteers on language immersion trips are housed with local families in a homestay.

Time Line: Global Works programs range from two to five weeks during the summer.

Cost: Program fees run from $3,195 to $6,695 and include room and board. Airfare costs are not included, but Global Works offers group flight options.

Getting Started: Prospective volunteers should visit the website listed above to complete an online application; most trips fill up by the March prior to departure. Short, friendly telephone interviews are required in order to clarify Global Works' expectations and guidelines with prospective volunteers. Training is provided in-country as a part of the program by the adult leaders and by local organizations.

Needed Skills and Specific Populations: Volunteers must be willing to challenge their typical comfort zones and have a desire to live, work, and travel with others. Volunteers with disabilities may be able to volunteer with Global Works, which will be determined on a case-by-case basis. Global Works programs are restricted to teenagers, but custom service trips for schools, universities, families, clubs, or organizations can be arranged throughout the year. Volunteers must be at least 14 years old and beginning the ninth grade.

Globalteer

54 Woodchester
Yate
Bristol BS37 8TX
United Kingdom
+855 (0)63 761 802
E-mail: volunteer.camkids@globalteer.org
Website: www.globalteer.org

Project Type: Community Development; Education; Natural
Conservation (Land); Orphans; Women's Issues; Youth
Mission Statement Excerpt: "To provide support to communities and projects in need; to raise awareness in developed
countries of the plight faced by poverty stricken countries;
educate locals and volunteers about environmental issues
and the need to protect wildlife."
Year Founded: 2006
Number of Volunteers Last Year: 380
Funding Sources: None
The Work They Do: Globalteer provides assistance to
community-based projects, including schools and orphanages, and works within hill tribe communities in remote
mountainous regions. In these projects, volunteers have the
opportunity to teach English or general studies, as well as to
work with children in the areas of sports, arts, and crafts.
Globalteer also promotes humane behavior toward animals
by providing appropriate care, protection, treatment, and
security for animals that are in need of attention due to
sickness, maltreatment, poor circumstances, or ill usage, and
educates the public in matters pertaining to animal welfare
in general and the prevention of cruelty and suffering
among animals. Globalteer collaborates with elephant and
wildlife projects, on which volunteers can help care for
animals and help to maintain the sanctuaries.

Project Location: Projects for children and adolescents are located in Siem Reap, Cambodia; Mondulkiri, Cambodia; Medellin, Colombia; and Cusco, Peru. Elephant projects are located in Mondulkiri, Cambodia, and Petchaburi, Thailand, while wildlife projects are located in Petchaburi, Thailand, and North Sulawasi, Indonesia. Volunteers are housed in private houses, hostels, or hotels, and travel to project sites by bicycle or public transportation.

Time Line: Volunteers are accepted year-round, though the elephant and wildlife projects have specific weekly start dates. Volunteers with children and elephants commit to a minimum of one week, while volunteers in wildlife centers commit to a minimum of two weeks. The stated maximum stay for all projects is three months, except for the Indonesia wildlife project (two months) and the Cambodia elephant project (one month). Volunteer time lines are often negotiable and may be extended.

Cost: Program fees vary by location and the length of the volunteer project, starting at $580 for one week at some sites and ranging up to a maximum of $3,455 for 12 weeks at other sites. Program fees include airport transfers and accommodations; the elephant and wildlife program fees also include all meals. None of the program fees include transportation to the country of service.

Getting Started: Prospective volunteers may apply through Globalteer's website; interviews are not required. Volunteers receive a predeparture orientation guide, information on their volunteer site, and, as applicable, a teaching guide. Once in-country, volunteers receive an orientation to their volunteer site and their local community, as well as teacher training in some sites.

Needed Skills and Specific Populations: Globalteer does not require specific skills but will try to find appropriate placements for volunteers who do have specific skill sets that they wish to utilize. Volunteers must be at least 18 years old, though children are welcome to volunteer with parents or as part of a group of family volunteers. Globalteer does

These volunteers work in a local day care center in Medellin, Columbia, teaching English and leading other activities. On this day, the children were thrilled to have a special excursion entitled "Off to the library!"—and off they ran! *Photo courtesy of Ashlee Chapman/Globalteer*

not have a maximum age for volunteers, though all volunteers must be able to cope with the physical challenges and weather conditions at each project. Volunteers with disabilities will be accommodated when possible.

Thank You, Teacher

By Mark Acres

Globalteer

Globalteer placed me in the town of Siem Reap, Cambodia, in a wonderful little grassroots school situation in the heart of a very poor local community. I had never taught before, but my growing enthusiasm to help these beautiful children quickly overcame any anxieties I had about teaching. In quite stark contrast to many children in the West, these children are so willing to learn, so dedicated to their studies, and so well behaved. They are simply a joy to be around. I was greeted every day by their smiling, welcoming faces.

Behind these warm smiles, however, there are many tragic stories of families struggling to feed and clothe themselves. We are talking about Cambodia, a developing country trying to forget a sad past but which is nonetheless enveloped by poverty and the hardships it creates. Parents often have to keep their children at home to help them with work and daily chores. For example, at the project where I taught, a little girl of five missed school regularly so that she could stay home and look after her one-year-old brother while her mother was at work. Sometimes parents cannot afford to send their children to state school, denying them the full education they require to help them escape the cycle of poverty and make better lives for themselves. A daily struggle to make ends meet is the sad reality most Cambodians face. But there is hope.

The project I helped with, called the Breakfast Club, is just one example of the great work being done within Cambodian communities to improve the lives of many families.

The Breakfast Club provides a morning meal to the poorest and most needy children, directly combating the malnutrition that so seriously threatens their health and growth. During my time with the project, I saw one four-year-old boy make great progress in the Club; his skin and hair no longer reflected the effects of undernourishment and he had more energy to join in and play with the other children.

Perhaps the words of one little girl I heard talking to the director represent the enormous difference we can make to the lives of many: "Teacher, much easier to learn when not feel hungry. Thank you, teacher."

Globe Aware

6500 East Mockingbird Lane, Suite 104
Dallas, TX 75214
(214) 824-4562 or (877) 588-4562; Fax: (214) 824-4563
E-mail: info@globeaware.org
Website: www.globeaware.org

Project Type: Community Development; Construction;
Economic Development; Education; Orphans; Rural Development; Youth
Mission Statement Excerpt: "Globe Aware seeks to promote
cultural awareness and sustainability by engaging in locally
chosen development projects that are safe, culturally interesting, and genuinely beneficial to a needy community."
Year Founded: 2002
Number of Volunteers Last Year: 1,500
Funding Sources: Fully funded by donations from individuals
The Work They Do: Globe Aware's main focus is to carry out
work that leads to greater independence and health for local
communities. For example, volunteers work with deaf orphans
in Peru to teach them a variety of life skills, from first aid and
hygiene to employable skills such as sewing and cooking. They
also fix playgrounds, paint murals, and give one-on-one attention and care to the orphans. In other programs, volunteers
build modified adobe stoves that reduce fuel consumption and
dramatically decrease the contraction of upper respiratory
disease from smoke inhalation. Globe Aware takes on a broad
spectrum of work projects at most sites.
Project Location: Globe Aware currently works in Latin
America (Mexico, Costa Rica, Peru, Brazil, and Cuba), Asia
(Thailand, Nepal, Laos, China, Cambodia, and Vietnam),
Africa (Ghana), and Eastern Europe (Romania). Work sites
vary tremendously. For example, the Cusco, Peru, work site,
where volunteers work with orphans, is a cobblestoned,
double-courtyarded facility with flushing toilets and hot
water. In Thailand, volunteers may teach in clean rural
classrooms or build homes in hot and humid (but beautiful)

outdoor environments. Volunteer accommodations vary by program and community, but all accommodations, food, and water while on the program are provided by Globe Aware. For example, at project sites in Thailand and Costa Rica, there is no hot water, but it is rarely missed due to the warm outside temperatures. In Cusco there are flushing toilets, running hot water, and access to electricity. In some programs volunteers stay at modest hotels, and in others there are homestays; a few programs offer on-site dormitory style accommodations.

Time Line: Each program is offered for at least one week every month, with the exception of the Thailand program, which is available November through May. Most programs last one week, Saturday to Saturday, but some of Globe Aware's volunteers choose to extend their programs by up to three weeks at an additional charge of $750 per additional week.

Cost: Program fees range from approximately $1,190 up to $1,390. Each fee covers the cost of meals, accommodations, on-site travel, emergency medical evacuation, medical insurance, donations to the various community projects, and an orientation package. Airfare is not included in the program fee.

Getting Started: An application is available on the organization's website, or Globe Aware can fax, mail, or e-mail the application to prospective volunteers; interviews are not required. Orientation materials are sent to volunteers upon registration, and the first day upon arrival is devoted to orientation activities.

Needed Skills and Specific Populations: No specialized skills are necessary to volunteer with Globe Aware. Volunteers under the age of 16 must fill out a special waiver. Senior volunteers are welcomed. Volunteers with disabilities are welcomed, though there are limitations within each program. For example, the program in Cusco may not suit those who use wheelchairs because the living accommodations and work place are on cobblestone. Globe Aware also encourages families volunteering together, as a way to expose children to cultural learning and promote cross-cultural awareness.

A Vacation for Soul, Mind, and Heart

By Francis Higgins

Globe Aware

My husband, son, daughter, and I flew to Mexico, committed to participating in a volunteer vacation as a family. We were sent to Chalcatzingo, where we stayed with a lovely host family, Octavio and Margarita. After only two days of helping and experiencing life in Chalcatzingo, we felt like this was our "second home." Our host family made us feel so welcome. During the day, we worked very hard to build a cistern to capture water that will then be used to irrigate crops. And then in the evening we had great, homemade meals in Octavio and Margarita's beautiful, cool garden with dogs, cats, bunnies, and birds all around us. Constantino and Lorena, the family who received the cistern, were very appreciative of all our hard work. We truly feel that our family helped their family in a sustainable way. This vacation was so much more than a mere holiday. It was a vacation for our souls, minds, and hearts.

Globe Shares

906 Chestnut Avenue
Richland, WA 99352
(856) 472-9744
E-mail: info@globeshares.org
Website: www.globeshares.org

Project Type: Construction; Economic Development; Education; Orphans; Professional/Technical Assistance; Rural Development; Trail Building/Maintenance

Mission Statement Excerpt: "Globe Shares exists to collect and distribute aid to those in need around the globe, to act as a conduit for charitable services domestically and abroad, and to provide domestic and international charity though direct representation."

Year Founded: 2009

Number of Volunteers Last Year: 4

Funding Sources: Private donors

The Work They Do: Globe Shares connects individuals interested in volunteering during their travels with opportunities around the world without charging a fee. They currently have 12 ongoing projects; if Globe Shares cannot find an existing project or potential opportunity in a location a volunteer is interested in working in, they will work to locate one. Volunteers have participated in projects such as teaching English to children at schools and in special sessions, creating and teaching math and science classes to refugees, designing and building homes for those in need, feeding the homeless, and translating. Globe Shares also provides an online presence for volunteers to blog, post photos, and list their projects and goals.

Project Location: Globe Shares helps connect volunteers to projects around the world but has particular expertise in Southeast Asia, China, and South America. The work environment and housing depend on the project. At some project sites, housing is provided for free by the host organization, while at others volunteers find and pay for their own accommodations. Most living situations have running water, electricity, Internet access, and beds.

Time Line: Volunteer opportunities are available throughout the year for a minimum of two weeks and a maximum of one year; the average length of a volunteer trip has been one month. Globe Shares requests that the travelers they assist spend at least one-third of their trip time volunteering.

Cost: Globe Shares does not charge a fee to connect travelers to volunteer opportunities. Volunteers are responsible for all of their travel expenses and food, but some volunteer opportunities may provide free accommodations or discounts on food.

Getting Started: Travelers who would like to add a volunteer component to their trip should contact Globe Shares via e-mail. Globe Shares does not have any application deadlines, as projects are constantly available. They do require an in-person or phone interview, and an orientation is provided at that time.

Needed Skills and Specific Populations: Globe Shares does not require any specific skills but will seek to place travelers in volunteer positions that utilize their talents and abilities. Volunteers should be at least 16 years old, and senior volunteers are encouraged. Globe Shares will work with volunteers with disabilities to find projects that can accommodate their needs. While Globe Shares has not previously worked with families, they are open to and encourage family participation.

Go Differently

Flat 1, The White House
24 Third Avenue
Hove BN3 2PD
United Kingdom
+44 1273 451372
E-mail: info@godifferently.com
Website: www.godifferently.com

Project Type: Agriculture; Community Development; Economic
   Development; Education; Historic Preservation; Natural
   Conservation (Land); Youth
Mission Statement Excerpt: "Go Differently offers small group
   and tailor made ethical vacations, volunteering, and voluntourism tours based on the appreciation and respect of the
   local people and the environment."
Year Founded: 2002
Number of Volunteers Last Year: 350
Funding Sources: Private individuals
The Work They Do: Go Differently offers opportunities both
   for "voluntourism"—two-week country tours that include
   both vacationing and volunteering—as well as single location volunteer projects that do not include travel and
   tourism. Their projects include living and working with
   elephants in Thailand, teaching English in village schools,
   and community development projects.
Project Location: Go Differently offers volunteer vacations in
   Thailand, Vietnam, Cambodia, and Laos. Volunteers typically stay with families, sometimes in quite basic conditions,
   or in small, locally owned hotels. Voluntourists, on the
   other hand, stay in a combination of both locally owned
   hotels and more luxurious facilities. Potential volunteers
   who have concerns about their level of comfort should
   discuss this in advance with Go Differently to ensure that
   they are choosing a suitable trip.
Time Line: Voluntourism trips are operated throughout the year

Natasha, six-year-old sister of Joe, who authored the following diary on Elephant Camp, leans down from her tall perch on top of her elephant, Sao noi, to share a treat. Natasha says, "My elephant is nice and big and I love her." *Photo courtesy of Sarah Blaine, mother of Joe and Natasha*

in small groups and on precise dates; see Go Differently's website for details. Volunteer projects that are not a part of a tour can be joined at any time. The minimum stay is one week, with most volunteers staying for two weeks. Longer volunteer stints can be arranged and may be eligible for a discount.

Cost: Volunteer projects start at $640 per week, and voluntourism trips begin at $1,700 for two weeks. The program fee includes accommodations, food, and logistical and linguistic support throughout the trip. Volunteers are responsible for the cost of their travel to the project's start point.

Getting Started: Prospective volunteers should contact Go Differently to discuss their specific interests and to check the availability of volunteer projects. Interviews are not required, but applicants do complete a Volunteer Questionnaire to ensure a proper match between volunteer and project. Go Differently does not provide formal training but does give each volunteer documentation that details the daily routine, a packing list, local contact information, and cultural considerations.

Needed Skills and Specific Populations: The only required skill is good spoken English for the English teaching positions, though sometimes other major European languages may be an acceptable substitute. While Go Differently encourages children to volunteer, all volunteers under the age of 18 must be accompanied by a parent or other responsible adult. Families may enjoy discounts for sharing rooms, as available. Go Differently welcomes volunteers of all nationalities, senior volunteers, and volunteers with disabilities, and will work to accommodate special needs when possible.

Joe's Diary on Elephant Camp

By Joe Blaine, Age Nine

Go Differently

Day 1: First, you have to do an opening ceremony; you won't understand it, but it is for good luck with your elephant. Next, you go off with your *mahout* (elephant handler) and feed your elephant bananas, after that you walk with your elephant to get to know her, and then you go back and give your elephant a drink. Now you go on another walk and stop to shower her. Next tourists come to see the elephants so you have to stop but you can stay the night at camp and put your elephant to bed; the best bit is that you have saved an elephant.

Day 2: My elephant is named Kwan muang. She is 35 years old. My *mahout* is called Tone. He is 27. Today I rode Kwan for the first time. You feel safer on the neck than in the seat. Me and Tone had lots of fun together. These are the commands for riding an elephant:

- come = *maa*
- back/slow = *toy*
- stop = *how*
- go = *uhhhhha*
- left = *ben sai*
- right = *benqua*

Day 3: Today I learned how to climb up on the back of an elephant by way of her foot. The elephant puts out her leg and you stand on the leg, hold onto the ear, and jump. To get them to put out their leg you shout "*zoom*." Something else cool happened; I got to ride Kwan all by myself.

Day 4: Today I woke up at camp at 5 AM to go grass cutting. You have to wear long trousers because the grass is long and sharp. You do grass cutting for food for your elephant. Then at 6 AM we went back to camp and put the elephants in their daytime place, and then you ride them and shower them.

Day 5 (Christmas Day): We had a lovely day with our elephants. I love riding; you don't feel like you are going to fall off because their backs are so wide.

Day 6: Today Daddy and I woke up at 5 AM to go grass cutting. Then we went to camp for our leaving ceremony. It was a sad day as I had to say good-bye to Tone and Kwan, my special elephant. ELEPHANT CAMP ROCKS!

Greenheart Travel

746 North LaSalle Drive
Chicago, IL 60654
(888) 227-6231; Fax: (312) 944-0728
E-mail: info@greenhearttravel.org
Website: www.greenhearttravel.org

Project Type: Community Development; Education; Natural
Conservation (Land); Orphans; Rural Development;
Women's Issues; Youth

Mission Statement Excerpt: "Our mission is to provide life-
changing travel experiences that lead to cultural
understanding, social responsibility, environmental awareness and personal growth. Through travel, we aim to foster
a more tolerant, peaceful and environmentally sustainable
world."

Year Founded: 1985

Number of Volunteers Last Year: Over 100

Funding Sources: None

The Work They Do: Greenheart Travel believes in connecting
people and the planet through youth development, environmental conservation, and women's empowerment projects,
partnering with organizations in economically developing
countries that need to develop a base of volunteers to keep
their projects sustainable. Additionally, they provide support
each year for underprivileged students in the US to travel to
a small project in the Costa Rican rain forest that is based
on eco-preservation and animal rescue. To increase the
number of volunteers and spread the project's environmental conservation work, Greenheart Travel sent a group
of students from the urban schools in Chicago to the project
to learn about environmental conservation and help the
project with its goals. Other Greenheart Travel volunteers
are involved in mentoring and tutoring children, painting
houses, teaching computer and business skills, reforestation
efforts, building and rebuilding trails, helping to conserve

sea turtles, and developing business skills in women in poverty.

Project Location: Greenheart Travel operates in Argentina, Australia, Brazil, Cambodia, Chile, Costa Rica, Ecuador, Georgia, Ghana, India, Kenya, New Zealand, Peru, Spain, Tanzania, and Thailand. Since most of Greenheart Travel's projects are in economically developing countries, amenities and lodging are usually rustic. Depending on the location, host communities may or may not have running water and electricity available at all times. When possible, Greenheart Travel houses volunteers with host families, though some volunteers stay in volunteer houses, always located close to a local market or town center.

Time Line: Volunteer opportunities are available throughout the year, with departure dates twice each month. Most volunteers opt for summer departures, so Greenheart Travel recommends an early-spring time line for applications for those dates, since they can fill up quickly. Volunteers must commit to two weeks, except in Costa Rica, which has a one-week minimum. There is a maximum stay of three months, and most volunteers stay for about three weeks.

Cost: Program fees range from $890 for two weeks in Ecuador to $4,470 for three months in India. Most program fees include all accommodations and meals; airfare is not included in any of the program fees.

Getting Started: Prospective volunteers may complete an online application, which includes a background check, and should do so at least eight weeks before their desired departure date. All applicants must complete a phone interview. Volunteers also complete a 30- to 45-minute predeparture orientation by telephone and have an in-country orientation upon arrival. Greenheart Travel provides a postdeparture orientation to help volunteers adapt to life back at home and figure out how to translate their international volunteer experience into a longer-term commitment to their home community.

Needed Skills and Specific Populations: Greenheart Travel only requires that volunteers have a love of travel and an adventurous spirit, though previous travel is always helpful. Volunteers must be at least 18 years old, with three exceptions: the Kenya program has a minimum age of 23, the Costa Rica program accepts teenagers, and the Brazil program accepts groups of teenagers but not individual teenagers. There is no maximum age, and Greenheart Travel encourages senior volunteers. Volunteers with disabilities will be placed according to their specific needs and the programs' abilities to accommodate them. Families are encouraged and receive a 5 percent discount for each person after the first.

Habitat for Humanity International's Global Village

P.O. Box 369
Americus, GA 31709
(229) 410-7530, or (800) HABITAT, ext. 7530;
Fax: (229) 410-7080
E-mail: gv@habitat.org
Website: www.habitat.org/gv

Project Type: Administrative; Community Development; Construction; Economic Development; Human Rights; Political Action

Mission Statement Excerpt: "Habitat for Humanity works in partnership with God and people everywhere, from all walks of life, to develop communities with people in need by building and renovating houses, so that there are decent houses in decent communities in which every person can experience God's love and can live and grow into all that God intends."

Year Founded: 1976

Number of Volunteers Last Year: Approximately 5,000 volunteers from the US-sending program of the Global Village program

Funding Sources: Individual donations, grants, corporate donations, and government funds

The Work They Do: One of the most well-known and beloved volunteer organizations in the United States, Habitat for Humanity International's Global Village program consists of short-term building trips designed to give concerned people a firsthand opportunity to observe and contribute to Habitat's work to eliminate poverty housing worldwide. Working alongside homeowners and local volunteers, team members assist low-income people in home-building and rehab projects. Through partnership with local families and local Habitat offices, Global Village volunteers learn about the need for affordable housing, the host culture, and Habitat's international work.

Project Location: Global Village volunteers work in approximately 50 nations around the world. Most work sites are in rural areas of economically underdeveloped countries and tend to be very basic. Team leaders and in-country Habitat hosts make arrangements for volunteers' food, accommodations, and local transportation. Accommodations vary by location, but generally include simple, decent, affordable hotels or guesthouses that have been approved by the locally based host program.

Time Line: Global Village trips run year-round for 10 to 20 days each.

Cost: Program fees range from $1,000 to $2,400. The program fee includes room and board, in-country transportation, travel medical insurance, and a donation to the host community's building program. Airfare to the host country is not included in the cost.

Getting Started: Prospective volunteers can apply online via the Habitat for Humanity International's Global Village website. Prospective volunteers must be interviewed by phone before being accepted into the program. Confirmed volunteers are given orientation manuals and are guided by a team leader in-country.

Needed Skills and Specific Populations: Volunteers do not need any prior experience or specific skills. Minors 16 years of age and older may participate as part of an institutional group, such as a school or church. Minors who are US citizens and at least 16 years of age may participate in a Global Village work team without accompaniment if the team is traveling to a non–disaster recovery site within the United States, and the minor has parental permission. Some projects or hosts may have a higher minimum age requirement; there is no maximum age limit. Senior volunteers are welcomed. Accommodations for volunteers with disabilities vary by work site and by disability. Participants must be in good health, as the work assignments often require strenuous manual labor.

Hands Up Holidays

61 Parkstead Road
London SW15 5AN
United Kingdom
(201) 984-5372 (US phone number)
E-mail: info@handsupholidays.com
Website: www.handsupholidays.com

Project Type: Administrative; Community Development; Education; Medical/Health; Natural Conservation (Land); Orphans; Trail Building/Maintenance

Mission Statement Excerpt: "Hands Up Holidays' mission is to provide inspiring tailor-made eco-luxury tours and exceptional service enabling its guests to experience incredible sights and blend that with meaningful volunteering and philanthropic opportunities."

Year Founded: 2006

Number of Volunteers Last Year: 220

Funding Sources: Individuals and companies

The Work They Do: Hands Up Holidays provides opportunities for individuals, couples, families, small groups, and companies to combine sightseeing with "a taste of volunteering." They cater to people who are "time-poor" but want to make a difference while on vacation. Hands Up Holidays consults with local communities to identify what projects enthusiastic volunteers could take on for an average of four or five days at a time or for a longer period of time, and then matches these with the volunteers' preferences. Most volunteers work in the areas of repairs and renovations, building, teaching, or environmental conservation, such as tree planting, turtle rescue, elephant conservation, or bird monitoring and tagging.

Project Location: Hands Up Holidays offers opportunities in 35 countries, mostly in Africa, Asia, and Latin America, as well as in Eastern Europe and the Pacific. Volunteers typically stay in four- or five-star lodging, with an emphasis on eco-

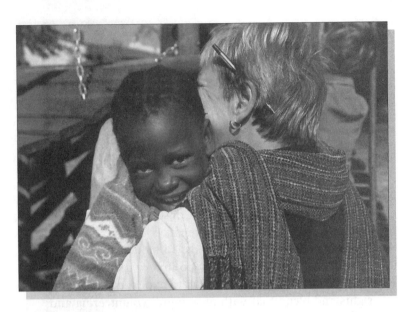

Volunteer Mary Chellar, age 64, embraces one of her little students. She taught in an elementary school in the Khayaletsha Township, Cape Town, South Africa. *Photo courtesy of Christopher Hill*

luxury accommodations where they are available. Volunteers can, however, be placed in homestays upon request in some destinations.

Time Line: Hands Up Holidays' trips are designed for each client, with no fixed schedule. They cater mostly to companies, families, and couples, although there are occasional scheduled trips for solo travelers. Most guests typically volunteer for 4 or 5 days, out of a total of 9 to 14 days, with the balance of time spent sightseeing.

Cost: Program fees include English-speaking guides, a donation to the project, accommodations, entrance fees, and meals as indicated in the itinerary. These fees range from $1,500 for 15 days in Nepal to $29,900 for 18 days in New Zealand; the average program fee is $3,000 per person for 10 days. Program fees do not typically include international airfare, though Hands Up Holidays can arrange air travel and include it in an expanded program fee.

Getting Started: Hands Up Holidays recommends that participants book their trip at least 60 days in advance to help ensure availability, but this is not always necessary depending on the time of year. Police background checks are required for volunteers who wish to assist with children. Interviews may be required for volunteers who wish to utilize special skills or who wish to travel for longer periods of time. A predeparture information packet is sent to volunteers, and a local guide provides an in-country orientation upon arrival.

Needed Skills and Specific Populations: While Hands Up Holidays does not require any specific skills, they can help to match projects for people who have specializations that they wish to utilize for the benefit of others. Unaccompanied volunteers must be at least 18 years old; volunteers under this age may be allowed if accompanied by an adult, though this is determined in consultation with the parents. Senior volunteers are encouraged but may need to provide a doctor's certificate if over the age of 60. If at all possible, Hands Up Holidays will accommodate the needs of volunteers with disabilities, but this may not be possible in all cases. Families are welcome to volunteer with Hands Up Holidays.

Health Volunteers Overseas (HVO)

1900 L Street NW, Suite 310
Washington, DC 20036
(202) 296-0928; Fax: (202) 296-8018
E-mail: info@hvousa.org
Website: www.hvousa.org

Project Type: Education; Medical/Health; Professional/Technical Assistance

Mission Statement Excerpt: "Health Volunteers Overseas is dedicated to improving the availability and accessibility of health care in developing countries through training and education."

Year Founded: 1986

Number of Volunteers Last Year: 494

Funding Sources: Donations from individuals, corporations, and foundations

The Work They Do: HVO provides clinical education and training in various disciplines including anesthesia, dermatology, hand surgery, hematology, internal medicine, oral health (including dentistry, oral surgery, and public health), nursing education, oncology, orthopedics, pediatrics, physical therapy, and wound and lymphedema management. HVO also provides needed education-related materials and equipment to program sites to reinforce educational programs. Volunteers are involved in a variety of activities, including clinical training, teacher training, curriculum development, and student and faculty mentoring. They lecture, serve as clinical instructors, conduct ward rounds, and demonstrate various techniques in classrooms, clinics, and operating rooms.

Project Location: Volunteer assignments with HVO are available in more than 25 economically developing countries in Africa, Asia, the Caribbean, Latin America, and Eastern Europe. Amenities and the comfortableness of the work sites and accommodations vary by location.

Time Line: HVO's programs are ongoing, and the organization accepts volunteers year-round. Volunteers typically serve for one month, though there are some stints on which volunteers can serve for two weeks. Longer placements are also available.

Cost: HVO does not charge program fees, but it does require participants to become members to help provide support for the organization's administrative costs. Volunteers are responsible for their international travel, and many sites provide room, board, and daily transportation.

Getting Started: Prospective volunteers should visit HVO's website or call the number listed above. Interviews are not required, but all volunteers have several conversations with both HVO recruiters and the program director. HVO has a predeparture orientation process that includes communication by phone, e-mail, and fax. All volunteers receive HVO's *Guide to Volunteering Overseas*, a booklet that contains information on international travel, safety and health precautions, and cross-cultural communication skills, as well as teaching and training tips. In addition, volunteers receive access to the HVO KnowNET, an online site that has a broad array of orientation materials, such as suggested packing lists, training and program details, and site-specific information on housing, travel, food, personal needs, and weather.

Needed Skills and Specific Populations: HVO volunteers must be fully trained and licensed health care professionals. In addition, HVO prefers volunteers with three to five years' professional experience, since activities include teaching and training. There is no language requirement for volunteers, although knowledge of Spanish or French can be useful on occasion. The most successful HVO volunteers are well-trained, flexible, adaptable, and open to new experiences. There is no minimum age required to volunteer with HVO, and senior volunteers are welcomed. Qualified volunteers with disabilities are welcomed, though they should work with HVO staff to assess the feasibility of assignments. Family members often accompany HVO volunteers, and in some sites may be able to volunteer as teachers, administrators, or in some other capacity.

Holy Land Trust (HLT)

529 Manger Street
P.O. Box 737
Bethlehem, West Bank
Palestine
+970 2 276 5930; Fax: +970 2 276 5931
E-mail: palestine@holylandtrust.org
Website: www.holylandtrust.org

Project Type: Administrative; Community Development; Human
  Rights; Political Action; Social Justice; Women's Issues;
  Youth
Mission Statement Excerpt: "Through a commitment to the
  principles of nonviolence, the Holy Land Trust seeks to
  strengthen and empower the Palestinian community in
  developing spiritual, pragmatic and strategic approaches
  that will allow it to resist all forms of oppression and build
  a future that makes the Holy Land a global model and pillar
  of understanding, respect, justice, equality and peaceful
  coexistence."
Year Founded: 1998
Number of Volunteers Last Year: 75
Funding Sources: Donations from a variety of sources
The Work They Do: HLT designs nonviolent resistance training
  programs for the community of Bethlehem as a "means to
  end the Israeli occupation of the West Bank." HLT volunteers participate in a variety of tasks, such as working with
  the Palestine News Network in editing news written in
  English, working on an independent research project,
  attending programs sponsored by HLT, and other office
  needs.
Project Location: HLT's offices are located in central Bethlehem
  near the Church of the Nativity; depending on their work,
  volunteers may also need to take public transportation to
  other parts of the West Bank. Volunteers are housed with
  host families in Bethlehem or in apartments, as arranged by
  HLT.

Time Line: Volunteers are welcome throughout the year. Longer-term volunteers are preferred, but HLT accepts volunteers for terms as short as one month. The average volunteer stay is three months.

Cost: HLT does not charge a program fee, but volunteers are responsible for all of their transportation and living costs. HLT will help arrange for a host family or other accommodations, but volunteers should expect to pay a reasonable fee for this housing. Volunteers who wish to spend more time in local communities outside of planned staff visits will need to bring extra funds for public transportation.

Getting Started: Volunteers should download an application from the HLT website and e-mail it to the organization. Interviews are required and may be conducted by phone or Skype. No formal orientation is provided upon arrival, but volunteers do meet with an HLT volunteer coordinator to discuss their work and expectations of volunteers and to designate their initial work before beginning.

Needed Skills and Specific Populations: Volunteers must speak English and commit to upholding HLT's vision and practice of universal nonviolence. Knowledge of Arabic and Palestinian culture is preferred but not required. Volunteers with administrative, IT, social media, or website experience are especially needed. Volunteers are generally over 18 years old, and there is no maximum age limit. HLT welcomes volunteers with disabilities, although their office is not accessible for volunteers with physical disabilities; instead, they will seek other offices or spaces to accommodate these volunteers. Volunteer families are welcome.

Iko Poran

Rua do Oriente, 280/201
Santa Teresa
CEP 20240-130 Rio de Janeiro/JR
Brazil
+55 21 3852 2916; Fax: +55 21 3852 2917
E-mail: rj@ikoporan.org
Website: www.ikoporan.org

Project Type: Community Development; Education; Medical/Health; Professional/Technical Assistance; Social Justice; Women's Issues; Youth

Mission Statement Excerpt: "To implement development projects and international volunteer programs that make a positive impact on local organizations, promoting intercultural exchanges and strengthening a constant and growing number of non-governmental organizations (NGOs) in Brazil."

Year Founded: 2002

Number of Volunteers Last Year: Approximately 300

Funding Sources: None

The Work They Do: Iko Poran serves as a bridge between 35 locally operated organizations and prospective volunteers, placing people according to their skill sets, talents, and wishes. Volunteers can take part in a range of activities with these organizations, including education programs for both children and seniors, sports, the arts, and language classes. Volunteers may also be able to assist the organization with administrative tasks or help to shape strategic decisions and directions that the organization takes.

Project Location: Iko Poran collaborates with organizations that are based in Rio de Janeiro, Brazil. Volunteers live in a house with other Iko Poran volunteers and travel by foot, bus, or subway to their work site. The house is described as roomy and has an outdoor kitchen; it is located in Santa Teresa, one of the most culturally active districts of the city.

Time Line: Volunteers are welcomed year-round, but must begin on the first or third Saturday of every month. Volunteers stay for a minimum of 3 weeks and a maximum of 24 weeks, depending on their visa, with most staying for 6 to 8 weeks.

Cost: Iko Poran's volunteers pay a minimum fee of BRL 2,100, which includes accommodations for four weeks, 20 hours of Portuguese lessons, and pickup at the airport (though volunteers are responsible for their own return to the airport). The program fee does not include meals, daily transportation, or international airfare to Rio. Up to 50 percent of the program fee goes directly to the organization that hosts the volunteer.

Getting Started: Prospective volunteers should apply via Iko Poran's website at least two weeks before arriving in Rio in order to make sure that Iko Poran has enough time to find an appropriate placement and to reserve accommodations in the volunteer house. Interviews are not required. Iko Poran provides a one-hour orientation soon after arrival, covering etiquette, navigation of the city, safety, and other pertinent topics.

Needed Skills and Specific Populations: Iko Poran does not require any specific skill sets, except for volunteers who wish to work in its circus project, who must have established circus skills and a performance background. Volunteers must be at least 18 years old; families are welcome only if all participants are at least this age. They do not have a maximum age for volunteers, though Iko Poran discourages senior volunteers during the summer months of December through February because of high temperatures. Iko Poran does not discourage volunteers with disabilities, but notes that Rio's public transportation system and sidewalks may not accommodate all disabilities.

Independent Living Alternatives (ILA)

Trafalgar House
Grenville Place
London NW7 3SA
United Kingdom
+44 20 8906 9265; Fax: +44 20 8959 1910
E-mail: PAServices@ILAnet.co.uk
Website: www.ILAnet.co.uk

Project Type: Community Development; Human Rights; Medical/Health; Social Justice

Mission Statement Excerpt: "To promote the right of disabled people to live independently."

Year Founded: 1989

Number of Volunteers Last Year: 35

Funding Sources: Service fees from clients

The Work They Do: ILA provides a comprehensive range of personal assistance services to disabled people. Volunteers provide personal assistance to disabled people to enable them to live independently; this might include personal assistance such as helping someone to get dressed, have a bath, and utilize a toilet, or more practical assistance such as shopping and housework.

Project Location: London and Cumbria, England. Volunteers live in the disabled person's home; during their time off, they reside in shared volunteer accommodations. ILA pays for the volunteer's room and board, travel expenses, and a living allowance.

Time Line: ILA does not have specific starting and end dates for volunteer projects. Volunteers commit to a minimum of four months and maximum of one year.

Cost: There is no cost to volunteer with ILA, but volunteers must pay for their own travel to London, insurance, and any visa costs.

Getting Started: ILA has an open application process, with no deadlines. Phone interviews are required of all prospective volunteers. ILA provides training as needed for volunteers in areas such as food safety, fire safety, first aid, and hygiene.

Needed Skills and Specific Populations: While not essential, volunteers will find a driver's license helpful. Volunteers must be at least 18 years old, and there is no maximum age for volunteers. Volunteers with disabilities may be able to volunteer with ILA, depending on their disability. Families may be able to volunteer together in some circumstances.

Indian Network for Development Exchange (Idex)

A 14 A, Indrapuri
Lal Kothi
Jaipur 302015
Rajasthan
India
+91 141 2742306; Fax: +91 141 2743409
E-mail: info@idex.in
Website: www.idex.in

Project Type: Community Development; Economic Development; Education; Orphans; Rural Development; Women's Issues
Mission Statement Excerpt: None available.
Year Founded: 2002
Number of Volunteers Last Year: 900
Funding Sources: None
The Work They Do: Idex supports development projects in India. Projects include teaching in primary schools, preparing teaching aids or tutoring through bridge courses, organizing health camps and awareness programs, post-flooding relief work, empowering adolescent girls and women, providing care to children living with HIV/AIDS, assisting children with developmental disabilities, and helping seniors. Idex volunteers work in one of three project areas—education, care, or empowerment—and usually work five days each week for three to five hours each day. Education volunteers assist teachers, run independent classes in English and math, and teach at special schools for children with developmental disabilities. Care volunteers assist at local child-care centers, serving pregnant women and providing a safe space for young children. Empowerment volunteers help young women overcome the gender gap by instructing them in English, computer, or vocational skills,

and also carry out women-focused health awareness campaigns. Outside of these three areas, volunteers may also work on HIV/AIDS projects and assist in environmental cleanup and beautification efforts.

Project Location: Idex's work takes place in three Indian states: Himachal Pradesh, Goa, and Rajasthan. Volunteers often have the opportunity to become deeply involved with their host organizations and communities, and may be asked to lead instead of merely assist in various projects, such as teaching. Most of Idex's placements are in rural areas. Idex arranges for all volunteer housing, and volunteers share comfortable yet simple accommodations.

Time Line: Volunteer programs are available year-round through Idex. Some programs have varying start dates, and others have set start dates. Volunteers commit to a minimum of 2 weeks and a maximum of 12 weeks, with most staying for one or two months.

Cost: Idex's program fee for a four-week volunteer stint begins at €900, which includes airport transfers, shared accommodations, and all meals; it does not include international airfare.

Getting Started: Interested applicants may e-mail Idex or complete the "contact us" information on Idex's website at least three weeks before they wish to volunteer. Interviews are not required, but Idex asks that volunteers send a motivation letter detailing their reasons for wanting to volunteer in India. Idex partners with organizations in various countries around the world to help guide the volunteer, place them in their Indian host site, and help finalize travel and logistical details. Volunteers receive an orientation that lasts from one to three days and covers Indian culture, Idex's volunteer code of conduct, health, personal safety, and other pertinent information.

Needed Skills and Specific Populations: Volunteers do not need to have a specific skill set—just the desire to utilize their talents and abilities to assist Idex in its community-based projects. Volunteers must be at least 18 years old, except those who are supervised by adult chaperones or who are accompanied by their parents. Senior volunteers are welcomed, but Idex cannot guarantee placement in a site that will utilize all of their work experiences or educational qualifications. Idex will consider placing volunteers with disabilities on a case-by-case basis. Families are encouraged to volunteer with Idex, and those who bring children under the age of 12 can be provided with special, child-friendly housing arrangements.

Institute for International Cooperation and Development (IICD)

P.O. Box 520
Williamstown, MA 01267
(413) 441-5126; Fax: (413) 458-3323
E-mail: info@iicd-volunteer.org
Website: www.iicd-volunteer.org

Project Type: Agriculture; Community Development; Education; Human Rights; Medical/Health; Orphans; Rural Development

Mission Statement Excerpt: "Move humanitarian development forward by working towards achieving the objectives outlined in the Declaration of Human Rights."

Year Founded: 1987

Number of Volunteers Last Year: 100

Funding Sources: Individuals and a private organization

The Work They Do: IICD takes on a number of projects, but is primarily concerned with fighting AIDS and improving education around the world. Most volunteers work in the areas of HIV/AIDS prevention work, the environment, agriculture, and education. In Brazil, volunteers work on poverty alleviation efforts through projects such as vegetable gardening, building a latrine, building playgrounds, teaching mothers' clubs about healthy food, and giving lessons in bee hiving or sustainable farming. In Africa, volunteers work in a wide range of volunteer activities, including training teachers for primary schools, working with farmers' clubs to create sustainable farms, working in childrens' villages, and combating HIV/AIDS. All of IICD's programs are completed in close cooperation with the local population.

Project Location: IICD works in Angola, Brazil, Malawi, Namibia, Zambia, Mozambique, and South Africa. Volunteers live at the work site, usually in rural areas without electricity or running water. However, volunteers can request an urban placement with more amenities. Volunteers typically live at the project site or at a house connected to the project.

Time Line: Volunteer projects start in February, May, June, August, October, and November. Some programs run for 9 to 14 months, and others run for 20 months.

Cost: IICD charges an enrollment fee of $350. The program fee is $3,950 for 9 to 14 months and $4,450 for 20-month programs.

Getting Started: Prospective volunteers should call or e-mail the office; IICD does not have application deadlines. Interviews are required and can be completed in person or on the phone. Every volunteer receives an extensive orientation and training, lasting for three months for volunteers in Brazil and six months for those in Africa.

Needed Skills and Specific Populations: IICD does not require any specific skills, just a lot of stamina. Volunteers must be at least 17 years old; couples are welcome, but children are not. There is no maximum age limit. IICD is very willing to try to accommodate volunteers with disabilities and has successfully worked with volunteers with sight disabilities. Volunteers from around the world are welcome, as long as they can obtain a visa for their country of service.

Intercultural Youth Exchange (ICYE)

Latin American House
Kingsgate Place
London NW6 4TA
United Kingdom
+44 20 7681 0983; Fax: +44 20 7916 1246
E-mail: info@icye.org.uk
Website: www.icye.org.uk

Project Type: Community Development; Education; Human
Rights; Natural Conservation (Land); Orphans; Women's
Issues; Youth

Mission Statement Excerpt: "Operating within an international
network of locally managed ICYE organizations, ICYE UK
encourages inter-cultural understanding and cooperation
through the exchange of people and ideas."

Year Founded: 1949

Number of Volunteers Last Year: 60

Funding Sources: Foundations

The Work They Do: ICYE offers a wide range of volunteer placements, including opportunities such as working with street
children in Brazil; promoting HIV awareness in Mozambique; assisting women's education and development in
India; and protecting sea turtle habitats in Costa Rica.
Volunteer assignments depend on the skills and interests of
the volunteers and the requirements of the project.

Project Location: ICYE works in Latin America, Africa, and
Asia. Volunteers usually live with local host families in
settings ranging from rural villages to large cities. ICYE
locates accommodations for volunteers.

Time Line: ICYE offers both short-term volunteer opportunities
of 3 to 16 weeks, which depart throughout the year, and
also long-term 6- or 12-month opportunities, which depart
in January and August.

Cost: Program fees for short-term volunteer opportunities begin
at £750, which covers international flights, accommodations,
food, health insurance, and airport transfers. Long-term

Stephanie adapts to life in Nepal by wearing traditional clothing alongside her host family. Stephanie volunteered for Aishworya Children's Home located in Kathmandu. *Photo courtesy of ICYE-UK*

volunteer programs are £3,795 for 6 months and £4,495 for 12 months; these fees include international travel costs, room and board, health insurance, training and orientation before departure and on arrival, 30 hours of language instruction, and pocket money. Part of the program fee helps to defray the costs of volunteers from Latin America, Africa, and Asia to operate in disadvantaged communities in the United Kingdom.

Getting Started: Interested volunteers should contact ICYE by e-mail; there are no application deadlines, and ICYE can conduct the required interview by phone. ICYE offers predeparture training, training in-country, and ongoing training during and after the volunteer experience.

Needed Skills and Specific Populations: Specific needed skills vary from project to project, but all volunteers must be enthusiastic, dedicated, and passionate. Volunteers must be at least 18 years old, and long-term volunteers may not be older than 30. ICYE welcomes volunteers with disabilities and will make appropriate living and project arrangements. Families may volunteer together as long as all members meet the minimum age requirement.

InterExchange

161 Sixth Avenue
New York, NY 10013
(212) 924-0446; Fax: (212) 924-0575
E-mail: workabroad@interexchange.org;
grants@interexchange.org
Website: www.interexchange.org

Project Type: Community Development; Education; Medical/
   Health; Natural Conservation (Land); Natural Conservation
   (Sea); Social Justice; Youth
Mission Statement Excerpt: "To ensure that the young people,
   businesses and families whom we serve enjoy life-changing,
   exceptional cultural exchange experiences."
Year Founded: 1968
Number of Volunteers Last Year: Fewer than 100
Funding Sources: None
The Work They Do: InterExchange facilitiates individualized
   experiences and placements for volunteers. Volunteers may
   work in the areas of environmental conservation, education,
   social work, health care, cultural affairs, hospitality, and
   media.
Project Location: InterExchange connects volunteers to placements in Argentina, Australia, Costa Rica, Ecuador, the
   Galapagos Islands, Ghana, India, and Peru. Volunteer
   housing tends to be with a host family or in a student residence or hostel.
Time Line: Project availability depends on the country; some
   countries offer year-round opportunities, while others are
   only available at certain times of the year. In some countries,
   volunteers may choose their start date; others require that
   volunteers begin on a preset date. The average InterExchange
   volunteer stays for four to eight weeks. Placements are from
   one week to eight months long.
Cost: InterExchange's program fees begin at $595 for one week
   in Australia, and range up to $2,595 for eight weeks in

Argentina. Program fees vary by country and often have a base price for a certain number of weeks, with additional weeks added on at further expense. Most programs include accommodations and some board, but arrangements are carefully detailed for each program on InterExchange's website. None of the program fees include international airfare. InterExchange also has two grants—the Christianson Grant and the Working Abroad Grant—that are available to defray the costs for some participants; details are available on its website.

Getting Started: Applications for all InterExchange programs are available on their website at www.interexchange.org /wa-volunteer. InterExchange generally conducts phone interviews, as well as in-person interviews when possible. They provide volunteers with predeparture materials and an orientation before departure. All volunteers also receive an in-country orientation upon arrival.

Needed Skills and Specific Populations: Volunteers must be at least 18 years old. InterExchange does not have a maximum age for volunteers, but their average volunteer is between 18 and 30 years old. As long as participants are physically able to perform the duties associated with their assigned or chosen project, InterExchange will allow them to apply. InterExchange volunteers are generally US or Canadian citizens. Couples traveling together may participate in the program, but InterExchange cannot guarantee that they will be placed together, especially in programs that utilize host families to house volunteers.

International Student Volunteers (ISV)

4848 Lakeview Avenue, Suite 100A
Yorba Linda, CA 92886
(714) 779-7392; Fax: (714) 777-4647
E-mail: info@isvonline.org
Website: www.isvonline.org

Project Type: Agriculture; Community Development; Construction; Education; Natural Conservation (Land); Orphans; Scientific Research

Mission Statement Excerpt: "To create an environment conducive to combining education, conservation, community development and recreation, into the most incredible experience of a lifetime while giving back to the local communities in the countries where we are travelling."

Year Founded: 1983

Number of Volunteers Last Year: 4,000

Funding Sources: None

The Work They Do: ISV has a range of projects focusing on conservation and community development. Each project is run in conjunction with local community-based host organizations that have long-term goals of sustainability. ISV has a wide range of available projects, including organic farming in Costa Rica, building playgrounds in Thailand, nutrition projects and education projects in the Dominican Republic, building schools for indigenous populations in Ecuador, habitat regeneration in Australia, and sports and English programs for children in South Africa.

Project Location: ISV operates programs in Australia, New Zealand, Costa Rica, Panama, Ecuador, the Dominican Republic, Thailand, South Africa, Croatia, Bosnia and Herzegovina, and Romania. Work sites vary by country and by project, but most are in isolated communities or ecosystems. Volunteers are provided with a range of different possible accommodations, which might include bunk houses, jungle cabins, hostels, and hotels. Homestays are available in community development projects in Costa Rica, Ecuador, and the Dominican Republic.

Time Line: ISV operates projects from May through September and from November through February. Length of available volunteer programs range from a minimum of two weeks to a maximum of three months. Most of ISV's volunteers combine two weeks of volunteering with two weeks of adventure travel.

Cost: The program fee for a two-week volunteer project is $1,995; there is an additional $1,300 to $1,400 fee to add on two weeks of adventure travel afterwards. An additional volunteer project costs $1,395, and an additional adventure tour costs $1,495. During volunteer projects, program fees include accommodations, all meals, and ground transportation. International and domestic air transportation is not included.

Getting Started: Prospective volunteers apply online via ISV's website; no interview is required. Training is provided once volunteers reach the project site and is followed up with additional training as needed.

Needed Skills and Specific Populations: No specific skills are required. ISV volunteers are generally 18 or older, though specialized programs for high school students are sometimes available. Most ISV volunteers are under the age of 35, but families and volunteers older than this age are accepted on a case-by-case basis. ISV reviews the needs of volunteers with disabilities with them before accepting them into a program. ISV can also set up specialized programs for larger groups, including community groups, seniors, families, and businesses.

An African Experience

By Chelsea Behymer

International Student Volunteers (ISV)

In summer 2009, I flew to South Africa to volunteer with the Race to End Extinction project. The project was at the Wild Cheetah and African Wild Dog Rescue and Rehabilitation Center just outside Johannesburg. We spent two unforgettable weeks eradicating invasive plant species, feeding wild cheetahs and African wild dogs, building temporary enclosures for the rehabilitation of endangered vultures, and so much more. We worked with the local people to reach out to the community, emphasizing the importance of protecting native species to preserve their society and resources as a whole.

The second two weeks in South Africa was spent touring the country and was jam-packed with unbelievable adventures like hiking up and rappelling down Table Mountain, bungee jumping off the world's highest bungee bridge, and seeing amazing wildlife at Kruger National Park.

We did and saw so many incredible things, but I will never forget the day spent touring the Cape Peninsula in Cape Town. After going to see the adorable African penguins, known as the black-footed penguin, at Boulder Beach and voyaging out to Seal Island to see the immense populations of Cape fur seals, we were driving back to the city when we suddenly stopped. As the setting sun lit up the scene ahead of us in a brilliant golden orange light, a troop of about forty baboons appeared on the road. As they crossed, African tribal music drifted out of our van, following the massive males and the cautious females with playful young on their backs into the grassy field to the side. It was surreal and left us all speechless as we watched them disappear with the setting sun.

I left South Africa with not only an appreciation for the incredible beauty of its landscape and people but also an understanding of the diversity of the country and the struggles it has overcome. South Africa has taught me that some of the most amazing animals thrive in seemingly the most difficult habitats, and that some of the most joyful and loving people come out of the most complicated circumstances. It comes down to your ability to adapt to your surroundings, to have eyes for the beauty around you, and to have hope for the future. So volunteer with an open mind for diversity, an open heart for the love that people have to offer, and open eyes for all that volunteering will show you—because there is *a lot* to see and learn!

International Volunteer HQ (IVHQ)

P.O. Box 8273
New Plymouth
New Zealand
+64 6 758 7949; Fax: +64 6 758 7949
E-mail: volunteer@volunteerhq.org
Website: www.volunteerhq.org

Project Type: Construction; Education; Human Rights;
Medical/Health; Orphans; Women's Issues; Youth

Mission Statement Excerpt: "IVHQ aims to provide volunteer
travelers with quality, flexible, safe and highly affordable
volunteering placements in developing countries."

Year Founded: 2007

Number of Volunteers Last Year: Over 5,000

Funding Sources: None

The Work They Do: IVHQ has a number of great volunteer
programs located in Africa, South America, Central
America, and Asia. Some example programs include
construction and renovation projects in Latin America,
human rights work in Cambodia, programs for the empowerment of women in India, panda conservation in China,
and surfing outreach in South Africa. Volunteers are placed
in schools, orphanages, hospitals, HIV/AIDS clinics, local
NGOs, and conservation areas. Individual tasks vary
depending on the specific placement.

Project Location: IVHQ operates in 18 countries, including
Brazil, Guatemala, Costa Rica, Colombia, Ecuador, Mexico,
Peru, Ghana, Kenya, Tanzania, Uganda, South Africa,
Nepal, India, Cambodia, Vietnam, Thailand, and China.
Living and work conditions tend to be basic; accommoda-
tions vary from program to program but can include home-
stays, dormitories, or guesthouses.

Time Line: Volunteer projects run throughout the year; project
length depends on the country, with a minimum of one
week and a maximum of six months.

Cost: Most programs start at $250 for one week. The majority of IVHQ's four-week programs are between $450 and $600, and long-term, 24-week placements range from $2,220 to $3,365. Program fees include accommodations and meals but do not include international airfare.

Getting Started: Prospective volunteers may apply online via IVHQ's website; interviews are not required. Volunteers receive an information booklet before departure, as well as an in-country orientation after they arrive.

Needed Skills and Specific Populations: Other than medical training for health-related projects, there are no required skills for volunteers. Volunteers must be at least 18 years old, with no maximum age. IVHQ will work with volunteers with disabilities to find appropriate placements and have also placed many groups of volunteers and volunteer families.

i-to-i Volunteering

61-63 Chatham Street, 5th floor
Boston, MA 02109
(800) 985-4852
E-mail: travel@i-to-i.com
Website: www.i-to-i.com

Project Type: Archaeology; Community Development; Construction; Education; Medical/Health; Natural Conservation (Land); Orphans; People with Disabilities; Rural Development; Youth

Mission Statement Excerpt: "To allow travelers from around the world to give something back to the communities they visit by contributing to worthwhile projects during their stay, sharing skills and experiences, and promoting cultural understanding, and to provide local projects in communities worldwide with a consistent supply of trained and committed volunteer workers who will work toward the project's own goals."

Year Founded: 1994

Number of Volunteers Last Year: 8,000

Funding Sources: No outside sources

The Work They Do: i-to-i Volunteering offers hundreds of projects in 21 countries; they are designed to help disadvantaged communities and ecosystems. Project offerings are quite diverse, and include protecting endangered pandas in China, rain forest conservation in Ecuador, working with endangered animals in Costa Rica, teaching English in Kenya, working in a community health center for early childhood development in Tanzania, protecting endangered lions in South Africa, building homes for families in Costa Rica, and care work, such as helping orphaned children or street youth in Brazil or India.

Project Location: Projects are offered by i-to-i in Argentina, Australia, Brazil, Cambodia, China, Costa Rica, Ecuador, India, Indonesia, Kenya, Laos, Malaysia, Nepal, Peru,

Stephanie Kwong, on the beach of Playa Buena Vista in Mexico, holds a baby sea turtle that emerged at around 7 AM, a rare time for turtles to hatch. *Photo courtesy of Stephanie Kwong*

Philippines, South Africa, Sri Lanka, Tanzania, Thailand, Vietnam, and Zambia. Accommodations depend on the project and range from volunteer houses to homestays.

Time Line: Projects run throughout the year and last from 1 to 12 weeks; the average volunteer serves for 2 to 3 weeks.

Cost: Program fees vary by location and length of the project, but a typical two-week placement with i-to-i costs $1,595, which includes accommodations and food, a welcome orientation, and, for some projects, a TEFL (Teaching English as a Foreign Language) course. Volunteers are responsible for providing their own airfare.

Getting Started: Prospective volunteers can call the toll-free number listed above to talk with a travel advisor and sign-up for projects or visit i-to-i's website for project details. Interviews are not required of prospective volunteers. Every trip includes a standard orientation session upon arrival in the country. The orientation session covers administrative issues, health and safety, code of conduct, expectations during the project, suggestions on how to succeed as a volunteer, and cultural tips. All of i-to-i's teaching projects include a 60-hour online TEFL course for volunteers before they leave for their projects. Additional Spanish language lessons are offered as needed.

Needed Skills and Specific Populations: Most of i-to-i's projects do not require specific knowledge or skills, but some media, marketing, and health projects require volunteers to submit their resumes in advance. Volunteers must be at least 16 years old, and senior volunteers are welcomed. Families with children who meet the minimum age requirement are welcome. Placement for volunteers with disabilities will be done on an individual basis in order to be 100 percent sure that the programs in which they are interested will be able to support them fully.

Pura Vida (Pure Life): Turtle Conservation in Costa Rica

By Stephanie Kwong

i-to-i Volunteering

I spent two weeks volunteering on a turtle conservation project in Costa Rica. We had no running water or electricity and lived in a two-story beach shack built by the previous volunteers. Believe it or not, we had it good. The previous volunteers lived in tents and were flooded every time it rained, so I was glad to be off the ground, even if it was a shack! Given these rustic conditions, how can anyone call this a vacation? Well, maybe it's not a vacation in the typical sense, but the impact this experience had on me was immense. I really learned to appreciate the small things in life; the things we take for granted in our large, crowded cities. Ticos (self-appointed slang for Costa Ricans) are generally very happy people. I envy their passion for life, friendships, family, and pride in their own culture and country. Even in a small, poor village like Samara, Ticos find purpose in doing the same simple activities every day, such as working with the turtles to preserve their lifestyle and habitat. The help of the volunteers is always very much appreciated by the locals.

The highlight of my trip involved the long, solitary nights of sitting watch at one of the two hatcheries. I would sit in the dark, listening to the howler monkeys (scaring the life out of me) while shoveling beach crabs and snakes (yes, snakes!) off the hatchery grounds. Not only was I protecting the hatchery, but I also did rounds up and down the rows of nests to check for movement. If there was any movement, that meant the babies were hatching. Seeing the babies emerge from the sand is the most incredible experience one can imagine. Waiting for them to make their way to the surface can take up to an hour or more. We place the babies into a bucket until they have rested enough to continue their journey towards the ocean. It is not an easy night for the turtles. They tend to fall asleep on their way up, and then climb a bit more, and many times they will fall back asleep once they reach the surface. Later, we release them on the beach a few meters away from the ocean and watch them run for the waves in the moonlight. Sitting there on the beach, I've never felt so much at peace with myself and fully able to enjoy the environment—the earth, the sand, the air—around me.

I also spent some nights patrolling the beach with another volunteer looking for the olive ridley turtle (nicknamed Lora for their Latin name *Leipidochelys olivacea*) that nests on these beaches in the dark. Patrolling was done by moonlight as flashlights were not allowed since the light scares the turtles back into the ocean, delaying the nesting process. We looked for turtle tracks that came out of the ocean and followed them to see where the turtles lay their eggs. If we spotted a turtle, we quietly worked around her, measuring her shell, tagging her fins, and collecting her eggs. We took the eggs back to the hatchery where we dug a new nest by hand and reburied them to protect them from poachers and predators. Seeing one of these giant sea turtles in person is an amazing experience; I couldn't believe how big these animals were, but at the same time, how gentle and peaceful. Working with these turtles and seeing them in their natural habitat is an experience that can't be described—I only hope you can experience it yourself.

Costa Rica was definitely a life-changing experience for me. With all the adventures I had, the people I met and the culture I tasted, it only took two weeks for me to fall in love with the country, making it my favorite place in the world. *Pura Vida*, a Tico term for "Pure Life" or "Life is good."

Jatun Sacha

Volunteer Program, Jatun Sacha Foundation
Casilla 17-12-867
Quito, Pichincha
Ecuador
+593 2 243 2240 or +593 2 331 7163;
Fax: +593 2 331 8156
E-mail: volunteer@jatunsacha.org
Website: www.jatunsacha.org/ingles/index.php

Project Type: Agriculture; Community Development; Education; Natural Conservation (Land); Natural Conservation (Sea); Rural Development; Scientific Research

Mission Statement Excerpt: "Jatun Sacha is dedicated to promoting the conservation of forest, aquatic, and *páramo* ecosystems of Ecuador through technical training, scientific research, environmental education, community development, sustainable management of natural resources, and the development of leaders with a high participation of ethnic groups and women to improve the quality of life of the community."

Year Founded: 1989

Number of Volunteers Last Year: 1,284

Funding Sources: Private sources, nonprofit organizations, and USAID

The Work They Do: Jatun Sacha focuses on biological conservation and cultural diversity through private reserves, environmental education, and the development of products and research that improve the lives of the people in its zones of influence and activities. The volunteer program offers opportunities in a variety of activities, including reforestation projects, habitat restoration, organic agriculture, agroforestry, construction, alternative animal production, forestry programs, community visits, community and health programs, environmental education, teaching experiences, productive projects, production of organic fertilizers, sustainable wood production, alternative energy programs, sustainable aquaculture, beach cleanups, research, phenology studies, natural regeneration studies, flora and fauna inventories, hummingbird and mammal feeding, and tending gardens of orchids, bromeliads, and medicinal plants.

Project Location: The volunteer program works with eight biological stations managed by the Jatun Sacha Foundation in national and internationally recognized reserves located in the four major regions of Ecuador. The reserves extend from sea level up to 4,000 meters in altitude. This range includes marine, intertidal, and mangrove ecosystems, as well as dry forest, rain forest, cloud forest, and pre-mountain and high-mountain forest, as well as the *páramo* and the Galapagos Islands. The reserves also work with local communities, each of which has its own history. Volunteers are housed at each station's facilities.

Time Line: Volunteers are accepted throughout the year for a minimum of two weeks and a maximum of one year. Jatun Sacha estimates that the average volunteer stays for one month.

Cost: Volunteers pay a $47 application fee ($67 for the Galapagos) and a program fee of $475 per month ($840 for the Galapagos). The program fee covers lodging and all meals. Volunteers are responsible for transportation and all other costs.

Getting Started: Prospective volunteers should send an application letter that indicates their experience in conservation activities, future interests, reasons for applying, and preferred station and participation dates, along with a CV or resume, a recent health certificate, a police record card, two passport-sized photos, and the application fee. Jatun Sacha provides an orientation meeting before volunteers travel to sites that consists of an overview of the foundation, its reserves, and its respective projects; volunteer activities; and directions to the volunteer's reserve. Once at the reserves, volunteers receive a more in-depth orientation on the activities in which they will participate, and they receive on-the-job training throughout their service.

Needed Skills and Specific Populations: Volunteers must have at least a basic knowledge of Spanish and be at least 18 years old. Senior volunteers who are physically fit are welcomed. Volunteers with disabilities are welcomed, provided that the necessary accommodations can be made. Families can volunteer with Jatun Sacha, but children may not be able to participate in all activities, and there are no day care centers available.

JustWorks

Unitarian Universalist Service Committee (UUSC)
689 Massachusetts Avenue
Cambridge, MA 02139
(800) 388-3920 or (617) 868-6600; Fax: (617) 868-7102
E-mail: justworks@uusc.org
Website: www.uusc.org/justworks

Project Type: Community Development; Human Rights; Social Justice

Mission Statement Excerpt: "The Unitarian Universalist Service Committee advances human rights and social justice around the world, partnering with those who confront unjust power structures and mobilizing to challenge oppressive policies."

Year Founded: The JustWorks program was established in 1996; the UUSC was founded in 1940

Number of Volunteers Last Year: JustWorks averages between 100 and 250 volunteers per year

Funding Sources: Individual donors and and the Veatch Fund of the Unitarian Universalist Congregation at Shelter Rock, Manhasset, NY

The Work They Do: JustWorks offers short-term service-learning experiences that help volunteers examine and understand the causes and damaging effects of injustice. Participants work directly with people in the communities they serve, experiencing social-justice struggles firsthand. Volunteers work directly with grassroots partners and are taught advocacy skills to address issues such as poverty, discrimination, and racism, while learning about human-rights issues and promoting intercultural understanding and reconciliation. Participants may then make use of these skills and newfound knowledge in their congregations, campuses, and communities when they return home. For example, Just Works projects have included helping survivors of the devastating earthquake in Haiti to rebuild their lives and communities. This project involved working with

UUSC's grassroots partners in their Haiti rebuilding efforts. Activities include construction projects, medical assistance, and education programs.

Project Location: JustWorks program locations change every year. They may be held anywhere in the United States or internationally. Accommodations depend on the project; in the past they have included RVs, dormitories, and tents.

Time Line: Most JustWorks projects last one week. They are usually held between March and October.

Cost: The program fee varies depending on the project, but generally ranges from $500 to $1,500. The program fee includes all accommodations, food, and local transportation during the project, but it does not include transportation to and from the project site. In general, JustWorks volunteers eat locally grown food prepared by local people.

Getting Started: To apply for a JustWorks project, prospective volunteers may download an application from UUSC's website or contact the office via e-mail or phone. Applicants are encouraged to submit their materials at least six to eight weeks before the project's start date; interviews are not required as a part of the application process. Orientation and training are provided on-site at the beginning of each camp.

Needed Skills and Specific Populations: Some camps may require or give preference to volunteers who have specific skills. In general, volunteers must be at least 15 years old, though some projects are designed specifically for youth and young adults, and some projects have a minimum age of 18. Many JustWorks camps are intergenerational, and senior volunteers are encouraged to apply. JustWorks is unable to accommodate individuals with disabilities. Families are encouraged to apply for the JustWorks camps.

Kiva Fellows Program

3180 18th Street
San Francisco, CA 94110
(415) 358-7500
E-mail: kivafellows@kiva.org
Website: www.kiva.org/fellows

Project Type: Community Development; Economic Development; Human Rights; Rural Development; Social Justice; Women's Issues

Mission Statement Excerpt: "To connect people, through lending, for the sake of alleviating poverty."

Year Founded: 2004

Number of Volunteers Last Year: 125

Funding Sources: Foundations, private individuals, grants, and corporate donations

The Work They Do: Kiva empowers individuals to lend to entrepreneurs across the globe. By combining microfinance with the Internet, Kiva is creating a global community of people connected through lending. The Kiva Fellows Program offers individuals an opportunity to travel abroad and witness firsthand the impact and realities of microfinance by working directly with a host microfinance institution (MFI). Daily volunteer tasks vary depending upon the assigned field partner but generally include facilitating connections between Kiva's borrowers and lenders, writing journals and blogs for online publication, interviewing businesses, collecting and posting borrower profiles for funding to Kiva's website, and creating documents for the MFIs.

Project Location: Kiva currently has a presence in over 50 countries. Volunteers work in the offices of the partner MFIs and often journey with loan officers to try to build connections between lenders and entrepreneurs. Volunteers are responsible for arranging their own housing, though some MFIs can help direct volunteers to various housing options. Past volunteers have arranged homestays, lived in private apartments, or stayed in a hotel.

Time Line: New Kiva volunteers are trained and depart three times annually, generally in January, May, and August. Volunteers must depart no longer than two weeks after completing the training. Volunteers commit to at least a 16-week stay and may stay longer, though they may then be placed with multiple MFIs.

Cost: Kiva does not charge a program fee, but volunteers are responsible for all of their own expenses, including transportation, accommodations, and food. Many MFIs are located in rural areas, which can lower the cost of living.

Getting Started: Prospective volunteers must complete an application online, which includes supplemental documents. Among these supplemental documents is a budget that estimates the volunteer's expenses for the duration of the fellowship and indicates how they plan to meet those costs. Prospective volunteers will be interviewed at least twice via Skype before being accepted. Before the start of the volunteer experience, Kiva requires a five-day in-house training session in San Francisco that covers the Kiva model, mission, tools, and resources, and well as overviews of microfinance, how to conduct trainings, and other skills needed to be a volunteer. During the volunteer experience, Kiva provides online PowerPoint presentations and reading materials, as well as complete online courses.

Needed Skills and Specific Populations: Kiva mostly encourages applicants with backgrounds in business, finance, and social development, but has accepted volunteers with a wide range of experiences. Volunteers must be at least 21 years old; while there is no maximum age, senior volunteers should be aware of the rigorous nature of the volunteer program. The average age of Kiva fellows is 30. If a couple applies and both people are accepted, they will be placed together, but volunteers are discouraged from bringing their children with them. Volunteers with disabilities are welcome to apply, but should be aware that not all MFI sites can accommodate all disabilities. Volunteers must speak English fluently.

Koke'e Resource Conservation Program (KRCP)

Project of the Garden Island Resource Conservation and
Development, Inc.
P.O. Box 1108
Waimea, HI 96796
(808) 335-0045; Fax: (808) 335-0414
E-mail: rcp@aloha.net
Website: www.krcp.org

Project Type: Natural Conservation (Land)

Mission Statement Excerpt: "Koke'e Resource Conservation
Program (KRCP) seeks to involve the public in protecting
native ecosystem resources by coordinating volunteers to
conduct essential removal of invasive noxious weeds in
selected areas."

Year Founded: 1998

Number of Volunteers Last Year: 1,532

Funding Sources: Government and private grants

The Work They Do: KRCP focuses on alien species control
projects in the forests of Koke'e State Park on Kaua'i Island,
Hawaii. About 1,000 acres are actively managed, and
KRCP removes ginger, guava, privet, and several other types
of plants. Other work, such as trail maintenance and
nursery planting, occasionally takes place. Volunteers join
staff members daily to hike and do off-trail work, treating
specific weeds, in a section of the park. The park has a
variety of forest ecosystems and weed problems, so work
does not become monotonous.

Project Location: All volunteers work in Koke'e State Park,
which is 3,000 to 4,000 feet above sea level and is made up
of swamp, wet forest, and dry forest. Conditions can be
muddy and involve steep terrain; hiking and off-trail bush-
whacking are common. Volunteers should be prepared for
rain, but they may be comforted to know that there are no
snakes. Lodging is in a 1930s bunkhouse, constructed by
the Civilian Conservation Corps as a part of the New Deal,

that has bunk beds, hot running water, and a communal kitchen.

Time Line: Volunteers are accepted year-round for a period of one day to four weeks. The average stay is two weeks. Volunteers work from 7:00 AM to 5:00 PM four days each week and have three days off.

Cost: There is no cost to volunteer with KRCP, and, as available, housing is provided free of charge. Volunteers are responsible for purchasing their own food, which is obtained in a town that is 45 minutes away from the site. Because transportation to Koke'e State Park is difficult, KRCP will provide transportation for volunteers to and from the airport and for all work-related purposes, but cannot provide recreational transportation on days off. KRCP recommends that, when feasible, volunteers plan to rent a car. Volunteers must also have health insurance.

Getting Started: Prospective volunteers should contact KRCP at the address listed above and request an application form. Interviews are not required before volunteering. Much of the first day of volunteering is spent in training and orientation, and more training is given daily as needed.

Needed Skills and Specific Populations: Anyone who can handle the strenuous off-trail work is welcomed, including senior volunteers and volunteers with disabilities. Volunteers are expected to work with mild herbicides and machetes. Volunteers under the age of 18 should be accompanied by their parents or volunteer as a part of a group, and they are not allowed to use herbicides or machetes. Families are welcome to volunteer with KRCP. There are no citizenship restrictions for volunteers.

La Sabranenque

Rue de la Tour de l'Oume
30290 Saint Victor la Coste
France
+33 466 500 505
E-mail: info@sabranenque.com
Website: www.sabranenque.com

Project Type: Historic Preservation; Rural Development

Mission Statement Excerpt: "La Sabranenque works toward the preservation of traditional Mediterranean architecture through work projects aimed at consolidating and rehabilitating sites and through teaching volunteers the construction techniques."

Year Founded: 1969

Number of Volunteers Last Year: 250

Funding Sources: No outside funding; La Sabranenque is self-funded

The Work They Do: La Sabranenque works on consolidating and rebuilding traditional regional architecture in southern France. Projects range from the paving of a village path to the consolidation of a Romanesque chapel to the complete reconstruction of a complex of houses. Volunteers take an active part in the restoration work, including clearing rubble, cutting stone, dry stone walling, paving paths, tiling floors or roofs, and plastering walls. The main construction technique used is stone masonry.

Project Location: Volunteers work in Provence, France. Work sites may be houses, chapels, or medieval castle sites, either within a village or on a hilltop. Volunteers are housed, two to a room, in the restored village of Saint Victor la Coste. Food is prepared by a chef and is described as one of the highlights of the experience.

Time Line: Volunteers are accepted May through October, and they can stay from one week to several months. The average volunteer stay is one to two weeks.

Cost: La Sabranenque's one-week program fee for May and October is $670; the two-week program fee from June through September is $850. The fee includes housing and full board, all activities, and pickup and drop-off at the Avignon train station. The program fee does not include international airfare or train costs to Avignon. La Sabranenque is run by volunteers, so approximately 90 percent of the program fee goes directly toward program costs.

Getting Started: Prospective volunteers should contact La Sabranenque and request a brochure and an enrollment form. Interviews are not required before starting to volunteer. All volunteers are trained in the traditional construction techniques used while on the job.

Needed Skills and Specific Populations: No construction skills are needed; La Sabranenque's volunteers rarely have experience in this kind of work. Volunteers must be at least 18 years old; there is no maximum age limit, and La Sabranenque regularly hosts volunteers who are in their 60s. Due to the layout of the village and the access to projects, La Sabranenque may not be able to accommodate people who have difficulty walking. Families frequently volunteer with La Sabranenque.

Malawi Volunteer Organisation (MVO)

P.O. Box 101
Monkey Bay
Malawi
+265 888 671 093; Fax: +265 999 187 709
E-mail: info@malawivolunteer.org
Website: www.malawivolunteer.org

Project Type: Community Development; Education; Medical/ Health; Orphans; Youth

Mission Statement Excerpt: "To place the volunteer where it counts, for the volunteers and the projects."

Year Founded: 2003

Number of Volunteers Last Year: 112

Funding Sources: Private donors

The Work They Do: MVO places volunteers in medical, education, public health, and sports/community projects. Medical volunteers work at a hospital and help run a wound and minor injuries clinic. Education volunteers work in one of two schools, assisting teachers with their exceptionally large classes, which can have over 120 students. Public health volunteers work on anti-malaria campaigns, including collecting data, distributing mosquito nets, and carrying out community education campaigns. Sports/community volunteers help coach local youth and organize sporting events.

Project Location: All projects take place in the Monkey Bay area of Malawi, mostly in the village of Namakoma, with transportation provided to nearby communities as needed. Volunteers stay in a shared house on the shores on Lake Malawi.

Time Line: Volunteers are accepted year-round, but typically begin on the second Monday of every month. The minimum stay is 4 weeks, and while there is no stated maximum, volunteers rarely stay longer than 12 weeks, with the average being around 6 to 8 weeks.

Cost: The program fee is £949 per month, which includes accommodations, meals, and local transportation. The program fee does not include international airfare.

Getting Started: Prospective MVO volunteers should complete an online request form; no interview is required. Once on-site, volunteers receive an orientation that includes a tour of the project sites and a visit to nearby communities.

Needed Skills and Specific Populations: It is helpful but not required for medical volunteers to have knowledge of first aid, and similarly helpful for teachers to have an education background. Volunteers must be at least 17 years old, and there is no maximum age. Malawi is not a particularly disability-friendly country, but MVO will do their best to accommodate volunteers with disabilities. Families are welcome, but all family members must be at least 17 years old.

Manna Project International (MPI)

P.O. Box 121052
Nashville, TN 37212
(615) 746-7487; Fax: (615) 296-4120
E-mail: info@mannaproject.org
Website: www.mannaproject.org

Project Type: Community Development; Economic Development; Education; Medical/Health

Mission Statement Excerpt: "To foster communities of young adults and to encourage them to use their passions and education in service to communities in need."

Year Founded: 2004

Number of Volunteers Last Year: 160

Funding Sources: Foundations and private donors

The Work They Do: MPI volunteers work in the areas of education, health care, business development and microfinance, community empowerment, and leadership training. Volunteers can either sign up for 13-month program director positions or for four- or eight-week summer volunteer programs. Program directors organize and run community initiatives and develop new projects and may also help with donor relations and financial management. Summer volunteers help with the daily operations of MPI's programs and teach lessons.

Project Location: MPI operates in the communities of Managua, Nicaragua; Chaquiyja, Guatemala; and Quito, Ecuador. Program directors all live together in shared quarters with another program director of the same gender. Summer volunteers are housed either at the same location as the program directors or in a nearby hostel.

Time Line: Program directors begin annually in July and serve for 13 months, until the following August. Summer volunteers serve for either four or eight weeks in May and June.

Cost: Program directors pay $8,500 for their 13 months of service but also receive a living stipend of approximately

$1,000. Summer volunteers pay $900 per four-week session. Accommodations and meals are provided for all volunteers, though international airfare is the responsibility of the individual volunteer.

Getting Started: Program directors must submit an application form, resume, undergraduate transcript, and two references. Summer volunteers submit an application form, resume, and one letter of recommendation. Deadlines for applications are generally in January and March. Applicants will be contacted no more than two weeks after the deadline. Program directors have an in-person training in Miami before departure and then have one month of overlap with the departing program directors. During this period, the new program directors attend language school and participate in homestays.

Needed Skills and Specific Populations: Program directors must have a bachelor's degree, and Spanish language skills are a plus. They must also demonstrate leadership and achievement, and be self-starters. All volunteers must be at least 18 years old; while there is no maximum age, almost all program directors are between 22 and 28 years old, and this age range is preferred in order to create a peer-based setting in the shared housing. Family members may apply as individual candidates, but MPI does not guarantee that they will be placed together.

Medical Ministry International (MMI)

P.O. Box 1339
Allen, TX 75013
United States: (972) 727-5864; Fax: (972) 727-7810
Canada: (905) 524-3544; Fax: (905) 664-8386
E-mail: mmitx@mmint.org
Website: www.mmint.org

Project Type: Medical/Health

Mission Statement Excerpt: "Medical Ministry International is an opportunity to serve Jesus Christ by providing spiritual and physical health care in this world of need."

Year Founded: 1968 as Medical Group Missions; became Medical Ministry International (MMI) in 1995

Number of Volunteers Last Year: 1,600

Funding Sources: Private sources and some faith-based organizations

The Work They Do: MMI sends volunteer teams of health care professionals to serve the world's poor who have little or no access to medical care. The health care MMI offers is usually all that is available to the recipients. Both medical and nonmedical volunteers are accepted, including dentists, primary care and specialty physicians, surgeons, optometrists, nurses, health educators, other health professionals, translators, technicians, handy people, and general helpers. To provide the very best possible care for patients, only qualified professionals participate directly in surgical or dental procedures. Medical and project directors assign each participant a role, matching his or her skills and training to the needs of the project. Days are full, and volunteers work hard as a team to see as many patients as possible during the week.

Project Location: The organization works regularly in over 30 countries around the world. Work sites vary; some involve a short-term clinic set up in a school or community center for the duration of a project, while others involve a clinic that is moved by volunteers to different areas every few days. Teams may also work at an existing hospital. Accommodations are usually in a hostel, dorm, or small hotel, all of which have bathroom facilities. MMI usually uses its own cooks to ensure that volunteers and staff members receive healthful food and water.

Time Line: One- and two-week projects are scheduled year-round, though most projects are for two weeks. It may be possible to stay longer than two weeks, but volunteers will need to work this out with the hosts on location. Some MMI volunteers add tourist travel to the end of their stay.

Cost: The program fee is $895 for a one-week project and $1,295 for a two-week project. All room and board costs are included in the program fee; volunteers must provide their own airfare to the country of service. Each project has a project director and a medical director who will work with volunteers to coordinate all needed medicines and supplies. More than 90 percent of the program fee goes directly into program services.

Getting Started: Prospective volunteers can apply online, download an application online, or request an application from the address listed above. MMI provides preparatory materials that outline how to plan for the trip and what to expect. Team orientation occurs on the first day in the host country.

Needed Skills and Specific Populations: Doctors, dentists, and surgeons must be currently licensed to practice. Volunteers aged 12 to 14 must be accompanied by a parent; youths 15 to 17 years old must be accompanied by a designated adult and need a notarized letter signed by both parents (or legal guardians) authorizing them to make the trip; volunteers under 18 years of age will not be allowed in operating rooms. People aged 18 and over are welcome to volunteer as adults. Families with children who meet the minimum age requirements listed above are welcomed, as are senior volunteers; spouses may accompany medical volunteers. Volunteers with disabilities are welcomed, provided they are able to travel in places that are not wheelchair-accessible; please contact MMI before applying.

Mercy Ships

P.O. Box 2020
Lindale, TX 75771
(903) 939-7000; Fax: (903) 939-7114
E-mail: jobs@mercyships.org
Website: www.mercyships.org

Project Type: Administrative; Community Development; Education; Medical/Health

Mission Statement Excerpt: "Mercy Ships, a global charity, has operated hospital ships in developing nations since 1978. Mercy Ships follows the 2000-year-old model of Jesus, bringing hope and healing to the world's forgotten poor."

Year Founded: 1978

Number of Volunteers Last Year: Approximately 1,600

Funding Sources: Faith-based, government, and private sources

The Work They Do: Mercy Ships provides medical care and training for long-term sustainable change in developing nations. As a global charity, Mercy Ships serves people without regard for ethnicity, gender, or religious preference. Mercy Ships is best known for its work in health care services, which are provided to patients free of charge. Their newest vessel, the *Africa Mercy*, includes six state-of-the-art operating rooms, an intensive care unit, X-ray and laboratory services, a CAT scanner, and ward bed space for up to 78 patients. On shore, mobile dental teams establish field clinics in nearby communities. A major focus of Mercy Ships is the support of training for national doctors and nurses in the countries it serves, to improve local health care delivery systems.

Project Location: The majority of Mercy Ships' projects are located in West Africa. In most cases, volunteers are fed and housed on a Mercy Ship. Volunteer lodging is dormitory style.

Time Line: Available positions are listed on the Mercy Ships website. Depending on the position, Mercy Ships volunteers commit to a length of service ranging from two weeks to several years; they may even make a career choice to be part of the Mercy Ships crew. Volunteers are considered short-term if they serve for less than two years.

Cost: Short-term volunteers pay an onboard living fee of $680 per month, which helps cover the cost of food and housing, and they are responsible for paying for their own travel expenses to and from the vessel. A discount is given to those who make at least a two-year commitment.

Getting Started: Prospective volunteers can download an application from the Mercy Ships website. Entry training is required for anyone wanting to serve for nine months or more and is offered at Mercy Ships' International Operations Center in Texas.

Needed Skills and Specific Populations: Mercy Ships offers both medical and nonmedical volunteer opportunities. Medical volunteers must be experienced, fully licensed, and certified and have at least two years of postgraduation experience. Volunteers must be at least 18 years old; there is no maximum age limit as long as the volunteer meets our health requirements. Due to the limited confines of the Mercy Ships vessels, the organization generally cannot accommodate short-term volunteer families or people with disabilities.

National Cooperative Business Association Farmer-to-Farmer (FTF) Program

1401 New York Avenue NW, Suite 1100
Washington, DC 20005
(202) 638-6222; Fax: (202) 347-1968
E-mail: ncba@ncba.coop
Website: www.ncba.coop/ncba-clusa/our-work
/farmer-to-farmer

Project Type: Agriculture; Community Development; Economic Development; Natural Conservation (Land); Professional/ Technical Assistance; Rural Development

Mission Statement Excerpt: "To develop, advance and protect cooperative business."

Year Founded: 1916

Number of Volunteers Last Year: 12

Funding Sources: Government and foundation support

The Work They Do: Farmer-to-Farmer fields short-term volunteers who provide technical assistance to farmers, farm groups, and agribusinesses in the areas of food security and agriculture. Through this program, funded by the US Agency for International Development, volunteers provide assistance and training in processing, production, marketing, and other agricultural disciplines to the targeted populations.

Project Location: FTF volunteers operate only in Senegal. Project sites are frequently shaded clearings in local villages. There is no electricity, Internet service, or running water. These volunteer assignments are physically demanding. The weather in Senegal can be very hot, with daytime temperatures exceeding 100°F. Volunteers need to be able to stand for long periods of time and walk two to four miles per day over rough terrain. Volunteers stay in hotels or guests houses that are arranged by FTF program staff. Accommodations are safe and air conditioned and sometimes have wireless Internet.

Time Line: Volunteer projects last for two to three weeks and operate year-round except for the month of Ramadan, which usually takes place in August or September.

Cost: The NCBA covers all assignment-related expenses; volunteers should not have to spend any of their own funds to participate.

Getting Started: Potential volunteers should send a letter of interest and a resume to the e-mail address listed on the "Available Assignments" section of the FTF website; a phone interview is required as part of the application process. Volunteers receive an orientation to the host organizations and to working in Africa, but are expected to already have professional expertise in the area of their assignment.

Needed Skills and Specific Populations: Volunteers are typically experts in cooperative development, marketing, soil conservation, agricultural production, processing, or other related disciplines. Volunteers must be at least 18 years old; senior volunteers are encouraged, but their health must be good enough to allow them to be successful in Senegal and Niger's physically challenging environments. Volunteers with disabilities will be considered on a case-by-case basis. FTF volunteers must be US citizens or permanent residents. Families may volunteer together for FTF assignments as long as each has a productive volunteer assignment; family members who do not have a volunteer assignment are discouraged from accompanying FTF volunteers.

National Trust Working Holidays

Heelis
Kemble Drive
Swindon SN2 2NA
United Kingdom
+44 844 800 3099
E-mail: working.holidays@nationaltrust.org.uk
Website: www.nationaltrust.org.uk

Project Type: Agriculture; Historic Preservation; Natural Conservation (Land)

Mission Statement Excerpt: "For ever, for every one."

Year Founded: 1895

Number of Volunteers Last Year: 4,000

Funding Sources: Individual donors

The Work They Do: The National Trust carries out conservation projects in historic homes and gardens and across the countryside. Volunteers assist in this mission through practical conservation tasks such as biodiversity surveys, helping with events, gardening, and educational activities.

Project Location: Volunteer projects take place throughout England, Wales, and Northern Ireland. Accommodations are provided and include a large range of options, depending on the project and location.

Time Line: Volunteer projects take place throughout the year for a minimum of 3 days and a maximum of 11 days.

Cost: Program fees start at £55 and go up to £350; all program fees include room and board. Volunteers are responsible for their own expenses en route to the project, including airfare to the United Kingdom.

Getting Started: Prospective volunteers can book a trip through the National Trust's website listed above; volunteers are not required to interview before beginning their booking. Each project begins with a health and safety talk that includes an orientation to the project and any tools to be used.

Needed Skills and Specific Populations: No specific skills are needed to volunteer with the National Trust. Volunteers must be at least 18 years old, and there is no upper age limit. Volunteers with disabilities should discuss this with the National Trust's booking office, as not all projects are accessible. The National Trust does offer specific Youth Discover holidays for those 16 to 18 years old, as well as family-friendly volunteer opportunities.

Naucrates

Via dei Ristori, 7
04010 Giulianello di Cori (LT)
Italy
+39 333 430 6643; Fax: +39 06 966 5018
E-mail: info@naucrates.org
Website: www.naucrates.org

Project Type: Community Development; Natural Conservation (Land); Natural Conservation (Sea)

Mission Statement Excerpt: "We work toward conservation of nature with particular interest in endangered species and habitats."

Year Founded: 2001

Number of Volunteers Last Year: 40

Funding Sources: Naucrates receives money from some private sources

The Work They Do: Naucrates takes on conservation, education, and scientific research projects, specifically in the areas of sea turtle survival and the protection of mangrove forests and Mediterranean woods. Volunteers help by walking the beach looking for sea turtle nests, taking weather measurements, participating in fundraisers, educating local schoolchildren, and planting new trees to restore mangrove forests and Mediterranean woods.

Project Location: Naucrates's work is mainly conducted on an island off the coast of Thailand, based at Lion Village (Pak Choke). Lodging in the local village is in homestays. Each house has toilets and a shower, and laundry is done on request by local ladies. Tap water at the village is not potable, but bottled water is always available. Electricity is available only between 6:30 PM and 10:00 PM. Food is cooked by a local woman, with a vegetarian option available on request.

Time Line: The Thailand project runs between December and April; volunteers must commit to a minimum of two weeks. Most volunteers stay for one two-week period.

Cost: The program fee is €695 for two weeks, which covers three meals a day, accommodations, coordination fees, and training. Travel expenses and insurance are not included.

Getting Started: Prospective volunteers can download an application from the Naucrates website or contact the organization to request one. Training is provided on the first day, and workshops are held throughout the stay.

Needed Skills and Specific Populations: Volunteers must be fit and able to work in a group. The minimum age for volunteers is 18; seniors are welcomed, provided they are in good physical health. Naucrates cannot host volunteers with disabilities.

New Era Galapagos Foundation (NEGF)

San Cristobal Island, Galapagos
Ecuador
E-mail: info@neweragalapagos.org
Website: www.neweragalapagos.org

Project Type: Community Development; Education; Natural
   Conservation (Land); Youth
Mission Statement Excerpt: "To conserve the Galapagos Islands
   by empowering local residents through educational pro-
   grams and environmental action projects."
Year Founded: 1998
Number of Volunteers Last Year: 65
Funding Sources: Private donations
The Work They Do: NEGF programs consist of educational and
   environmental action projects, including foreign language
   training and art and environmental education programs. All
   of these empower local residents with the skills and awareness needed for the long-term conservation of the Galapagos
   Islands, while simultaneously providing human and social
   development opportunities that enable the local population
   to benefit from conservation. Specific projects include
   running a summer camp for children and teens, teaching
   courses in English as a foreign language, camping with the
   Eco Scouts, teaching gardening skills to teens, and helping
   with coastal cleanups. Volunteers usually work 20 to 25
   hours per week.
Project Location: All of NEGF's projects are located on San
   Cristobal Island, Galapagos, Ecuador. The building in which
   English as a foreign language and environmental education
   courses take place has year-round electricity and Internet
   access. Volunteers live in a friendly, low-key community,
   surrounded by wildlife, and should not expect much in the way
   of nightlife. Volunteers typically live with local host families.
Time Line: The "summer camp" runs from the first week of
   February until the second week of March and offers volunteer opportunities in educational areas, including environ-

mental art, English language, and guiding field trips. The English for All volunteer program is also educational in nature, and volunteers assist with or lead classes Monday through Friday in the months of April through December. Volunteers in this program must stay for a minimum of one month, though volunteers are requested to stay for at least two months if possible. One-day Saturday environmental cleanup and education programs are also available.

Cost: There is no program fee. Volunteers must cover all of their own costs, including airfare.

Getting Started: Prospective volunteers can either fill out the online application form at the NEGF website or send a resume with a cover letter to the e-mail address listed above, specifying their area of interest, level of Spanish, and dates available for volunteer work. This information should arrive at NEGF no less than two months prior to the start date of the project in which they are interested. NEGF provides a general overview of its programs and basic introductions to the volunteer program. For the summer camp, volunteers arrive a minimum of one week in advance to design and prepare the various programs. All volunteers, regardless of the programs in which they are involved, are encouraged to arrive one week before their programs start.

Needed Skills and Specific Populations: Most volunteers have previous ESL teaching experience, though exceptions are made for fluent English speakers when resources are limited. Basic Spanish (at a minimum) is preferred, but is not required for the English as a foreign language program. Volunteers who teach environmental education typically also have a background in this area or in the natural sciences. NEGF requires all volunteers to be at least 21 years of age and to have a positive attitude with a good sense of humor. NEGF encourages senior volunteers and volunteers with disabilities to participate in its programs, and it has hosted several volunteers from each of these populations.

NGOabroad

P.O. Box 2034
Vashon, WA 98070
E-mail: info@NGOabroad.com
Website: www.NGOabroad.com

Project Type: Community Development; Economic Development; Education; Medical/Health; Professional/Technical Assistance; Women's Issues; Youth

Mission Statement Excerpt: "NGOabroad is a unique service that helps you enter or advance in international humanitarian work and provides frugal, customized international volunteer opportunities."

Year Founded: 2003

Number of Volunteers Last Year: 124

Funding Sources: No outside funding sources

The Work They Do: NGOabroad offers two services: international volunteer opportunities and assistance entering or advancing a career in humanitarian work with international nongovernmental organizations (NGOs). NGOabroad offers both established volunteer programs as well as individualized, customized opportunities, such as setting up opportunities for a French citizen to work with refugees in Miami and for a Hungarian man who wanted to work with people with autism-spectrum disorders in Malta. Examples of established programs include launching and marketing village enterprises with Congolese refugees, combating domestic violence in Cameroon, coaching soccer in Ghana, and assisting with a medical clinic in Peru, art therapy with kids in Honduras, and IT education in Sri Lanka.

Project Location: NGOabroad works in Africa (Uganda, Kenya, Ghana, Cameroon, and Sierra Leone), the Americas (Costa Rica, the Dominican Republic, Peru, Honduras, Bolivia, and Ecuador), and Asia (India, Sri Lanka, and Nepal). Most of the work environments are very simple offices, which may have Internet connections, though most of the volunteers'

269

time is spent outside the office, working among the people. Medical clinics have basic equipment. Volunteers often stay with host families, whom they join for meals and help with household chores; many of the houses in Africa may utilize pit toilets. In post-conflict Uganda, which has a housing crunch, volunteers stay in local guesthouses.

Time Line: Volunteer projects are available year-round. Exact dates for each volunteer's experience is determined by the volunteer in consultation with NGOabroad and the community being served, in order to take into account school schedules, the harvest season, or other activities of the host organization. Most volunteers stay for two or three months; others stay for years.

Cost: Program fees are $750 to $800, plus $12 per day for lodging and meals. Program fees do not include airfare or insurance.

Getting Started: Prospective volunteers should visit the organization's website to complete an online questionnaire and send it with a resume or CV to NGOabroad. While NGOabroad requests that volunteers, especially those interested in Africa, complete an application at least six months before departure, it has successfully placed volunteers on much shorter time lines. NGOabroad does require a phone interview with each prospective volunteer in order to determine the best placement in advance. Volunteers going to Africa are given a two-hour travel consultation before departing, which mostly covers health and safety issues.

Needed Skills and Specific Populations: NGOabroad does not require specific skill sets but does have placements available for many different kinds of trained professionals who seek to transfer their skills to an international setting. Mostly, NGOabroad seeks volunteers who have "an attitude of service and humility, of cultural graciousness, and the ability to roll with the punches." They welcome volunteers of all ages, including families, as well as volunteers with disabilities where those disabilities make them the "resident expert" on how to assist others with similar conditions.

Oceanic Society

Quarters 35N, Fort Mason
San Francisco, CA 94123
(800) 326-7491 or (415) 441-1106; Fax: (415) 474-3395
E-mail: info@oceanicsociety.org
Website: www.oceanicsociety.org

Project Type: Education; Natural Conservation (Land); Natural Conservation (Sea); Scientific Research

Mission Statement Excerpt: "The mission of the Oceanic Society is to protect marine wildlife and oceanic biodiversity through an integrated program of scientific research, environmental education, volunteerism, and the establishment of nature reserves."

Year Founded: 1969

Number of Volunteers Last Year: 216

Funding Sources: Private sources, including individual donors and foundations

The Work They Do: The Oceanic Society's work is focused on conservation. It primarily conducts conservation research that includes geographic information systems to help establish nature reserves. For example, in Belize, research project results will be used for an ecologically sustainable management plan. The society also provides training for Belizean students on its projects and works closely with local groups and agencies. In the past, volunteers have collected data on dolphins, manatees, crocodiles, seabirds, sea turtles, and coral reefs, and they have helped to map the distribution of various species of wildlife. They have also mapped habitats and conducted transects to monitor reef health.

Project Location: Most of the Oceanic Society's volunteer projects are located in Belize, Suriname, Micronesia, Baja California, and Costa Rica. Volunteers work in remote areas. They should be prepared to face obstacles such as heat and sometimes insects. All volunteer accommodations include hot water and electricity, and they are usually double-occupancy cabins. Food is primarily of the local cuisine.

Time Line: Volunteer projects are available year-round for a minimum of seven days and a maximum of three weeks. On average, volunteers stay for eight days.

Cost: The average program fee is $1,970, which covers all costs except airfare to the host country, non-meal refreshments, and tips for local guides.

Getting Started: Prospective volunteers should carefully review the project descriptions on the organization's website, complete an application form (which is also available on the website), and submit it with a $400 deposit. Interviews are not required. The Oceanic Society provides all volunteers with a detailed research plan listing goals, objectives, and methods. It also sends, in advance of a volunteer's departure date, an outline of specific volunteer tasks and sample data sheets. Tutorials are sometimes provided on its website. Once on-site, formal briefings and training are provided by the researcher prior to beginning the field work. Equipment trials are run before data is collected.

Needed Skills and Specific Populations: Some projects require snorkeling abilities before beginning the volunteer assignment. There are a variety of tasks associated with each project, and the Oceanic Society matches each task to the volunteer's abilities and interests. Most projects have a minimum age of 16, though some require volunteers to be at least 18 years old. Some projects, but not all, accept senior volunteers. Some projects are directed at families with a minimum age of 10. Volunteers with disabilities are welcomed as locations allow.

OmniMed

81 Wyman Street
Waban, MA 02468
(617) 332-9614; Fax: (617) 332-6623
E-mail: ejoneil@omnimed.org
Website: www.omnimed.org

Project Type: Community Development; Education; Medical/
  Health; Rural Development; Social Justice
Mission Statement Excerpt: "To promote health equity through
  service training programs abroad."
Year Founded: 1998
Number of Volunteers Last Year: 20
Funding Sources: Foundations, private donors
The Work They Do: OmniMed trains and maintains community
  health workers in rural Uganda. Volunteers can help train
  the community health workers, conduct focus groups and
  home visits, develop the program's infrastructure, and coordinate with government officials.
Project Location: OmniMed operates only in Mukono, Uganda.
  Volunteers should expect a truly rural experience, including
  pit latrines and bucket showers.
Time Line: Volunteers are accepted year-round for no more and
  no less than four weeks each.
Cost: OmniMed estimates that the total cost of volunteering
  with them is around $3,500 for one month, including
  airfare. The program fee is $1,500, airfare is between
  $1,200 and $1,700, and accommodations and food total
  about $350 for one month.
Getting Started: Prospective volunteers should contact
  OmniMed and submit a resume or CV. There is no application or application deadline. Volunteers who pass an initial
  paperwork screening must also complete a phone interview.
  Training is provided online, including an overview of health
  inequality issues.

Needed Skills and Specific Populations: A background as a trained health professional is preferred, but not required. All volunteers must be willing to spend time before departure learning about the program and how best to support and maintain the community health workers. Volunteers must be at least 21; there is no maximum age for volunteers, as long as they are willing to accept the austere, challenging conditions under which they will live and work in Uganda. Volunteers with disabilities who can ride public transportation and navigate independently are welcome. Families cannot volunteer with OmniMed.

Operation Crossroads Africa (OCA)

P.O. Box 5570
New York, NY 10027
(212) 289-1949; Fax: (212) 289-2526
E-mail: oca@igc.org
Website: www.operationcrossroadsafrica.org

Project Type: Agriculture; Community Development; Construction; Economic Development; Education; Medical/Health; Rural Development; Women's Issues

Mission Statement Excerpt: "Make a difference for others, see the difference in yourself."

Year Founded: 1957

Number of Volunteers Last Year: Approximately 250

Funding Sources: None; OCA is self-funded

The Work They Do: Through OCA, groups of 8 to 10 volunteers of diverse backgrounds work together with local people on community-initiated projects. Projects tend to be physical in nature and fall into one of five categories: community construction and development (such as constructing youth training centers, health centers, and wells); health and medical outreach; agriculture and reforestation (such as clearing land, planting seeds, and digging ditches); education and training (in which volunteers might teach ESL, help with youth recreation events, or give computer lessons); and women's development (primarily income generation and microenterprise projects).

Project Location: As its name indicates, OCA works in Africa. Specific host countries change each year, but in past years OCA has operated projects in 35 African nations including Ethiopia, Ghana, Kenya, Gambia, Lesotho, Malawi, Namibia, South Africa, Tanzania, Uganda, Benin, Mali, Niger, Senegal, and Togo. Volunteers live communally, often in very basic conditions and almost always in rural areas.

Time Line: All of OCA's projects run during the summer. Volunteers spend six weeks working on a volunteer project, followed by one week of travel in the host country, during which local transportation is used.

Cost: OCA's program fee is $3,800. This program fee is remarkably inclusive, in that it takes care of the volunteer's international airfare and all in-country transportation, food, accommodations, visas, and international health insurance during both the volunteer experience and the week of travel afterward.

Getting Started: A program application is available on OCA's website; requirements include a two-page autobiographical essay and responses to five questions. Applications are due in February, and no interview is required. OCA requires volunteers to complete three days of orientation and training before departure.

Needed Skills and Specific Populations: OCA volunteers must be at least 18 years old. Except for those volunteers who wish to work in the areas of medicine and health, no special skills are required. Racial, gender, ethnic, regional, and educational diversity are primary goals of OCA, and groups are structured to be as inclusive as possible.

Outreach360 (formerly Orphanage Outreach)

6611 West Robert E. Lee Street
Glendale, AZ 85308
(800) 876-5678; Fax: (602) 714-8231
E-mail: info@outreach360.org
Website: www.outreach360.org

Project Type: Agriculture; Community Development; Construction; Education; Orphans; Youth

Mission Statement Excerpt: "The mission of Outreach360 is to transform individuals, families, communities, and countries through the education and development of orphaned, abandoned, and disadvantaged children. As we release the hero within these children, we release the hero within each person involved with Outreach360."

Year Founded: 1995

Number of Volunteers Last Year: 2,400

Funding Sources: Foundations and individual donors

The Work They Do: Outreach360 collaborates with the community to meet real needs. They teach in grade schools and operate community centers supporting K–12 students by teaching English, literacy, public health education, and environmental sustainability. Volunteers can also be involved with summer learning camps and assist with agriculture and construction projects. Multiweek and long-term volunteers can assist with a leadership development program.

Project Location: Outreach360 offers opportunities in the Dominican Republic and Nicaragua. In the Dominican Republic, they work in three small villages on the northwest part of the island: Monte Cristi, Jaibon, and Manzanillo. Volunteers in the Nicaragua program work in a town named Jinotega, known as the "City of Mist." Volunteers stay in simple, comfortable summer camp facilities owned by Outreach360, with bunk beds, showers, and buffet meals.

Chris Goffnett blows bubbles with kids at a day care center in Nicaragua. *Photo courtesty of Bryson Adams*

Time Line: Volunteer projects take place year-round. Volunteers commit to a minimum of one week. Most volunteers serve one or two weeks, but they can stay as long as two years.

Cost: Program fees are $800 for a week, $1,800 for a month, and $2,800 for two months; additional months after the first two are $500 each. Scholarships are available for groups, early registration, and families. The program fee includes all accommodations and meals, in-country transportation, in-country staff support, and insurance. Volunteers are responsible for their own travel expenses to and from the Dominican Republic and/or Nicaragua.

Getting Started: Prospective volunteers should first complete an online form, available at Outreach360's website, and should do so at least 30 days before they want to depart. Phone interviews are only required for those planning to volunteer for two months or longer. Volunteers receive an online volunteer guide, as well as more training in their host country.

Needed Skills and Specific Populations: No specific skills are required, though volunteers should be enthusiastic, flexible, and creative. Families are encouraged to volunteer, though children under the age of 18 must be accompanied by a parent or temporary legal guardian. Senior volunteers are welcomed, as are volunteers with disabilities; each volunteer should discuss any specific needs with Outreach360 staff prior to registering.

Our Family Volunteer Vacation

By Chris Goffnett

Outreach360 (formerly Orphanage Outreach)

During spring break 2010, our family of eight traveled to the Dominican Republic for a family volunteer vacation. We were placed in Jaibon. Our kids made fast friends with the boys at the orphanage and were quickly involved in baseball games, playing with puppies, and enjoying the time with their new friends.

During the week we spent in Jaibon, our group went to various neighborhoods nearby to organize activities with the local children. We taught the children songs, we colored, we played games, and we read stories. In each neighborhood, happy children and grateful parents welcomed us. The children were out of school for Holy Week, and they were very enthusiastic for organized activity.

One afternoon, we spent time at Batey Libertad, a Haitian migrant camp. At Batey Libertad, many of the children lacked shoes, and many of the younger boys wore almost no clothing at all. At some of the other locations we had worked that week, we experienced spending time with children who were mired in poverty. But at Batey Libertad the poverty was much, much worse. Yet the children of Batey Libertad were energetic and excited to spend time playing, coloring, and singing with us. For our children it was an opportunity to learn that joy does not come in a package or in some clothes, but joy comes from experiencing life with one another.

Our experience volunteering in the Dominican Republic gave us time to unplug from the fast pace of our lives. We were able to clear away all of the distractions that put demands on our lives and focus on our family. Without the demands of work, school, sports schedules, etc., we were able to enjoy time with one another and with the communities in which we were working. Working with children in Jaibon and the surrounding communities was a deeply rewarding experience. I felt that we were there to give them hope; the hope that there are people in the world who care about them, who want the best for them, and who are willing to come and meet them where they are.

Pacific Crest Trail Association (PCTA)

1331 Garden Highway
Sacramento, CA 95833
(916) 285-1846; Fax: (916) 285-1865
E-mail: info@pcta.org
Website: www.pcta.org

Project Type: Trail Building/Maintenance

Mission Statement Excerpt: "The mission of the Pacific Crest Trail Association (PCTA) is to protect, preserve and promote the Pacific Crest National Scenic Trail (PCT) as an internationally significant resource for the enjoyment of hikers and equestrians, and for the value that wild and scenic lands provide to all people."

Year Founded: PCTA was founded in 1977, though precursors of the group date back to the 1930s

Number of Volunteers Last Year: Last year, over 1,400 volunteers donated more than 132,000 hours of their time

Funding Sources: PCTA receives funding from both private and corporate foundations, donations, and the federal government

The Work They Do: PCTA volunteers work together to carry out a wide variety of trail maintenance, construction, and reconstruction projects. Projects may include brushing, blowdown tree removal, tread rehab and construction, and the creation of rock and log structures and bridges. On overnight projects, volunteers are expected to assist with camp chores, such as cooking and cleaning.

Project Location: Volunteers work along the 2,650-mile Pacific Crest Trail, which runs through the coastal ranges of Washington, Oregon, and California all the way from Canada to the US-Mexico border. Work sites range from low-lying deserts to temperate rain forests, and from wilderness backcountry sites to easily accessible locations. Lodging ranges from developed campgrounds to backcountry tent sites.

Time Line: Projects are available year-round, though not in all locations, due to weather and elevations. Volunteer projects include one-day, weekend, and weeklong commitments.

Cost: There is no program fee to volunteer with PCTA. Tools and safety equipment are provided to volunteers at no cost throughout the duration of a project. On overnight projects, all meals and designated camp fees are also covered. Volunteers will need to arrange their own transportation to and from the meeting site; bring water bottles, a day pack, and sturdy boots; and, on extended trips, provide their own camping gear.

Getting Started: Prospective volunteers should start at PCTA's website, where they can learn about the organization, the trail, and current volunteer projects. Volunteers will need to submit an application, which can also be found online. Volunteers are accepted throughout the year, and interviews are not required. All volunteers receive a safety orientation and project-specific training from trail crew leaders.

Needed Skills and Specific Populations: Volunteers do not need prior experience in trail work to participate, but should be capable of traveling through and living temporarily outdoors. Volunteers must be at least 16 years old, but volunteers aged 14 and 15 can participate with a parent or guardian. There is no maximum age to volunteer on a trail crew. PCTA welcomes volunteers with disabilities as long as they can carry out the project tasks safely.

Passport in Time (PIT)

P.O. Box 15728
Rio Rancho, NM 87174
(800) 281-9176; Fax: (505) 896-1136
E-mail: volunteer@passportintime.com
Website: www.passportintime.com

Project Type: Archaeology; Historic Preservation; Scientific
Research
Mission Statement Excerpt: "The goal of Passport in Time (PIT)
is to preserve the nation's past with the help of the public."
Year Founded: 1988
Number of Volunteers Last Year: 1,500
Funding Sources: The US Forest Service, an agency within the
US Department of Agriculture, sponsors PIT, and projects
are also now run through the Bureau of Land Management
and some state parks
The Work They Do: PIT is a volunteer cultural heritage preservation program on public lands throughout the United
States. PIT volunteers work with professional archaeolo-
gists, anthropologists, paleontologists, and historians on
such diverse activities as archaeological survey and excavation, rock art restoration, archival research, historic structure restoration, gathering of oral histories, analysis and
curation of artifacts, and much more. What sets PIT apart
from other public heritage programs is that volunteers are
helping professionals with the daily job of historic preservation and research on public lands.
Project Location: PIT projects take place on public lands across
the United States. Some work sites are in towns or communities, but most are in woodland, and often remote, areas. A
few projects provide group meals or a camp cook and ask
volunteers to contribute to group meals. In most cases,
volunteers camp out near the project areas. Facilities range
from campgrounds to bunkhouses, guard stations, and
primitive campsites. In addition, some projects are located

close to towns, making it possible for volunteers to stay in hotels. Project leaders provide selected volunteers with a complete list of facilities, food, and lodging options, and prospective volunteers will find a project overview listed for each project on the PIT website when they apply.

Time Line: Projects take place year-round. Projects vary in length, but most are five days long. Many offer the option of staying for two five-day sessions. Project commitments vary greatly. Some require a minimum time commitment of one day, and a few have longer-term needs that span months. Minimum commitments are listed in each project's description on the PIT website.

Cost: There are no program fees to volunteer with PIT. Volunteers provide their own transportation to the projects and, usually, their own meals and lodging. Out-of-pocket expenses vary widely, depending on the type and length of the project and whether volunteers are camping or staying in local hotels.

Getting Started: Prospective volunteers fill out applications on PIT's website for any and all projects they find interesting, and can realistically attend, and submit the applications by the respective projects' deadlines. All applications are then submitted to the project leader, and selected volunteers are contacted within approximately three weeks. Application does not guarantee selection, but, unless specified, everyone is considered on an equal basis, regardless of experience with PIT or possession of any technical/professional skills. For regular program updates, interested volunteers can sign up for the e-Traveler newsletter by contacting the PIT Clearinghouse or through the "subscribe" link on the PIT website. PIT volunteers receive training on-site from agency professionals during the projects.

Needed Skills and Specific Populations: Most projects do not require specific skills; those that do note this in their project descriptions. Volunteers must be at least 18 to participate without an adult, but many PIT projects accept children who are accompanied by an adult. The program encourages participation by families, and it is pleased with the increasing number of grandparent-grandchild pairs who serve on PIT projects. Senior volunteers are "absolutely" encouraged to work with PIT. Many of PIT's projects are in locations that are fully accessible to volunteers with disabilities, and the toll-free number listed above includes TTY. Volunteers with special needs are encouraged to contact PIT directly to see if the projects they are interested in can accommodate their needs. International volunteers can apply to work with PIT using a tourist visa.

Peacework

209 Otey Street
Blacksburg, VA 24060-7426
(540) 953-1376 or (800) 272-5519
E-mail: mail@peacework.org
Website: www.peacework.org

Project Type: Community Development; Economic Development; Education; Rural Development; Women's Issues; Youth

Mission Statement Excerpt: "Peacework is dedicated to meeting humanitarian needs, promoting global understanding, expanding personal awareness of the world's cultures, and integrating the resources of educational institutions and corporations where strategic and enduring partnerships can address conditions of poverty and development."

Year Founded: 1989

Number of Volunteers Last Year: Approximately 400

Funding Sources: Projects and donors

The Work They Do: Peacework arranges and manages global projects in collaboration with indigenous community development organizations and educational or corporate partners. Projects include construction, education, medical services, health education, business and entrepreneurship, and other humanitarian and community development efforts. Almost all of Peacework's project arrangements are tailored for groups, such as those from a university or a professional service organization; there are no minimum or maximum group sizes. In some limited cases, projects can be arranged for individuals in disciplines such as health care and education. Peacework's primary focus is the Peacework Village Network, in which a long-term partnership is organized between an institution of higher education and one or more villages around the world so that the cross-section of disciplines, resources, and affiliates of the university or college are integrated with resources and needs in the developing community.

Project Location: Projects are located in Russia, Vietnam, Belize, Honduras, South Africa, Ghana, the Dominican Republic, the People's Republic of China, Haiti, the Czech Republic, Guatemala, Costa Rica, Mexico, St. Lucia, Cambodia, and Malawi. Work sites and accommodations vary depending on the locations, but they are arranged with the host community and are consistent with their resources. Accommodations are comfortable and safe.

Time Line: Projects can take place at any time of year. There is no minimum or maximum duration. Typical projects run for one to two weeks.

Cost: In general, program fees run from $1,400 to $2,800 per person and cover international airline travel, accommodations, meals, visas as required, in-country travel costs, liability insurance, and medical insurance.

Getting Started: Organizations should contact Peacework or complete the "Getting Started" form found on its website. Peacework collaborates with group leaders or administrators to plan an orientation in advance of a volunteer project and then works with in-country hosts to provide a group briefing on-site at the beginning of a project.

Needed Skills and Specific Populations: Projects are available for any level or type of skill, experience, age, physical ability, and background, and are also available for families.

Projects Abroad

347 West 36th Street, Suite 903
New York, NY 10018
(888) 839-3535; Fax: (212) 244-7236
E-mail: info@projects-abroad.org
Website: www.projects-abroad.org

Project Type: Community Development; Education; Human
  Rights; Medical/Health; Natural Conservation (Land);
  Natural Conservation (Sea); Orphans
Mission Statement Excerpt: "Projects Abroad sends volunteers
  to 25 different developing countries to do service projects
  and internships."
Year Founded: 1992
Number of Volunteers Last Year: 7,000
Funding Sources: No outside funding sources
The Work They Do: Projects Abroad offers a wide range of
  volunteer and internship programs, including teaching,
  helping in a health clinic or a hospital (including opportuni-
  ties for pre-med students), working in orphanages, assisting
  print and television journalists, doing environmental conser-
  vation work, taking care of animals, doing archaeological
  work, providing business expertise, and coaching sports.
Project Location: Volunteer placements are available in
  Argentina, Bolivia, Brazil, Cambodia, China, Costa Rica,
  Ethiopia, Fiji, Ghana, India, Jamaica, Mexico, Moldova,
  Mongolia, Morocco, Nepal, Peru, Romania, Senegal, South
  Africa, Sri Lanka, Tanzania, Thailand, Togo, and Vietnam.
  In most cases, volunteers stay with host families and have
  their own rooms, although sometimes the rooms are shared
  with another volunteer. The host families also provide all
  meals.
Time Line: Volunteers are accepted throughout the year for
  between one month and one year. The average volunteer
  works for one to three months.

Cost: Program fees vary, but range from $1,995 to $5,995, depending on the duration and location of the volunteer program. The program fee covers accommodations, food, health and travel insurance, and airport transfers. Airfare is not included in the program fee.

Getting Started: Prospective volunteers can apply online via Projects Abroad's website, over the phone, or by requesting a brochure and completing the application form contained therein. An interview is not required for the application, but applicants must provide contact details for someone who can serve as a reference. Volunteers receive their own personal MyProjectsAbroad web page which contains predeparture information about what to bring and how to prepare for their trip. Volunteers are also given a one-day, in-country orientation to the area of service and to the host culture.

Needed Skills and Specific Populations: Volunteers must be at least 16 years old, and senior volunteers are welcomed. Projects Abroad accepts volunteers of all nationalities. No specific skills are required, though volunteers must be self-reliant, mobile, and able to withstand significant levels of culture shock. Projects Abroad can reasonably make accommodations for volunteers with disabilities, given the circumstances in each specific country. Families with young children are able to volunteer with some of Projects Abroad's programs.

ProWorld Volunteers

600 California Street, 10th floor
San Francisco, CA 94108
(877) 429-6753 or (415) 434-5464; Fax: (415) 434-5480
E-mail: info@proworldvolunteers.org
Website: www.proworldvolunteers.org

Project Type: Administrative; Construction; Education; Human
Rights; Medical/Health; Natural Conservation (Land);
Women's Issues; Youth

Mission Statement Excerpt: "The mission of ProWorld is to
empower communities, promote social and economic development, conserve the environment, and cultivate educated,
compassionate global citizens."

Year Founded: 1998

Number of Volunteers Last Year: 820

Funding Sources: Government, foundations, and private donors

The Work They Do: ProWorld offers volunteer and internship
opportunities with local nonprofit organizations that are
tailored to the individual volunteer's skills and goals for the
experience. In general, volunteer projects are available in the
areas of health care, education, the environment, microbusi-
ness, appropriate technology, women's rights, construction,
journalism, and the fine arts. Examples of specific projects
include constructing schools, installing drinking-water
systems, providing shelter and counseling for victims of
domestic violence, teaching small-business management
skills, and supporting the educational initiatives of local
schools.

Project Location: Volunteers work in Cusco and Sacred Valley
of Peru; in tropical rain forest and coastal communities of
Belize; in Oaxaca, Mexico; in Udaipur, India; in Chiang
Mai, Thailand; in Salvador, Brazil; in Quito and the
Amazon in Ecuador; in San Jose, Costa Rica; in Kathmandu, Nepal; and in Cape Coast, Ghana. ProWorld selects
project and program locations based on multiple factors,

including participant safety, community need, community interest, and quality of participant experience. Volunteer accommodations are with families in homestays.

Time Line: Volunteers are accepted throughout the year for volunteer or internship opportunities that last from one week to six months. Programs start the first Saturday of every month except December.

Cost: A one-week volunteer program costs approximately $1,445, with a $290 program fee for each additional week. Room and board with a host family, health and travel insurance, project funding and support, domestic transportation, and cultural and adventure trips are included in the program fee. Volunteers in Peru, Mexico, Ecuador, and Costa Rica also receive intensive Spanish language classes, and volunteers in Brazil receive intensive Portuguese classes. Volunteers must pay for their own international airfare, as well as for individual travel outside the program.

Getting Started: Prospective volunteers can complete an online application, which is available on the ProWorld website. Volunteers whose applications are received at least three months prior to departure are given priority for project and location placement. The deadline for applications is one month prior to departure. Each volunteer must also complete an interview as a part of his or her application. Volunteers receive online training before departure and then have a two-day on-site orientation that includes information on health, safety, cross-cultural education, and projects, as well as excursions. Throughout the volunteer experience, ProWorld provides a "ProWorld Global Citizen Initiative," which includes education modules covering service-learning, social enterprises, international volunteering, cultural awareness, sustainable development, the role of nonprofit organizations, and reentry issues.

Needed Skills and Specific Populations: Volunteers must be at least 18 years old and in good health; there is no maximum age, and senior citizens are encouraged to volunteer. ProWorld can make accommodations through partner organizations for volunteers who have visual and auditory disabilities; they have had physically disabled participants in the past. ProWorld does not have any citizenship restrictions for volunteers. They have also hosted a few families over their history; children under the age of 18 must have a parent or guardian on the program with them, and pricing for children under the age of seven will be determined based on the care that they require during the program.

Raleigh

207 Waterloo Road, 3rd floor
London SE1 8XD
United Kingdom
+44 20 7183 1270; Fax: +44 20 7504 8094
E-mail: info@raleigh.org.uk or
volunteermanagers@raleigh.org.uk
Website: www.raleighinternational.org

Project Type: Community Development; Natural Conservation
(Land); Natural Conservation (Sea); Rural Development;
Scientific Research; Youth

Mission Statement Excerpt: "Raleigh is a youth and sustainable
development charity that provides adventurous and
challenging expeditions for people from all backgrounds,
nationalities and ages, especially young people. Our volunteers develop key skills, explore the world and make a real
difference to local communities and their environment."

Year Founded: 1984

Number of Volunteers Last Year: Approximately 1,200

Funding Sources: Foundations, government sources, and individual donors

The Work They Do: Raleigh runs adventure and challenge expeditions. Volunteers between the ages of 17 and 24 complete
sustainable community and environmental projects, plus
have the opportunity to participate in an adventure
challenge. Volunteers older than that age range are able to
lead and facilitate the expeditions, fulfilling a range of roles.
These volunteer managers fulfill roles such as project
manager, medic, finance manager, administrator, communications officer, adventure/trek project manager,
photographer, Spanish interpreter, artist, logistics manager,
and driver.

Project Location: Raleigh runs expeditions in Borneo, India,
Costa Rica, and Nicaragua. Their projects are based within
national parks and rural communities, which gives volun-

teers greater access to remote areas and the people who live there.

Time Line: Volunteer projects run for 5 to 10 weeks throughout the year. Volunteer managers receive training in-country, so their commitment is an additional two to three weeks.

Cost: Raleigh program fees for volunteers between the ages of 17 to 24 range from £1,750 to £2,995. Program fees for volunteer managers range from £1,350 to £1,950. The program fees include medical insurance, food and accommodations, in-country travel, specialist equipment, training, and support. Program fees do not include flights, vaccinations, or any required visas.

Getting Started: Prospective volunteers can attend an open event to find out further information if based in the United Kingdom or access an online application on Raleigh's website. Volunteers aged 17 to 24 do not need to complete an interview, but volunteer managers need to either attend an assessment weekend, if based in the United Kingdom, or complete a telephone interview.

Needed Skills and Specific Populations: Raleigh strives to make international volunteer opportunities open to as many people as possible. The only requirements are that prospective volunteers must desire an adventure, want to make a difference by volunteering overseas, and understand that they will learn about themselves and different cultures. Due to the nature of the environments, the remote locations, and work that Raleigh undertakes, any applicants with special medical or mobility requirements will be discussed individually during the application process to determine whether Raleigh can achieve the necessary safety requirements while also trying to account for the needs and wishes of the individual. Raleigh does not offer volunteer opportunities for families.

Sustainable Projects in India

By Owen White

Raleigh

After completing his management and economics course at university, Owen White decided to take a full gap year combining individual and group travel. Owen joined Raleigh's ten-week expedition in India in spring 2010 working on a variety of sustainable projects.

I was going to be traveling for a year during my gap year, and I wanted to mix it up so that I did some traveling on my own but also spent some time working with a group; Raleigh allowed me to do this by placing me in two different projects in India. My decision to take some time off after university was because I wanted to see something completely different and have a different experience while doing something worthwhile. I wanted to get out of the typical tourist routes, and Raleigh gave me this opportunity.

First I was placed in Kudimery, a remote hamlet in India, on a tribal housing project to benefit the Paniya Indigenous Tribal Group. Our project aims were to refurbish their homes, which were in considerable disrepair. We undertook tasks such as painting, plastering, cementing, and repairing roofing with the assistance of skilled masons. The project took place on a hill in the middle of a tea plantation in an absolutely stunning location.

It was interesting to see how the tribal people were treated by other members of Indian society, and I definitely observed a hierarchy within their culture that I hadn't anticipated. As we were the first project of many to come to Kudimery, it was important to make first contact with the tribal community and to establish trust between them and ourselves. This project was the first time the villagers were exposed to Western people, so cultural awareness was key in order for us all to live in harmony; winning their trust was significant. We enjoyed bonding with the local families and playing with their children. Trust from the village was given as we started to teach their children. Teaching was both a useful and enjoyable experience.

My next project was in the heart of the Cauvery Wildlife Sanctuary located in the mountains of the Mysore district of India, about 50 miles from Bangalore. Camping in the national park right by the river, deep in elephant and tiger territory, our group worked with the local forest department to construct an anti-poaching camp. Rock, sand, and water were required for the construction of the camp. Our location was so remote that we had to pull these resources from the river ourselves before we could start construction. Being in the national park was genuinely one of the best times of my life; we were cut off from anyone and everything for three whole weeks, and it was amazing to be just with the team. We spent a long time moving the materials from the river up a very steep hill to the campsite, so when we actually started building and using these materials it all felt really worthwhile and rewarding.

Concerning the team, we were all thrown in together and each group was made up of a random selection of people that would never normally associate with each other in day to day life. This was an excellent learning curve for me and it really flipped the stereotypes that I had in my head. It was funny, as the people I thought I wouldn't be great friends with were generally the people that I ended up getting on best with. I consider that, being integrated with lots of different types of people, I have developed my leadership skills. I have also developed my communication skills. I have dealt with people on all different levels and have managed situations when people are tired and drained, which I think is an important life skill.

Traveling and volunteering has taught me a number of things. I have learned by meeting so many different people that there is not one regimented path that you need to take in life. You can go out and experience so many different things in life and not just have a nine-to-five job. To sum up my Raleigh experience, it is a once in a lifetime opportunity that has definitely surpassed all of my expectations.

Reef Check

P.O. Box 1057
17575 Pacific Coast Highway
Pacific Palisades, CA 90272
(310) 230-2371 or (310) 230-2360; Fax: (310) 230-2376
E-mail: rcinfo@reefcheck.org
Website: www.reefcheck.org

Project Type: Natural Conservation (Sea); Scientific Research
Mission Statement Excerpt: "Reef Check's objectives are: to educate the public about the value of reef ecosystems and the current crisis affecting marine life; to create a global network of volunteer teams trained in Reef Check's scientific methods who regularly monitor and report on reef health; to facilitate collaboration that produces ecologically sound and economically sustainable solutions; and to stimulate local community action to protect remaining pristine reefs and rehabilitate damaged reefs worldwide."
Year Founded: 1997
Number of Volunteers Last Year: More than 1,000
Funding Sources: Both governmental and private sources
The Work They Do: Reef Check is the only volunteer-based organization that measures reef health using a standard method on a global scale. Its programs focus on building a global community of reef stakeholders and helping them at the grassroots level to improve reef health. Most volunteers participate in a reef monitoring survey, either by establishing their own Reef Check team or by joining an already established team. Reef Check surveys include collecting data on substrate materials, fish, and invertebrates. Volunteers help deploy transect lines, set up surveys, collect data, ensure dive safety, and record information about the reef location being surveyed. Reef Check also offers expeditions around the world to help monitor coral reefs.
Project Location: Reef Check has had teams in more than 90 countries and territories around the world, and there is potential for volunteers wherever there is a coral reef.

Conditions vary depending on the location and the team's setup, but volunteers should expect that their "work site" will be the ocean, as most Reef Check volunteers spend their days diving and actively looking at reefs. Volunteers are responsible for their own accommodations; some teams may be associated with a particular resort or hotel that can offer a discounted package.

Time Line: Volunteers can work with Reef Check throughout the year, depending on weather conditions. Volunteer assignments are usually for a minimum of one week, but they can vary depending on the monitoring period established by the team. The average volunteer stint with Reef Check is two weeks.

Cost: There is no program fee to volunteer with Reef Check, but there may be a small fee for training or other required classes. Volunteers, therefore, are responsible for all of their own costs. Average costs for a volunteer vacation with Reef Check vary depending on location, lodging, length of stay, and dive expenses. Reef Check offers memberships starting at $25 per year, but membership is not a prerequisite to volunteering. All costs are the responsibility of the volunteer unless otherwise arranged with their team.

Getting Started: Prospective volunteers should e-mail Reef Check at the address listed above. Some teams require a phone interview in advance of the volunteer's service. Reef Check offers trainings that typically last for three days and include both land-based and ocean components.

Needed Skills and Specific Populations: To work with Reef Check, volunteers should be certified scuba divers with excellent buoyancy control. Some surveys may be able to be done via snorkel. Additional skills may be required, depending on the team. As long as the diver demonstrates the needed skills and can understand the survey protocol, there are no age or ability limits on who can volunteer with Reef Check. Families are welcome to volunteer with Reef Check, but to participate in a reef survey, all members must be experienced scuba divers. Some dive sites require various language abilities in order to communicate with local workers.

Restless Development

7 Tufton Street
London SW1P 3QB
United Kingdom
+44 20 7808 1784
E-mail: info@restlessdevelopment.org
Website: www.restlessdevelopment.org

Project Type: Community Development; Education; Human Rights; Medical/Health; Natural Conservation (Land); Rural Development; Youth

Mission Statement Excerpt: "Restless Development works to put young people at the forefront of change and development."

Year Founded: 1985

Number of Volunteers Last Year: More than 1,000

Funding Sources: Restless Development receives some funding from international governments, private foundations, and individuals

The Work They Do: Restless Development is dedicated to making young people central to the development process. Through Restless Development's International Placements, young American, European, and Australian volunteers live and work alongside African and Asian volunteers who are recruited from the host country. Restless Development's emphasis is on training these volunteers (all aged 18 to 28) to create a sustainable framework for development that responds to the needs of each community. Restless Development volunteers work in rural communities, where volunteers coordinate with schools and community leaders to identify and resolve key health or environmental issues. Health volunteers accomplish this goal through teaching health classes, providing skills training, and organizing community health workshops. Environmental volunteers introduce and encourage sustainable use of natural resources, waste management, appropriate technologies, and income generation projects.

Project Location: Volunteers work in rural communities in Nepal and Uganda. (Restless Development also administers programs in other countries, but these are run by national volunteers and do not accept international volunteer applications at this time.) Living conditions are very basic, as volunteers live the same way that the community members do. Transport around the community is generally by foot. Most villages do not have running water or electricity. Volunteers live in a family's home or in pairs in one house in the village. Accommodations will be arranged in advance by Restless Development but will be at the discretion of the community, so volunteer lodging may be in a school, an empty house, or a local family's home. Volunteers purchase food from local shops and markets, and they are generally responsible for cooking for themselves.

Time Line: Generally, volunteers depart in January, though those volunteering in Nepal will depart in October or November. Programs run from five to eight months, with the first month devoted to training. Holidays and time off varies by program, but volunteers can expect to have one or two days off each week (though they will generally stay in the village); long-term volunteers receive one to two weeks' midterm holiday.

Cost: Restless Development's program fee is $6,800. In return, the organization covers the cost of a round-trip flight to the placement country, comprehensive travel and health insurance, visas acquired by in-country staff, training, food, accommodations, in-country work-related travel expenses, and predeparture and in-country support. Restless Development books volunteers on 12-month return flights, so many volunteers travel independently or in small groups after the program ends.

Getting Started: Restless Development's application process is selective, and places on programs are limited. Restless Development recommends applying 6 to 12 months before departure to maximize choice of programs. Applications are accepted on a first-come, first-served basis. Prospective volunteers can download an information packet from the website or can request an application form from the office. Regular information sessions are held by phone. Applicants are interviewed by Restless Development through phone interviews. All volunteers participate in predeparture training conference calls, which provide an opportunity for volunteers to talk with returned volunteers and Restless Development staff. Once in-country, all volunteers will receive three to six weeks of training (depending on the length of the program), which will include program-specific information, training in nonformal education techniques and appropriate rural technologies, participatory rural appraisal skills, and information on language, health, and safety.

Needed Skills and Specific Populations: Restless Development volunteers must have graduated from high school and be at least 18 years old. The maximum age for volunteers is 28. People with disabilities should contact the Restless Development office to discuss their specific circumstances. There are no restrictions on citizenship. Restless Development was formerly known as Students Partnership Worldwide (SPW).

Seeds of Learning

P.O. Box 2107
Sonoma, CA 95476
(707) 939-0471; Fax: (707) 939-1951
E-mail: info@seedsoflearning.org
Website: www.seedsoflearning.org

Project Type: Community Development; Construction; Education; Rural Development; Social Justice; Youth

Mission Statement Excerpt: "Seeds of Learning is dedicated to promoting conditions for quality learning in developing communities of the Americas while educating its North American constituents about the rich cultural diversity and the educational and social needs of poorly resourced communities in Central America."

Year Founded: 1991

Number of Volunteers Last Year: 220

Funding Sources: Private donors, faith-based organizations, and foundations.

The Work They Do: Seeds of Learning sends 18 groups of volunteers to Central America annually. These groups of volunteers spend between 7 and 14 days partnering with communities in Nicaragua and El Salvador to erect or improve a school building while also forming relationships and exploring one another's cultures. On the construction sites, volunteer tasks include digging, mixing concrete, laying bricks, roofing, and painting. Volunteers also have opportunities to interact with the host community through cooking, reading to children, and other activities.

Project Location: Seeds of Learning works in a range of rural locations in El Salvador and Nicaragua, but all of their communities include simple living and rustic lodging. Work sites tend to be hot and humid, and can sometimes be wet. Volunteers are generally housed in nearby towns or cities in a hotel or hostel and travel to the work site by bus or truck.

Time Line: While most volunteers travel to Central America in the summer, Seeds of Learning places volunteers from February through November. Volunteer projects generally last from 7 to 14 days, with an average of 10 days.

Cost: The program fee is $1,300, which includes all meals, accommodations, in-country transportation, emergency travel insurance, and airport transfers, but not international airfare to the country.

Getting Started: Prospective volunteers may complete an online application via Seeds of Learning's website, or may print one off, complete it, and mail it in. Interviews are not required. Seeds of Learning provides an online educational packet for volunteers, and group leaders hold preparatory meetings in advance of the trip.

Needed Skills and Specific Populations: Seeds of Learning does not require any specific skills but asks that all volunteers come with a desire to work alongside others with an open mind. They do not have a minimum or maximum age for volunteers and encourage youth volunteers and families by offering a $100 discount on program fees to children under 16. Seeds of Learning also welcomes volunteers with disabilities.

Sierra Club Outings

85 Second Street, 2nd floor
San Francisco, CA 94105
(415) 977-5522; Fax: (415) 977-5795
E-mail: national.outings@sierraclub.org
Website: www.sierraclub.org/outings/national

Project Type: Archaeology; Historic Preservation; Natural
Conservation (Land); Natural Conservation (Sea); Scientific
Research; Trail Building/Maintenance

Mission Statement Excerpt: "Explore, enjoy, and protect the
planet."

Year Founded: The Sierra Club was founded in 1892, and the
first Sierra Club Outings were undertaken in 1901

Number of Volunteers Last Year: Approximately 1,000

Funding Sources: None; the Sierra Club Outings program is run
entirely on program fees, and it does not receive any funds
from outside organizations or from the Sierra Club itself

The Work They Do: Sierra Club Outings offers a range of
volunteer activities focused on the outdoors and environmental work. Volunteer opportunities include, but are not
limited to, archaeological digs, animal and habitat restoration projects, trail work, and invasive plant removal. All
service trips include at least one day with no activities
scheduled to allow volunteers to explore the surrounding
wilderness areas. The leaders of Sierra Club Outings projects are volunteers themselves who scout, propose, plan,
and run all of the trips. Sierra Club Outings stresses the
importance of building a strong community as a group, so
volunteers may feel more of a bond with their fellow participants than volunteers do with other organizations.

Project Location: Outings are offered throughout the United
States and in Puerto Rico, the Virgin Islands, and Canada.
Work sites vary from national parks and wilderness areas to
animal sanctuaries in Maui and parks in major American
cities. Accommodations are provided, usually either through

camping or in a rustic lodge, though some trips stay in B&Bs or cabins.

Time Line: Outings are offered almost every month of the year, and most last for one week.

Cost: In general, program fees are between $350 and $600, with a few both above and below this range. The program fee includes all room and board, work equipment, and group activities. Volunteers who are 18 or older must be members of the Sierra Club. The program fees do not cover travel costs to the volunteer sites, and volunteers typically need to bring their own camping gear.

Getting Started: Information and application forms for prospective volunteers are available at the website listed above. Volunteers register for a specific trip online or by calling the Sierra Club. After registration, they interview by phone with the trip leader, who determines whether or not they are approved for the trip, mostly based on whether or not the volunteer has the physical capacity to safely participate in the trip. Acceptance is not competitive, and the interview is not designed to weed out prospective volunteers. Training in specific tools and methodologies is provided on-site.

Needed Skills and Specific Populations: Most work sites are "moderately strenuous," but there are trips that can be undertaken by anyone in decent physical shape. Usually the minimum age for volunteers is 18, but this can be waived if the project leader agrees and if the minor's parent or guardian also volunteers on the project. There are also a few trips designed specifically for families with children, such as a trail-building trip near California's Trinity Alps and a family archaeology trip in Dixie National Forest, Utah. The largest demographic group for Sierra Club Outings is people aged 40 to 70 years old, so senior volunteers are very much welcomed. Sierra Club Outings also offers special-interest service trips for multigenerational families, teens, seniors, and women. Specific work sites may be able to accommodate volunteers with disabilities, depending on what disabilities are involved.

Righting the Cemetery

By Marty Joyce

Sierra Club Outings

It took us about an hour to bounce along the jeep trail five miles to the Sewell Cemetery, where we were to start a new project: restoration of a historic cemetery. There were 21 of us and a ranger. The site was 10 acres and not the open meadow we imagined. It looked like 50 years of second-growth forest. The tombstones were not apparent. But as we searched, we found more and more evidence of the talisman to eternal life.

Our task was to remove any trees less than six inches in diameter to open the burial ground to the Appalachian canopy. We also were to clear undergrowth and reset headstones. The first two tasks were old hat to this group of volunteers. The last required respect and a crash course from the ranger.

> *Darling*
> *A precious life from us is gone*
> *A voice we loved is stilled*
> *A place is vacant in our home*
> *Which never can be filled.*

First, you had to level the base stone with a mixture of sand and pea gravel. Once the base was level, pennies were set at corners to provide a space for the epoxy to set properly. Lincoln's beard was always placed up! The stone then had to be precisely lifted onto the base so the epoxy would not smear. The final touch was a rolled sealant around the perimeter between the stone and the base to keep moisture out. Gravestones are much heavier than they look.

> *Shes gone to worlds above*
> *Where saints and angels meet*
> *To realize our Saviours love*
> *And worship at his feet*

As we toured the site, like ghosts in our midst, more and more gravestones appeared. We soon realized that the two days set aside for this project would not enable us to rebuild all these stairways to heaven, which numbered 300.

> *Dear husband Thou art gone to rest*
> *Thy sins are all forgiven*
> *And saints in light have welcomed*
>   *thee*
> *To share the joy of heaven*

The headstones all faced east according to the Biblical guide. Every stone told part of a story. We were constantly trying to fill the gaps in these stories. Was there a plague in 1912 that led to so many tender flowers fading too soon?

> *Our darling baby*
> *Donovan Haynes*
> *Born Dec 11th 1912*
> *Dies Dec 29th 1913*
> *Sleep on sweet baby and take*
> *thy rest. God called thee home*
> *He thought*
> *it best*

For example, how and why did SS Propps drown on January 26, 1896, at age 27 yrs 1 mo 9 dys? The spirits of miners, lumberjacks, and railroad workers, their wives and children, were our soulmates as we toiled for two days in an effort to refurbish their heritage. Every tombstone reappointed to the sky was our affirmation that they had once lived. We were joined to the deceased through a few words of epitaph and our sweat mingled with their dirt.

Death is an intimate human experience. So if a graveyard is restored in the remote woods, so far back that no beer cans were found, does anyone care? Does anyone benefit? Yes. We all benefit by honoring the dead and remembering their lives. Our work was temporary, because they who lie there shall sleep, but not forever. They can rest assured, like Samual T. Surface, that they remain gone but not forgotten.

> *A loved one from us has gone*
> *A voice was loved is stilled*
> *A place is vacant in our home*
> *Which never can be filled.*

Sunseed Desert Project

Apdo. 9
04270 Sorbas
Almeria
Spain
+34 950 525 770
E-mail: sunseedspain@arrakis.es
Website: www.sunseed.org.uk

Project Type: Agriculture; Construction; Natural Conservation
(Land); Rural Development; Scientific Research
Mission Statement Excerpt: "Sunseed Desert Project aims to
develop, demonstrate, and communicate accessible low-tech
methods of living sustainably in a semiarid environment."
Year Founded: 1986
Number of Volunteers Last Year: 200
Funding Sources: The organization receives a few donations
from individuals
The Work They Do: Sunseed Desert Project demonstrates a
sustainable lifestyle by using and developing low-tech
methods that have the least detrimental environmental
impact as an appropriate alternative to other, often less
accessible technologies and techniques. Program areas
include appropriate technology, eco-construction and maintenance, dryland and water management, organic growing,
food preservation, education, publicity, and fundraising.
Volunteers can work in all of Sunseed's departments, both in
research and in community activities, such as gardening,
housework, and building. Longer-term volunteers may
undertake their own individual projects, choosing an idea
from Sunseed's Project Pack or designing a project
themselves in consultation with the organization. Examples
of past such projects include setting up an urban garden,
investigating the use of seed pellets, constructing a thermal
compost water heater, producing a study of local ecology,
and looking at erosion control techniques. Volunteers may

also join weekly activities, such as seminars, tours, Spanish lessons, and documentary screenings, and a monthly visit to other projects.

Project Location: Sunseed Desert Project is based in a small rural village located in a valley in the semiarid landscape of southeast Spain. Living and working conditions are basic and shared, but they are comfortable. Sunseed Desert Project volunteers follow a vegetarian diet (no milk or cheese; free-range eggs available once a week).

Time Line: All of Sunseed's projects are ongoing and accept volunteers and interns throughout the year. Volunteers may either be part-time, working four hours per day and six days each week, or full-time, working seven hours per day and five days each week.

Cost: Program fees vary by time of year and length of stay, but they range from €74 to €94 per week. Each program fee covers room, board, and the materials for individual projects, but not travel to or from Spain.

Getting Started: Prospective volunteers should check Sunseed's website and contact Sunseed's administrator by e-mail. All training is done on-site, and work is supervised as needed.

Needed Skills and Specific Populations: Volunteers under 16 years of age must be accompanied by an adult. Volunteers aged between 16 and 18 years must provide a written statement from an adult testifying to the volunteer's maturity and ability to volunteer. Senior volunteers are welcomed, but they should recognize the difficulty of the terrain at the center. While Sunseed tries to accommodate as many volunteers as possible, people with restricted mobility may have difficulty navigating the center, as it is not wheelchair accessible.

Sustainable Harvest International (SHI)

779 North Bend Road
Surry, ME 04684
(207) 669-8254; Fax: (207) 669-8255
E-mail: smallerworld@sustainableharvest.org
Website: www.sustainableharvest.org

Project Type: Agriculture; Economic Development; Natural
Conservation (Land); Rural Development
Mission Statement Excerpt: "The mission of Sustainable
Harvest International (SHI) is to provide farming families in
Central America with the training and tools to preserve our
planet's tropical forests while overcoming poverty."
Year Founded: 1997
Number of Volunteers Last Year: Over 300
Funding Sources: Support from foundations, faith-based organi-
zations, private donors, and corporations and businesses
The Work They Do: SHI works with families in rural farming
communities in Belize, Honduras, Nicaragua, and Panama.
Using organic vegetable gardens, wood-conserving stoves,
biogas digesters, and a host of other projects, SHI has local
field trainers who work with families, individuals, and
communities to preserve tropical forests while overcoming
poverty. SHI also operates Smaller World Tours, which
allows a group of 8 to 15 volunteers to work alongside
SHI's local staff and their participant families on a wide
range of projects. Volunteers are involved in hands-on projects such as building wood-conserving stoves, constructing
irrigation systems, and planting gardens.
Project Location: SHI's projects take place in rural communities
in Belize, Honduras, Nicaragua, and Panama; volunteers
should expect to live without some basic amenities, such as
electricity or in-home running water. Accommodations vary,
but options include homestays, community lodges, hotels,
and luxury eco-lodges, though most volunteers opt for
homestays with families who participate in SHI's projects.

Natalie, a volunteer, assists field trainer Estevan on chicken-coop construction in a Trio village in Belize. Many rural farming families want to diversify and raise chickens as well as crops. Sustainable Harvest International provides some of the materials to build *gallineros* (chicken coops) as well as the technical support and information the families need to turn their flocks into a sustainable part of their farms. Not only do the chickens provide eggs, but they also produce manure that families use to organically fertilize their fields. Free-range chickens that have a coop to roost in at night are less susceptible to diseases and predators, they provide more eggs, and they produce a larger amount of fertilizer. *Photo courtesy of Greg Bowles/Sustainable Harvest International*

SHI volunteers are always housed with at least one other volunteer in the homestay, and host families provide meals as well as a culturally and linguistically immersive setting for volunteers.

Time Line: SHI runs its Smaller World Tours on a set schedule, which changes annually and is available on their website; they can also plan a custom trip for a group of volunteers. SHI's trips are usually one to two weeks in length.

Cost: SHI's program fees vary by country and length of stay, but average around $1,500 per volunteer; youth under the age of 15 who travel with a family member pay only $675. The program fee does include all meals and accommodations but does not include airfare to the host country.

Getting Started: Trip schedules and deadlines change every year, so prospective volunteers should see SHI's website for a schedule and application. Interviews are not required as a part of the application process. SHI volunteers receive a predeparture orientation packet as well as an on-site orientation after arrival, which covers language and cultural training, along with a farm tour. During the volunteer experience, local staff and participant families work alongside the volunteers, providing hands-on instruction and training.

Needed Skills and Specific Populations: SHI does not require that its volunteers have any specific skill set, and it also does not have any minimum or maximum age. Senior citizens and families are encouraged to take part in SHI tours, provided that children are accompanied by a parent, legally appointed guardian, or designated chaperone. Volunteers with disabilities are also welcome, provided that they are aware that the work settings are in rural, physically demanding settings; accommodations will be made on a case-by-case basis. SHI also has a role for designated group leaders, who serve as liaisons between volunteer groups and SHI staff. Group leaders also assist with recruitment, pre-trip orientation activities, and some leadership responsibilities during the trip in exchange for having their program fees waived.

Tethys Research Institute

Viale G.B. Gadio, 2
20121 Milan (MI)
Italy
+39 02 7200 1947; Fax: +39 02 8699 5011
E-mail: tethys@tethys.org
Website: www.tethys.org

Project Type: Natural Conservation (Sea); Scientific Research

Mission Statement Excerpt: "The Tethys Research Institute is dedicated to the preservation of the marine environment. It focuses on marine animals and particularly on cetaceans inhabiting the Mediterranean Sea, and it aims to protect its biodiversity by promoting the adoption of a precautionary approach to the management of natural resources."

Year Founded: 1986

Number of Volunteers Last Year: Approximately 250

Funding Sources: Tethys is funded largely by faith-based and private sources

The Work They Do: Tethys does scientific research to identify the threats affecting Mediterranean cetaceans, and it proposes solutions to these problems. Volunteers actively collaborate in the collection of field data on cetaceans, and they are requested to help in all project activities. These may include recording navigation data, plotting sighting positions on a navigation chart, loading data in the computer, collecting ecological and behavioral data, noting photo-identification data, and helping with the identification of individual whales and dolphins. Volunteers and researchers alike take part in cooking and cleaning shifts.

Project Location: In the Ligurian Sea, Tethys has a 21-meter (69-foot) research ship that normally stays in the harbor of Portosole, San Remo, Italy. Volunteers sleep and live onboard during the research project. There are five cabins on board, which can host 16 people: the captain and one researcher each have a single bed in the bow and share one bathroom, and there are two four-bed cabins and a large room for six people (two double and two single beds), each with private bathroom, shower, and hot water.

Time Line: Volunteers are accepted from May through October for six days; volunteers can sign up for more than one project.

Cost: Program fees range from €850 to €925. The program fee covers all lodging and food, though volunteers must provide for their own travel expenses. Students under the age of 26 are offered a discount on some programs.

Getting Started: Prospective volunteers should call or fax the Milan office at the numbers listed above between 9:30 AM and 12:30 PM, Monday through Friday, from January to September, and during other months on Monday, Wednesday, and Friday (please remember to adjust for time zones). They will then complete an application form and send the program fee, which will secure the reservation. Interviews are not required to volunteer with Tethys. During each project, researchers give daily lectures on cetaceans and conservation issues. Practical training is also provided during the research project.

Needed Skills and Specific Populations: Volunteers must be able to swim, and they must be at least 18 years old, though minors accompanied by family members will be considered on a case-by-case basis. Volunteers should be able to speak enough English to be able to communicate with other project participants and team members. They should be in good physical condition and able to tolerate hot weather, sun, and long periods on a boat. Anyone in good physical condition is welcome to volunteer, including seniors. Prospective volunteers with disabilities should contact the organization's office and will be considered on a case-by-case basis.

Theodore Roosevelt Medora Foundation

P.O. Box 1696
Bismarck, ND 58502-1696
(701) 223-4800; Fax: (701) 223-3347
E-mail: volunteer@medora.com
Website: www.medora.com

Project Type: Administrative; Community Development; Economic Development; Historic Preservation; Museum; Youth

Mission Statement Excerpt: "Preserve the values and traditions of the Old West embodied in the pioneer cattle town of Historic Medora and the 'Bully Spirit' of Theodore Roosevelt."

Year Founded: 1986

Number of Volunteers Last Year: 485

Funding Sources: Individual donors

The Work They Do: The historic town of Medora, North Dakota, offers a number of historical tourist destinations that work collectively to keep the history of the Old West alive and to present it to thousands of visitors each year. Volunteers help in the preseason by helping to clean, paint, stain, and prepare flower beds, and by planting flowers. During the heavy tourist season, volunteers work in the information center, theater, restaurant, heritage center, campground, gift shop, and musical stage. End-of-season volunteers help clean up, work in food establishments, and assist with grounds and maintenance positions.

Project Location: Medora is a small town located in North Dakota's Badlands, near Interstate 94 and the Theodore Roosevelt National Park. Volunteers who bring their own camper or RV are housed in a local campground; others find accommodations in a local hotel or a residence built especially for volunteers, by volunteers.

Time Line: The preseason begins in mid-May and lasts about two weeks, and volunteers work for at least five days, beginning on a Monday. In-season volunteers are welcomed between June and August, beginning on Mondays for eight days. End-of-season volunteers have 11-day commitments in August and September.

Cost: There is no program fee. Volunteers are provided with all of their meals and lodging, and receive discounts for local retail shops, entertainment, and museums. Volunteers must provide their own transportation to Medora and to volunteer sites that are not within walking distance.

Getting Started: Prospective volunteers can request information and an application by mail or e-mail; the foundation asks that prospective volunteers do not call for information. There are no deadlines, but volunteer positions do fill up quickly, and volunteers should submit their application by January 15. No interview is required. The selection of volunteers is completed in March. Volunteers go through orientation (usually for about eight hours) on the day they arrive, which covers basic information about Medora and on-site training for specific tasks.

Needed Skills and Specific Populations: Volunteers must be cheery and welcoming, with a positive attitude, and be willing to "tackle any task with a smile!" Most of Medora's volunteers are aged 50 to 85, so while there is no minimum age to volunteer, children are not encouraged to volunteer, and families with children are a rarity in the volunteer corps. Volunteers with disabilities are welcome.

Transformational Journeys

480 Northeast Martin Boulevard
Kansas City, MO 64118
(816) 808-3668
E-mail: info@tjourneys.org
Website: www.tjourneys.org

Project Type: Community Development; Construction; Education; Professional/Technical Assistance; Rural Development; Social Justice; Youth

Mission Statement Excerpt: "To introduce individuals to experiences that can inspire compassion, develop understanding and promote generosity through mutual service with people of other cultures."

Year Founded: 1997

Number of Volunteers Last Year: Approximately 225

Funding Sources: Private sources

The Work They Do: Volunteers with Transformational Journeys carry out short-term projects, such as building homes, community centers, schools, and churches for economically disadvantaged communities in developing countries. Volunteers lead recreational projects, teach, build, paint, repair, and pour foundations. Some examples of projects include teaching dance or crafts to the children in a community in Brazil; erecting a multipurpose center for a Mayan village in Guatemala; building homes or small home repair in the Dominican Republic in partnership with local families; participating in the daily life activities of Haitians, and working with a local school in Tanzania.

Project Location: Volunteers can currently work on projects in Brazil, the Dominican Republic, Guatemala, Haiti, Tanzania, and Peru. Work sites range from very urban environments in Brazil and Kenya to rural Mayan villages in Guatemala's mountains to a Caribbean seaside community in the Dominican Republic. Lodging varies by country and ranges from dormitory-style accommodations, homestays, guesthouses, simple hotel rooms with shared or private bath to a possible four-star hotel in Brazil.

Time Line: Projects follow set time lines as specified by Transformational Journeys' country partners and run throughout the calendar year. Contact Transformational Journeys to find out about upcoming dates. Volunteer trips range from a minimum of 9 days to a maximum of 15 days.

Cost: Transformational Journeys' program fees include international travel costs and are priced on a per-trip basis. Because of this, program fees may fluctuate as air costs change. Estimated costs range from $1,700 to $3,550 for a 10-day program, depending on the country of service. Beyond international airfare, the program fee also covers medical travel insurance and most in-country expenses, such as hotels, transportation, and meals. Volunteers are responsible for visa fees, which can range from $40 to $100, depending on the country, obtaining their own passport, vaccinations when required, and one or two meals during excursion days.

Getting Started: Prospective volunteers should e-mail or call Transformational Journeys to request a travel schedule. Participation in an orientation session is required prior to departure, which includes instruction about the culture, language, politics, religion, and sociology of the destination country. Work training is provided on-site.

Needed Skills and Specific Populations: Volunteers' ages range from young children to seniors, and families are welcome. Minors must be accompanied by a parent or guardian. Some trips require specific activity levels due to site conditions or terrain. The work projects are identified prior to trip scheduling, in order to allow prospective volunteers to evaluate their ability to perform the tasks the project requires. Work training is provided on-site, and therefore no special skills are required for participation on a trip. Transformational Journeys will make every effort to accommodate volunteers with disabilities. A detailed interview will assist Transformational Journeys in assessing the volunteer's specific needs for in-country requirements, which will allow their in-country partners to determine their ability to handle these accommodations.

Travellers Worldwide

2A Caravelle House
17–19 Goring Road
Goring-by-Sea
Worthing BN12 4AP
United Kingdom
+44 1903 502595; Fax: +44 1903 708179
E-mail: info@travellersworldwide.com
Website: www.travellersworldwide.com

Project Type: Community Development; Education;
Medical/Health; Natural Conservation (Land); Natural
Conservation (Sea); Orphans; Youth

Mission Statement Excerpt: "Travellers makes a positive and
lasting impact upon the environments, communities, institutions, volunteers and all stakeholders that we work with, by
providing placement opportunities whilst ensuring that our
own ethical standards are met."

Year Founded: 1994

Number of Volunteers Last Year: Over 1,000

Funding Sources: None, outside program fees

The Work They Do: Travellers Worldwide offers over 250 projects in over 20 countries around the world, primarily in the
areas of teaching, conservation, health care, and sports.
Volunteers can take part in projects ranging from coaching
youth in Cape Town; to teaching children and adults in
Guatemala; to working in conservation, sustainability, and
education efforts in the Peruvian rain forest.

Project Location: Volunteer projects are located in 20 different
countries around the world. Volunteers are usually housed
in homestays or youth hostels.

Time Line: Volunteers are welcome throughout the year, in projects ranging in length from one week to one year.

Cost: Program fees start at £675 for some two-week programs
and rise depending on the program and length of stay.
Room and board is generally included in the program fee.

Getting Started: There are no deadlines for applications, which are accepted throughout the year and are available on Travellers Worldwide's website. Travellers Worldwide offers an orientation before the trip and upon arrival; one- and two-day training courses are also available for teaching projects. Prospective volunteers need to complete a phone interview as a part of the application process.

Needed Skills and Specific Populations: Volunteers must be at least 17 years old, but there is no maximum age for volunteers. Some of Travellers Worldwide's projects are suitable for volunteers with disabilities, but this requires discussions between the volunteer and Travellers Worldwide before registering. Families are welcome, as long as all children are at least 16 years old.

United Action for Children (UAC)

P.O. Box 177
Muvuka, South West Region
Cameroon
+237 772 0418
E-mail: unitedactionforc@yahoo.com
Website: www.unitedactionforchildren.org

Project Type: Administrative; Economic Development; Education; Youth

Mission Statement Excerpt: "To create a caring and sustaining environment for children and young people through innovative programs."

Year Founded: Organization was founded in 1996; first volunteers arrived in 2001

Number of Volunteers Last Year: Approximately 15

Funding Sources: Several governmental, foundation, and private donor organizations

The Work They Do: UAC operates a number of programs for children and young people in Cameroon, including elementary education, vocational training, a Community Sports for Development program that uses soccer to motivate productive initiatives, and a School on Wheels program in rural villages. Volunteers are able to assist in the nursery and primary schools, organize remedial reading programs, teach basic computer skills and music, paint murals, assist local staff in organizing sports, help with administrative work, become involved in local work, or get involved in fundraising, both locally and internationally.

Project Location: All volunteers work at UAC's project sites in Buea or Mamfe, Cameroon. Volunteers are housed in locally rented accommodations, which are included in the project fee. Volunteers take all meals at the project director's house.

Time Line: Volunteers are accepted throughout the year, though only 10 volunteers are allowed at any given time. UAC prefers that volunteers stay for a minimum of two months and requires that volunteers work at least five hours each day, beginning at 8:30 AM, excluding weekends.

Cost: UAC's program fee is $350 for volunteers who stay less than one month; $400 for one month of volunteering; $600 for two months' work; and $200 for subsequent months. The program fee includes airport transfers, accommodations, and meals. Volunteers must pay for their own airfare to Cameroon.

Getting Started: Prospective volunteers can apply directly to UAC via the website listed above. No interview is required.

Needed Skills and Specific Populations: Volunteers must be at least 18 years old, but there is no maximum age limit for volunteers. Although specialized skills in UAC's program areas are an advantage, they are not required.

United Planet

11 Arlington Street
Boston, MA 02116
(800) 292-2316 or (617) 267-7763; Fax: (617) 267-7764
E-mail: quest@unitedplanet.org
Website: www.unitedplanet.org

Project Type: Community Development; Human Rights;
Medical/Health; Orphans; Rural Development; Social
Justice; Women's Issues; Youth

Mission Statement Excerpt: "The mission of United Planet is to
foster cross cultural understanding and friendship in order
to unite the world in a community beyond borders."

Year Founded: United Planet was founded in 2001 and is the US
associate member of the International Cultural Youth
Exchange Federation, which was formed more than 60
years ago, after World War II

Number of Volunteers Last Year: More than 400

Funding Sources: United Planet receives donations from the
public as well as grants for specific projects

The Work They Do: United Planet runs many kinds of volunteer programs in more than 40 countries worldwide. Some
examples of projects undertaken by United Planet volunteers
include helping with sea turtle conservation efforts in Costa
Rica; assisting in public schools in Kathmandu, Nepal;
working at health clinics in Guatemala; repairing the homes
of senior citizens in a small village in northern Iceland; and
assisting with daily activities in an orphanage in Romania.
After the volunteer experience, participants are encouraged
to share their experience in their schools and communities
at home through the United Planet Cultural Awareness
Project and on the Internet via the United Planet online
community. This passing on of knowledge is seen as critical
to United Planet's mission.

Project Location: Volunteers can work in urban and rural
settings around the world. Work sites vary widely from site

Antoine takes "Raja the King" for a walk. Antoine had a teaching experience in Sungal, Himachal Pradesh, India. *Photo courtesy of Antoine Cassar*

to site, as do accommodations, which may include home-stays, guesthouses, or residential accommodations at the project.

Time Line: Volunteers can work with United Planet year-round, either through 1- to 12-week short-term projects, or long-term projects that run for six months or one year.

Cost: Program fees start at $945. Each program fee covers all meals, lodging, insurance, orientation, cultural activities and excursions, in-country transportation, and, in many cases, language classes. Longer-term commitments carry greater benefits.

Getting Started: Prospective volunteers can enroll in a project via United Planet's website. United Planet requires that all prospective volunteers complete an interview so that the organization can better understand the applicant's background and motivation for volunteering. Short-term volunteers with United Planet complete a predeparture training that takes place on the phone and online. Long-term volunteers take part in a weekend-long training twice per year.

Needed Skills and Specific Populations: No specific skills are required to volunteer with United Planet, but if a volunteer has a specialized skill, such as medical or dental, computer, educational, or environmental training, the organization will try to place the volunteer in a position that utilizes this skill. United Planet encourages volunteerism by people of all ages, so there is no minimum or maximum age. This philosophy of inclusion extends to volunteers with disabilities, as United Planet does its best to include everyone. United Planet is also open to non–US citizens and can organize volunteer programs for groups. Many families have volunteered through United Planet, mostly in orphanages, schools, and in environmental conservation programs; United Planet offers a family discount.

A Poem of Hospitality

By Antoine Cassar

United Planet

After the early-morning dose of spirituality and sweetness (a yoga session led by Sanji, followed by Auntie Ji's cinnamon tea and scrumptiously simple banana *chapathi*), it's time to prepare the day's lessons. I spend the mornings with a group of seven boisterous, sprightly, and extraordinarily respectful mentally challenged kids, teaching them simple English and math, singing songs and, weather permitting, playing sports and going for walks in the nearby forest. If I were to say that I have never before seen children so jubilant to attend school, I would not be exaggerating in the least. Highly affectionate from the second I met them, the energy that their hyperactivity drained out of me each morning would quickly be replenished with their smiles and laughter. No material comforts are needed: there are no tables and chairs, for example—only a mat rolled out on the hard floor, which you quickly become accustomed to, and which, I eventually discovered, has a double advantage: not only are teachers and pupils on the same level, but it is easier to sit in a circle, so that no child feels distant from the center of the action.

We are playing a card game I invented on the spot, to practice the order of numbers in English and in Hindi, counting backwards and revising simple addition and subtraction. Raja, a usually quiet seven-year-old boy with Down Syndrome, is thoroughly enjoying himself, throwing his cards down with joyful force, bringing out all the contagious charisma he usually hides. "Raja" is the Sanskrit word for monarch, and his tough, lively character quickly earns him the nickname of Raja the King. On a couple of occasions, his over-enthusiasm leads him to pick a fight with his two older companions, Lekhraj and Anish; I swiftly carry him outside to sit in the garden and calm him down. After a couple of minutes, we become friends again, as he turns to look at me with the face of a bashful angel. At that very moment, I realize how excruciatingly difficult it will be to leave him only days later.

After Aunty Ji's nourishing lunch and an enchanting Hindi lesson with Rushika, I am taken to Padhiarkhar, a tiny collection of houses down the road, almost floating within a sea of rice paddies. Out on the patio of one of the homes, with a backdrop of fields leading to the mountains, I teach a group of bright teenage girls who apparently, until only months before, had never had the opportunity to go to school. Yet they are far from illiterate, and their level of English is astounding. Together with another volunteer, we introduce each lesson with a geographical memory game. With the help of a transparent, inflatable globe, each girl "adopts" a country beginning with the same letter as their name: Anjeli chooses Argentina, for example, and Jamuna sets her eyes on Jordan. Regrettably, none of the girls' names begin with M, so there is nobody to adopt tiny Malta (my home country). They note the particular shape of their adopted countries, as well as the typical animals and fruits of each place; on the final day, after two weeks of throwing the globe to one another and testing each other's memory, completing the world map jigsaw I very luckily came across at the camp is as easy as *daal* (traditional lentil dish).

One of the simplest, most meaningful everyday aspects of my stay in India was the fact that all buildings—including the classrooms and the outdoor patio in Padhiarkhar—were to be entered barefoot. I found this custom to be of special significance when later visiting families in Shantiniketan and Bangalore. There is something very mystical in the act of removing your sandals to enter a family home, feeling the cool floor against the soles of your feet, the same floor that the hosts walk on, work on, sleep on, live on. The true poem of hospitality, I was to discover, was not the one I had written a year before that resulted in my winning the opportunity to volunteer and teach in India. The true poem of hospitality does not need to be composed in several languages, nor even in a single tongue. The earthy coolness of those floors, the warm and convivial gestures exchanged with the members of the family, the generous aromas of chai and spices slowly filling the room, prove more than strong enough to bridge the differences between the two meeting cultures. I slowly learned that such is the profound charm of hospitality: the beauty of humanity welcoming itself.

Via International

717 Third Avenue
Chula Vista, CA 91910
(619) 426-9110; Fax: (619) 426-6664
E-mail: info@viainternational.org
Website: www.viainternational.org

Project Type: Agriculture; Community Development; Construction; Economic Development; Education; Rural Development; Women's Issues

Mission Statement Excerpt: "Creating paths to self-reliance for an interdependent world."

Year Founded: 1974

Number of Volunteers Last Year: 1,259

Funding Sources: Government, foundation, and private donors

The Work They Do: Via International undertakes community development projects, including family health and food security initiatives such as nutrition, ecology, and garden programs; family financial security programs, including microcredit and microenterprise; and community leadership education. Volunteers have opportunities to work in the areas of school improvements, agriculture, community construction, education, murals, translation, and evaluation or documentation of projects.

Project Location: Via International works in Mexico (Mexicali and Tijuana); San Diego, California; Santa Fe and Taos, New Mexico; the Navajo Nation; and Guatemala. Project sites tend to be rustic and focused on construction or environmental work, though they may be located either in urban or rural areas. Volunteers are housed in group accommodations, sometimes in hotels.

Time Line: Via International's projects take place year-round. Volunteers have the option of working with Via International from 1 day to 2 years, though the average is about 10 days.

Cost: Program fees are approximately $100 per day, but vary depending on the duration and location of the volunteer experience. The program fee includes accommodations and all meals, but does not include transportation to the project site.

Getting Started: Individual volunteers should contact Via International's main office; groups of volunteers should contact the organization's booking coordinator, whose information is on Via International's website. Long-term volunteer applicants are required to complete an application and a phone interview. Training and orientation is provided to volunteers both prior to arrival and during the first day of the experience.

Needed Skills and Specific Populations: Though no specific skills are required of volunteers, many will find Spanish language skills to be useful. Volunteers under the age of 18 are welcome if accompanied by school personnel or parents. Groups of volunteers, families, and senior volunteers are also welcome. Via International will also attempt to accommodate volunteers with disabilities.

VISIONS Service Adventures

321 East Main Street, Suite 426
Bozeman, MT 59715
(406) 551-4423 or (800) 813-9283; Fax: (406) 551-1525
E-mail: info@visionsserviceadventures.com
Website: www.visionsserviceadventures.com

Project Type: Community Development; Construction; Education; Natural Conservation (Land); Natural Conservation (Sea); Youth

Mission Statement Excerpt: "Through service work and dynamic experience, VISIONS offers new perspectives and deep learning while working for and with under-resourced communities."

Year Founded: 1989

Number of Volunteers Last Year: 312

Funding Sources: Some funding from youth organizations

The Work They Do: VISIONS works on community-based projects in partnership with local host organizations. Service work is construction oriented, and social and environmental projects are also part of many programs. A focus in recent years has been on water access, including potable water systems, water conservation, and irrigation. VISIONS volunteers do hands-on construction work, including carpentry, masonry, and adobe. Skilled staff carpenters and other labor professionals provide training, and volunteers are involved in all aspects of the construction process, including building and doing technical labor.

Project Location: VISIONS operates programs in Peru, Ecuador and Galapagos, Nicaragua, the Dominican Republic, Dominica, Guadeloupe, British Virgin Islands, Mississippi Gulf coast, Montana Native reservations, Alaska Native communities, northern Vietnam, Cambodia, and Ghana. Their work takes place in underresourced communities, where volunteers will work shoulder to shoulder with local partners, therefore sharing their language, customs, and daily routines. Accommodations are basic but adequate and safe, and include community buildings such as schools, community centers, hostels, and rented homes. Volunteers live as a group and always as part of the neighborhood in the host community. Accommodations are split by gender and include a kitchen, common area, and bathrooms with running water and showers.

Time Line: Established summer programs run during July and August for three or four weeks; custom programs run year-round for a minimum of one week and a maximum of three months. VISIONS's Gap Year and College Internship Program in Cambodia runs year-round.

Cost: Program fees run between $1,500 and $5,450 for one- to four-week programs, depending on the length and location of the volunteer program. Accommodations and food are included in the program fee; transportation is not included.

Getting Started: Prospective volunteers can apply through the VISIONS website; applications are accepted as long as spaces for volunteers are available. Interviews are only required when VISIONS has questions about whether the applicant is good fit with their programs. All volunteers have an on-site, daylong orientation to the host community, carpentry/manual labor orientation, and continuing on-the-job training.

Needed Skills and Specific Populations: VISIONS does not require any previous skills or training. VISIONS accepts volunteers as young as 11 years old through their middle school programs. Other VISIONS programs, such as their summer high school program, gap year, and college internships, have other age guidelines. Custom programs are open to people of any age, including senior citizens. VISIONS can accommodate volunteers with disabilities at many of their work sites, and families are welcome on custom programs.

Vitalise

Shap Road
Kendal
Cumbria LA9 6NZ
United Kingdom
+44 845 330 0148; Fax: +44 1539 735567
E-mail: volunteer@vitalise.org.uk
Website: www.vitalise.org.uk

Project Type: Medical/Health; People with Disabilities
Mission Statement Excerpt: "To enable disabled and visually
impaired people to exercise choice and to provide vital
breaks for careers and inspirational opportunities for
volunteers."
Year Founded: 1963
Number of Volunteers Last Year: Approximately 4,000
Funding Sources: Various charitable organizations
The Work They Do: Vitalise works to provide disabled and
visually impaired people, who are referred to as guests, the
opportunity for respite and breaks in a holiday environ-
ment. Volunteers assist in this work by providing personal
and social support to guests and by helping with activities
and outings.
Project Location: Vitalise has three centers in the United
Kingdom, which are located in Essex, Southampton, and
Southport. These centers were built specifically to host
Vitalise guests and volunteers.
Time Line: Vitalise accepts volunteers year-round for a
minimum of one week and a maximum of one year.
Cost: Vitalise does not charge any program fee and provides
room and board free of charge to volunteers. Volunteers are
responsible for providing their own transportation to the
center.
Getting Started: Prospective volunteers must complete a
booking form, provide references, and agree to a
background check; no interview is necessary. Volunteers

receive training in health, safety, and moving and handling guests.

Needed Skills and Specific Populations: Volunteers must be reasonably fit and have a good command of the English language. The minimum age for volunteers from the United Kingdom is 16; from other countries it is 18. Senior volunteers are welcomed, and volunteers with disabilities will be considered, depending on their individual circumstances. Families are welcome, as long as all members meet the minimum age requirements.

Volunteer Africa

P.O. Box 24
Bakewell
Derbyshire DE45 1YP
United Kingdom
E-mail: support@volunteerafrica.org
Website: www.volunteerafrica.org

Project Type: Community Development; Construction; Rural Development

Mission Statement Excerpt: "Volunteer Africa has been established to give people from around the world the opportunity to work on community-initiated projects in developing countries."

Year Founded: 2001

Number of Volunteers Last Year: 132

Funding Sources: None; Volunteer Africa is self-funded

The Work They Do: Volunteer Africa offers volunteer opportunities in the Tanzanian province of Singida on community development projects. In Singida, volunteers work in rural villages on building projects, such as the construction of school classrooms or medical clinics.

Project Location: Volunteers work in the Singida region of Tanzania. In Singida, volunteers stay in a camp in the village they are working in with 4 to 12 other volunteers. Life is similar to that of local villagers: the conditions are basic with no electricity or running water. Volunteers are involved in daily camp duties such as fetching and purifying water and cooking.

Time Line: May to November, during the Tanzanian dry season. Volunteers participate for 2, 4, 7, or 10 weeks.

Cost: Participation for 2 weeks costs $900, 4 weeks costs $1,980, 7 weeks costs $2,590, and the program fee for 10 weeks is $3,215. Each program fee covers food, accommodations, language training, and in-country travel, but does not include insurance or travel to Tanzania. Approximately

60 percent of the program fee goes toward direct program costs and is therefore invested in the community being served.

Getting Started: Applications are available only online or via e-mail; Volunteer Africa does not maintain a phone or fax line so as to cut down on costs. An interview is required of all prospective volunteers, either by phone or in person. Volunteers receive an extensive guide for predeparture arrangements.

Needed Skills and Specific Populations: No specific skills are required, but volunteers should be able to live with a close team for 2 to 10 weeks and have good communication skills and the ability to problem solve. Volunteers must be at least 18 years old, and senior volunteers are welcomed. Applications from volunteers with disabilities will be screened for appropriate placements, just as any volunteer would be. Volunteer Africa has had a number of families volunteer.

Volunteer Bolivia

Casilla 2411
Cochabamba
Bolivia
+591 4 452 6028; Fax: +591 4 452 9459
E-mail: info@volunteerbolivia.org or
volunteerbolivia@gmail.com
Website: www.volunteerbolivia.org

Project Type: Education; Medical/Health; Social Justice; Youth

Mission Statement Excerpt: "Volunteer Bolivia . . . will match your skills and interests to local needs in order to provide you with an unforgettable cross cultural experience."

Year Founded: 2002

Number of Volunteers Last Year: 65

Funding Sources: Individual donors

The Work They Do: Volunteer Bolivia, located in Cochabamba, Bolivia, offers two types of placements: short-term volunteers, who work for one to five months, serve as aides to Bolivian educators, and long-term volunteers, who serve for five or more months, work in an area of their own expertise that matches the needs of communities in Bolivia. Short-term volunteers might help children with homework, design arts and crafts projects, or assist in a classroom. Examples of long-term volunteer placements include working in health professions, physical therapy, or graphic design; teaching advanced computer skills; or assisting with project development and administration.

Project Location: Most volunteers work in the city of Cochabamba, Bolivia, but Volunteer Bolivia can also place volunteers in other parts of the country. Volunteer placement sites have basic infrastructure, such as electricity, and may have running water. Volunteers typically stay in homestays with a private room and shared bath, or they may choose to rent a house or apartment.

Time Line: Volunteer Bolivia accepts volunteers throughout the year for a minimum of one month. They do not have a maximum time limit for volunteers.

Cost: Volunteer Bolivia's program fee for 4 weeks is $1,670, increasing up to $2,450 for 12 weeks, and $385 for each additional 4 weeks beyond the first 12. The program fee includes airport transfers, an in-country orientation, Spanish language classes (80 hours), a homestay with all meals, and the volunteer placement. Volunteers are responsible for their international airfare to Bolivia and insurance fees, as well as visa fees if applicable.

Getting Started: Prospective volunteers can apply online via Volunteer Bolivia's website; applications are accepted throughout the year. Interviews are not required. A basic orientation is provided upon arrival.

Needed Skills and Specific Populations: Long-term volunteers must have at least intermediate Spanish skills prior to volunteering. Volunteers must be at least 18 years old, with no maximum age. Volunteer Bolivia welcomes volunteers with disabilities and gladly hosts families, as they have found families "to be a great addition to the program."

Volunteer Honduras

P.O. Box 7523
Fredericksburg, VA 22404-7523
(540) 322-3471
E-mail: trips@volunteerhonduras.org
Website: www.volunteerhonduras.org

Project Type: Community Development; Construction;
Economic Development; Education; Medical/Health;
Orphans; Youth

Mission Statement Excerpt: "We are dedicated to improving the
quality of life for Hondurans through a combination of
volunteering and tourism."

Year Founded: 2010

Number of Volunteers Last Year: 90

Funding Sources: Private donors

The Work They Do: Volunteer Honduras partners with
children's homes, small communities, and local governments
to take on construction projects that benefit those in need,
such as communal bathrooms and renovations to school-
rooms. For example, in one project, volunteers installed
speed bumps and signage in front of five elementary schools
in a small town to help cut down on accidents involving
school children on this busy road. Volunteers typically
participate in light to moderate construction work during
the day and tutor children during the evenings.

Project Location: Volunteer Honduras's projects take place
mostly in the northern coastal regions of Honduras. Volunteers generally work outdoors, performing manual labor,
though the organization always provides water, snacks, rest,
and shade during projects. Volunteers are housed in comfortable hotels that have air conditioning and hot water.

Time Line: Volunteer Honduras sends volunteers for one-week
trips in organized groups at specific times of year. Typically,
three or four trips will go during the summer, one during
the Thanksgiving weekend, three during the winter, and

three in the spring. Volunteers commit to at least one one-week trip, though they may sometimes be able to string two or three weeks together at once. Volunteers generally spend five days volunteering and two days exploring Honduras as tourists in an organized group.

Cost: The program fee for one week is $725, with discounts for students, families, and those who take multiple trips (either consecutively or within a year). Program fees include airport transfers, accommodations, all meals, use of phones and Internet, and refreshments during the project. International airfare and insurance are not included in the program fee.

Getting Started: Prospective volunteers can complete an online application via Volunteer Honduras's website; applications must be received at least two weeks before the volunteer trip. Interviews are not required, except for those who wish to partake in the "Ultimate Honduras Roadtrip," which only operates once per summer and takes only three or four people. Volunteers who will spend time at children's homes also need to complete a background check. For orientation, volunteers rely on Volunteer Honduras's website and touch base with the organization two weeks before departure to answer any final questions.

Needed Skills and Specific Populations: No specific skills are required, though volunteers should have a strong work ethic, a positive attitude, and a desire to help others. Volunteers are generally at least 18 years old; volunteers under this age are welcome if accompanied by a parent or legal guardian and if they have the maturity and ability to handle a week of labor in an economically developing country. Senior citizens and volunteers with some disabilities are welcome, as long as they are able to perform light construction work; however, Volunteer Honduras's work sites are generally not capable of hosting volunteers who utilize wheelchairs. Families are strongly encouraged to participate and receive discounts off the program fee.

Volunteering Solutions

1735, Sector 45
Gurgaon 122003
Delhi NCR
India
(888) 790-3096; Fax: +91 124 4378572
E-mail: info@volunteeringsolutions.com
Website: www.volunteeringsolutions.com

Project Type: Community Development; Education; Medical/
Health; Natural Conservation (Land); Orphans; People with
Disabilities; Women's Issues

Mission Statement Excerpt: "To provide meaningful and fully
researched volunteer programs abroad, benefit local
communities by providing volunteer support, strengthen the
travel experience by providing cross-cultural experiences to
our volunteers, and use the funds and develop the communities and people we work with."

Year Founded: 2006

Number of Volunteers Last Year: 920

Funding Sources: None

The Work They Do: Volunteering Solutions offers over 100
projects in 17 countries around the world, including child-
care programs in Peru, women empowerment programs in
India, elephant orphanage programs in Sri Lanka, and
programs teaching monks in Thailand. People can volunteer
at schools, hospitals, orphanages, HIV/AIDS clinics,
women's groups, and other organizations that ask
Volunteering Solutions for assistance. Volunteering Solutions
aims to work closely with local communities.

Project Location: Volunteering Solutions offers projects in India,
Nepal, Sri Lanka, Thailand, China, Vietnam, Cambodia,
Philippines, Kenya, South Africa, Ghana, Malawi, Tanzania,
Honduras, Costa Rica, Ecuador, Peru, and Bolivia. In most
locations, volunteers stay with host families, though some
stay in designated volunteer houses.

Time Line: Projects are available year-round, and most volunteers begin their project on Mondays. Volunteers can sign up for a minimum of 1 week and a maximum of 24 weeks.

Cost: Volunteering Solutions' program fee begins at $200 and ranges up to $3,500 for 24 weeks. The program fee includes airport transfers, accommodations, and food; international airfare is not included.

Getting Started: Prospective volunteers complete an online application at Volunteering Solutions' website. Applications include a $200 application fee, photo, and resume; interviews are not required. Volunteers receive orientation upon arrival, including information on safety, local customs, and the local culture.

Needed Skills and Specific Populations: Volunteers must speak English; they must also speak Spanish if volunteering in a Spanish-speaking country. Volunteers in health and HIV/AIDS programs must be pre-med or medical students, nurses, or doctors. Volunteers must also be between the ages of 16 and 65, and Volunteering Solutions cannot place volunteers with disabilities. Families are welcomed.

Volunteers for International Partnership (VIP)

70 Landmark Hill, Suite 204
Brattleboro, VT 05301
(802) 246-1154; Fax: (802) 246-1154
E-mail: info@partnershipvolunteers.org
Website: www.partnershipvolunteers.org

Project Type: Education; Medical/Health; Natural Conservation (Land)

Mission Statement Excerpt: "Volunteers for International Partnership (VIP) provides volunteer service opportunities for individuals or groups by combining the most important aspects of cross-cultural education with the values of service and commitment."

Year Founded: 2004

Number of Volunteers Last Year: 300

Funding Sources: None

The Work They Do: VIP's volunteer projects are generally in the areas of social services, including work with the homeless and those with disabilities as well as with organizations that provide child and family support services; health education and public health; teaching and education; and environment and conservation. For example, in Turkey, volunteers may work at an organization that seeks out and supports immigrant families, students, the homeless, the unemployed, single mothers, and the elderly. Volunteers in Nigeria take part in public education campaign programs, collect data, and assist with research projects with an organization whose mission is to improve the quality of life of the population through innovative approaches to family health care delivery as well as women's development.

Project Location: VIP programs are available in 20 countries: Albania, Argentina, Brazil, Chile, China, Ecuador, Ghana, Great Britain, Guatemala, India, Ireland, Mexico, Morocco, Nepal, New Zealand, Nigeria, Peru, South Africa, Turkey, and the United States. Work sites vary considerably from country to country and project to project. In general, volunteers should be prepared for very basic accommodations with few amenities and should understand that many organizations operate with extremely limited resources. It is typical for a volunteer to work six to eight hours per day, five days per week. In most cases, volunteers will stay with host families, but some programs include residential accommodations.

Time Line: Volunteer placements are generally available all year round, and volunteers can choose their start and end dates; some countries specify a weekly or monthly arrival date. Volunteer placements are generally available in multiples of 4 weeks, up to 24 weeks. Special requests for shorter or longer programs can be accommodated in most cases. Most volunteers stay for two to three months.

Cost: Program fees vary by country and project. At the low end, a two-week program in Morocco is just under $1,000. More typically, four-week programs range from $1,380 in Nigeria to $2,470 in the United Kingdom. An eight-week program will range from $1,910 in Guatemala to $2,770 in Brazil. For those interested in longer volunteer experiences, 12-week programs range from $1,700 in Morocco to $3,410 in Argentina and 16-week programs range from $1,830 in Nigeria to $3,595 in Chile. Program fees include airport transfers, meals, and accommodations, but do not include international airfare.

Getting Started: Applications are accepted throughout the year via VIP's website, and interviews are required, typically by phone. All VIP programs include an in-country orientation.

Needed Skills and Specific Populations: VIP does not require that volunteers have specific skill sets, but they do look for people who are mature, flexible, enthusiastic, reliable, and sensitive, and who have common sense. US citizens must be at least 19 years old to volunteer; non-US citizens may be 18 years old. Children accompanied by their parents are also welcome, and VIP will work to meet the needs and desires of families. VIP does not have a maximum age limit for volunteers and will work with volunteers with disabilities to accommodate their needs.

Volunteers for Outdoor Colorado (VOC)

600 South Marion Parkway
Denver, CO 80209
(303) 715-1010; Fax: (303) 715-1212
E-mail: voc@voc.org
Website: www.voc.org

Project Type: Natural Conservation (Land); Trail Building/
Maintenance

Mission Statement Excerpt: "Volunteers for Outdoor Colorado's
(VOC's) mission is to motivate and enable citizens to
become active stewards of Colorado's natural resources."

Year Founded: 1984

Number of Volunteers Last Year: Approximately 3,600

Funding Sources: Individual donors and members, foundations,
corporations

The Work They Do: Every year, VOC offers dozens of opportunities for volunteers to take part in a variety of outdoor
stewardship projects in exciting locations throughout the
state. Examples of VOC's projects include building urban
and wilderness trails, planting trees in public places, and
preserving historic structures on public lands. Specific
volunteer activities may include digging, cutting, and
smoothing new trail; closing trails for revegetation; planting
and transplanting seedlings, shrubs, and trees; moving and
placing rocks for trail walls and steps; installing water diver-
sion structures; light construction of benches, bridges, and
fences; removing invasive weeds and plants; and preserving
historic wood structures by shaping replacement logs,
applying chinking, and reroofing.

Project Location: VOC projects take place throughout the state
in settings that include urban parks, state parks, wetlands,
high alpine areas, and forested mountain areas. Weather
conditions are highly variable in Colorado, and volunteers
should be prepared for weather conditions that range from
hot and sunny to snow showers. Some sites are open with
little shade and others are in heavily forested areas. Volun-

teers may choose to camp in tents or stay in nearby accommodations, and food is provided by VOC.

Time Line: VOC offers numerous outdoor volunteer projects every month from March or April through October. Volunteers can choose from daylong, weekend, and weeklong experiences. Most VOC volunteer experiences include meals, outdoor and social activities, and environmental learning opportunities; many involve camping and local entertainment.

Cost: There is no program fee to participate in most VOC volunteer experiences; however some wilderness projects may have an associated fee. Stewardship Adventures trips, which combine adventure travel with stewardship work, will have a fee; these fees will typically range between $15 and $250, depending on the project, and will be discussed in the online project description. Most of the food is provided for volunteers. Volunteers must provide their own transportation to the work site, tents and sleeping bags, and any personal food needs.

Getting Started: Prospective volunteers should visit VOC's website and browse the project calendar to see the variety of projects scheduled for the year; they can then register for projects by using the online registration or by calling VOC. Volunteers must register beforehand, preferably at least two weeks prior to the project's starting date. Any training needed is done on-site during the project.

Needed Skills and Specific Populations: Volunteers do not need to have prior experience or skills. VOC offers a variety of volunteer experiences designed for a range of populations, including youth, families, adults, individuals, groups/teams, and outdoor enthusiasts. VOC's minimum age for volunteers depends on the project and ranges from 8 to 16 years old. Senior volunteers are welcomed. Volunteers with disabilities are welcomed as long as they can perform moderate to hard physical work at altitudes as high as 12,000 feet. Some projects may require applicants to file a brief application or verification of physical health. Families and youth are encouraged to volunteer with VOC, provided children meet the minimum age requirements.

Volunteers for Peace (VFP)

7 Kilburn Street, Suite 316
Burlington, VT 05401
(802) 540-3060
E-mail: info@vfp.org
Website: www.vfp.org

Project Type: Agriculture; Community Development; Construction; Economic Development; Education; Natural Conservation (Land); Social Justice; Youth

Mission Statement Excerpt: "Volunteers for Peace (VFP) . . . provides programs where people from diverse backgrounds can work together to help overcome the need, violence, and environmental decay facing our planet."

Year Founded: 1982

Number of Volunteers Last Year: Approximately 1,100

Funding Sources: VFP is primarily a membership-based organization, but also receives a limited number of donations from individuals

The Work They Do: VFP primarily provides placements for two- to three-week service programs by recruiting volunteers and linking them with programs, but also offers opportunities up to a year in duration. VFP organizes and subsidizes 40 to 60 international work projects each year with over 100 nonprofits, environmental organizations, parks and recreation departments, and community organizations. Volunteers usually engage in physical, hands-on work, such as environmental cleanups, agricultural assistance, working with kids or disabled people, creating arts, and renovating and constructing community buildings. In the last 29 years, VFP has exchanged more than 28,000 volunteers in international voluntary service projects worldwide. In previous years, more than 3,400 projects have been listed annually. A typical project finds 10 to 15 volunteers from 5 or more countries working together for 30 to 40 hours per week. VFP's programs have a stated goal of fostering international education, voluntary service, and friendship. As an example, a recent project took place in Kenya, about four hours outside of Nairobi, where volunteers assisted the Amkeni Women's Group with tree planting, farm work, weaving, terracing, and brick making.

Project Location: VFP operates in more than 100 countries around the world. Work sites vary widely and range from developed cities to very rural communities; some locations are much more rustic than others. Accommodations are usually in a house, a community center, a school, or tents. Volunteers share cooking and cleaning responsibilities as a group. Unless otherwise specified, volunteers must bring a sleeping bag.

Time Line: Most of VFP's projects take place May through September, although some are offered year-round. An online directory lists all available projects and is regularly updated. Most programs last for two to three weeks, though some medium-term projects are available for one to six months, and VFP offers a few long-term, six-month to two-year projects.

Cost: VFP's basic fee is $300, which covers lodging, food, and work materials; for volunteers under the age of 18, the project fee is $500. Programs in developing countries often charge an additional fee upon arrival in the range of $150, to help offset the cost of the program. Volunteers must pay their own transportation costs and must be members of VFP to apply for a program; the annual membership is $30.

Getting Started: Prospective volunteers usually browse the Open Project List on VFP's website to find projects they are interested in. Once they have decided on a project, they complete the online registration form and pay the $300 registration fee. A downloadable registration form is available for those with limited Internet access. Most volunteer positions do not require interviews, except those that involve work with youth and disabled people, in which case the interview is usually completed via an online video tool. Once the volunteer is placed in a work project, VFP will e-mail an acceptance letter and information sheet that details how to get to the project and what to bring. VFP volunteers are responsible for educating themselves about their destination country, though a basic orientation is provided upon arrival in the first days of all projects.

Needed Skills and Specific Populations: No special skills are required, though VFP stresses that volunteers need to be motivated, cooperative, flexible, and culturally sensitive. Though some projects for teens exist in France, Germany, and a handful of other countries, most programs require volunteers to be at least 18 years old. Senior volunteers are welcomed, though they should be aware that the large majority of VFP's volunteers are in the 18–28 age group, and some programs have maximum age limits. Volunteers with disabilities are encouraged to apply, as work camps are designed to provide everyone with an opportunity to help; VFP will make reasonable accommodations. VFP primarily places US and Canadian citizens, but it will also place citizens of countries in which it does not have a partner organization. VFP has several family-friendly programs, which are published on its website at the end of March each year; the family placement fee is fixed at $500 regardless of the family's size.

Volunthai: Volunteers for Thailand

86/24 Soi Kanprapa, Prachacheun Road
Bang Sue
Bangkok 10800
Thailand
+66 44 812 346
E-mail: info@volunthai.com
Website: www.volunthai.com

Project Type: Community Development; Education; Orphans; Rural Development; Youth

Mission Statement Excerpt: "Volunthai is a not-for-profit volunteer organization that gives rural Thai students an opportunity to learn English and gives foreign volunteers the opportunity to experience life in a rural Thai community."

Year Founded: 2001

Number of Volunteers Last Year: 100

Funding Sources: No outside sources; program fees only

The Work They Do: Volunthai offers individual volunteers and school groups a chance to teach English in rural schools in Thailand. Volunteers also have the opportunity to try extracurricular activities, such as language study, meditation, and cooking. Volunthai is a small, independent organization run by an American and his Thai family.

Project Location: Volunthai operates in northeastern Thailand, in the area near Cambodia and Laos. Volunteers are expected to live and eat as local Thais do; this means simple accommodations, cold showers, and eating primarily Thai food. Volunteers are hosted by the local school, often living with the head English teacher's family or in a teachers' dorm on the school's campus.

Time Line: Volunteers are welcomed year-round, with the exception of Thailand's school holidays in September, March, and April. Volunteers usually commit to at least one month, and most volunteers stay for two or more.

Cost: Volunthai has a program fee of $375 for one month and

$200 for each additional month. This fee includes all room and board during the homestay; volunteers are responsible for their own transportation and personal expenses outside of the room and board.

Getting Started: Applications are available by e-mail via the website above. Volunteers can apply as little as one week before starting to teach. Volunteers are met in Bangkok for an orientation before traveling by bus to Chaiyaphum Province for a brief cultural training. From there they go to their homestay.

Needed Skills and Specific Populations: Volunteers must be flexible, open-minded, and enthusiastic about Thai culture and must speak English clearly. Except in special preapproved circumstances, volunteers must be at least 18 years old, though there is no maximum age limit. Families and non-native speakers of English are welcome to apply. Volunthai is unable to accommodate volunteers with disabilities.

Volunteering in the Thai Countryside

By Yvonne Blokland

Volunthai: Volunteers for Thailand

In 2010, I volunteered to teach English in Thailand for four weeks. Trakan Phuetpon is a small town not far from the Mekong River in the remote province of Ubon. The students I worked with were eager to learn but also shy and afraid to make mistakes. Also, they were not used to hearing English spoken by a foreigner (rather than a Thai teacher). This challenge is well known to the teachers and they are trying to overcome it in many different ways. One way they are coping with this problem is by working with foreign volunteers. Despite their insecurity, the students are very enthusiastic. In fact, the most successful interactions I had with students were outside the classroom. In informal settings, students were a lot less shy. They would come up to me in the hallways and ask me questions or tell me about themselves.

Everyone in the English department went out of their way to make my time there as nice as possible. All this kindness and attention was heartwarming and made my time at the school very, very enjoyable. My only complaint, at first, was that sometimes there was a lack of communication, and it was unclear to me when I was supposed to go somewhere. But this shouldn't be considered too big of an issue; I think it really comes down to a cultural difference. Western people tend to be very rigid and precise when it comes to appointments, and in Thailand people are much more relaxed. To be honest, I prefer the latter!

My time wasn't just spent in the classroom. The country-side of the Ubon Province is breathtaking, and I really enjoyed all the sightseeing trips people took me on: a national park, rice fields, a silk farm, and many, many temples. Every day I was presented with another type of Thai fruit or food that I had never seen before, and in most cases there was only one possible response: *Arroy mahk mahk* (delicious)! It has been a very interesting experience to see so much of Thai culture and to get to know something about the Thai educational system.

I realize I have probably learned a lot more myself than I was able to teach the students, but I hope that my visit was useful to both the students and the school!

Volunteers Without Borders (VWB)

22/8 Moo 4, Mahidol Road
NongHoi, Amphur Muang
Chiang Mai 50000
Thailand
+66 53 801 674
E-mail: info@track-of-the-tiger.com
Website: www.track-of-the-tiger.com

Project Type: Agriculture; Community Development; Construction; Economic Development; Education; Scientific Research; Trail Building/Maintenance

Mission Statement Excerpt: "The Voluntourists Without Borders Initiative aims to use the skills and funding of paying volunteers alongside the labour of the rural community to develop a sustainable ecotourism industry of world class standard, that is owned by the host community, and operated under a fixed length development contract with a private sector tour operator."

Year Founded: 2005

Number of Volunteers Last Year: 350

Funding Sources: Private donors

The Work They Do: VWB operates two projects, one at the Pang Soong Nature Trails and the other in the town of Sanpatong. At Pang Soong, volunteers can teach English to rural schoolchildren, assist in biodiversity monitoring and revenue stream development, or take on small construction projects. In Sanpatong, volunteers have the opportunity to teach English to rural schoolchildren and college students, assist in sustainable agriculture development as a revenue source for underprivileged students, engage in small construction tasks, or assist in the development of community-based tourism products.

Project Location: Volunteers work in northern Thailand, specifically in and around the city of Chiang Mai. The Pang Soong

Nature Trails project is located in a remote area one hour from Chiang Mai near the village of Ban Mae Lai, and accommodations are provided in a lodge and field studies center. The Sanpatong project is located in a rural village near an agricultural college established primarily for economically struggling Thai and ethnic minority students, one hour west of Chiang Mai. Volunteers at Sanpatong stay with host families.

Time Line: Programs run all year round, beginning on Sundays and ending on Saturdays. Most volunteers start for two weeks in Pang Soong, followed by two weeks in Sanpatong.

Cost: VWB's program fee is approximately 20,000 Thai baht per week, which includes accommodations and meals. It does not include international airfare.

Getting Started: Prospective volunteers should visit VWB's website for an application. Online orientation materials are provided once registration is complete.

Needed Skills and Specific Populations: VWB volunteers should be good communicators, hard workers, positive thinkers, creative, proactive, able to work independently and in teams, culturally aware, and committed. The project will most likely appeal to those who have a strong interest in environmental, development, and ecotourism fields. Volunteers of all ages are welcome, with no minimum or maximum age limit; children are welcome with their parents, but parents should talk with VWB in advance. VWB welcomes volunteers with disabilities in their Chiang Mai office or as "virtual volunteers."

Winant Clayton Volunteers

The Church of the Epiphany
1393 York Avenue
New York, NY 10021
(212) 737-2720, ext. 31; Fax: (212) 737-3217
E-mail: winantclayton@gmail.com
Website: www.winantclaytonvolunteers.org

Project Type: Community Development
Mission Statement Excerpt: "Winant Clayton Volunteers'
    mission is to: further goodwill and partnership between the
    communities in the two countries through an exchange of
    service, further the Anglo-American cooperation that the
    program founders had in mind, and offer personal growth
    and life changing experience to an individual through
    community service, working with vulnerable populations in
    another culture."
Year Founded: 1948
Number of Volunteers Last Year: 12
Funding Sources: Foundations and individual donors
The Work They Do: Winant Clayton Volunteers fulfills the
    vision of the late John G. Winant, US Ambassador to Great
    Britain during World War II, and the late Reverend Philip
    "Tubby" Clayton, vicar of All Hallows Church in London
    and private chaplain to the Queen Mother. Following World
    War II, these two men envisioned teams of volunteers
    composed of people from the United Kingdom, known as
    Claytons, and from the United States, known as Winants,
    who would travel to each other's countries to volunteer and
    learn about life there. Winant volunteers from the United
    States are placed in full-time volunteer positions on projects
    dealing with people of all ages with a variety of needs.
    Specific examples of volunteer work sites include commu-
    nity settlement clubs for the elderly, children, immigrants,
    and teenagers at risk; drop-in service centers for people with
    HIV/AIDS; psychiatric rehabilitation centers; and summer

day care programs for inner-city children. Placements range from structured to self-structured, but all require energy, enthusiasm, initiative, and flexibility. Volunteers may be placed alone or with another Winant volunteer.

Project Location: Winant volunteers serve primarily in the East End of London. Housing is provided to volunteers in the form of host-family accommodations, flats, or dormitory rooms.

Time Line: Winant volunteers work full-time, five days per week, for seven weeks. This volunteer experience is then followed by two weeks of independent travel. The program begins in mid-June and ends in late August.

Cost: Winant Clayton Volunteers does not charge a program fee to participate, but volunteers must pay for their own airfare to and from London, which is arranged through Winant and Clayton. Volunteers must travel as a group from New York City. Housing is provided to volunteers at no charge. A volunteer who stays with a host family will be fed by that family; all other volunteers are provided a small stipend of approximately $70 a week for food. If a volunteer is required to use public transportation to travel to and from a work site, those travel costs will be covered. A small amount of financial aid is available.

Getting Started: Prospective volunteers can download an application from the organization's website or write or call the office at the address and phone number listed above for information and an application. Applicants must submit applications, two references, and a nonrefundable $50 application fee by the deadline date. Each applicant will be interviewed, either in New York City or by a former Winant volunteer who lives near the applicant. Accepted volunteers must submit a deposit by mid-April to pay for their group flight, with the balance due by the end of that month. Once accepted into the program, volunteers receive an orientation on living and volunteering in London before they fly to London.

Needed Skills and Specific Populations: Winant volunteers must
be at least 18 years old and must be US citizens; there are
no specific skills required to be a Winant volunteer, just the
right attitude and the desire to work hard for a good cause.
There is no upper age limit, though families are not able to
volunteer through this organization. Winant Clayton Volunteers accepts volunteers with learning disabilities or small
physical disabilities; volunteers with other disabilities should
contact the organization prior to beginning the application
process.

Winrock International

2101 Riverfront Drive
Little Rock, AR 72202-1748
(501) 280-3000; Fax: (501) 280-3090
E-mail: volunteer@winrock.org
Website: www.winrock.org

Project Type: Agriculture; Community Development; Economic
Development; Natural Conservation (Land); Professional/
Technical Assistance; Rural Development; Women's Issues

Mission Statement Excerpt: "Winrock International is a
nonprofit organization that works with people in the United
States and around the world to empower the disadvantaged,
increase economic opportunity, and sustain natural
resources."

Year Founded: 1985

Number of Volunteers Last Year: 200

Funding Sources: Government and foundation grants, as well as
private donors

The Work They Do: Winrock International focuses on three
program areas: enterprise and agriculture, empowerment
and civic engagement, and the environment. Winrock volunteers collaborate with farmers, businesses, organizations,
and governments in the areas of agricultural development,
economic growth, natural resource management, renewable
energy, democracy and governance, enterprise development,
and women and youth empowerment by providing training
and technical assistance to meet the specific needs of the
target beneficiaries. Examples of volunteer tasks include
training beneficiaries in modern agriculture production and
processing technologies, assisting a private enterprise to
develop a business or strategic plan, helping a group to
understand the structure and function of cooperatives and
associations, and providing training in business management
skills.

Project Location: Winrock operates volunteer projects in Bangladesh, Cambodia, Egypt, El Salvador, Ethiopia, Ghana, Kenya, Lebanon, Mali, Nepal, Nicaragua, Nigeria, and Sudan. Volunteers are generally housed in local hotels or apartments.

Time Line: While Winrock recruits throughout the year, volunteer assignments have specific starting and ending dates. The average volunteer assignment is from two to six weeks, though occasionally they have volunteer opportunities for six months or longer.

Cost: All volunteer expenses, including accommodations, food, and international airfare, are covered by Winrock International.

Getting Started: Volunteer applications are available online through Winrock's website, and there are no deadlines. Prospective volunteers may complete an application detailing their experience and expertise, which will be kept on file until an appropriate placement can be found. Applicants must complete a phone interview with a Winrock recruiter. Orientation materials are provided in advance of volunteer travel.

Needed Skills and Specific Populations: Volunteers must have a developed skill set specific to the project area. Winrock does not have a maximum age for volunteers, but all volunteers must submit a health certificate indicating that they are healthy enough to complete the volunteer assignment. Applications from volunteers with disabilities will be placed on a case-by-case basis to ensure proper accommodations. Most of Winrock's opportunities are only available to US citizens or permanent residents, but there are limited opportunities for citizens of other countries. Winrock does not have family volunteer opportunities.

Women in Progress (WIP)

P.O. Box 18323
Minneapolis, MN 55418
(800) 338-3032; Fax: (612) 781-0450
E-mail: info@womeninprogress.org
Website: www.womeninprogress.org

Project Type: Community Development; Economic Development; Women's Issues

Mission Statement Excerpt: "Women in Progress works to achieve economic independence of women and alleviate poverty at a grassroots level in Africa through the sustainable growth of small women-owned businesses and at the same time establishes mutual understanding among people of diverse cultures."

Year Founded: 2003

Number of Volunteers Last Year: 60

Funding Sources: Revenue from the sales of fair-trade products, donations

The Work They Do: WIP works with small women-owned microbusinesses that produce a line of high-quality fair-trade goods. WIP's primary program is to penetrate international markets in order to generate increased income. WIP offers a holistic approach to business development that enables business women to "pull it all together" with measurable income generation through exports and hands-on, personalized business assistance. Examples of volunteer activities include introducing a woman entrepreneur to computer applications; helping a small business create a marketing plan and execute it by designing and creating brochures; generating new product ideas for successful export to the United States and Europe; and assessing business practices of cooperative members against fair-trade principles to determine whether they will receive a fair-trade certification.

Project Location: All of WIP's projects are located in Ghana. Housing is very simple, with electricity and running water most of the time. Houses include kitchen facilities and mosquito netting. Volunteers generally share a bathroom and perhaps a bedroom. Internet access is available on-site or nearby. Volunteers may also stay with a nearby host family for an additional charge.

Time Line: WIP's projects run year-round, and volunteers establish their own dates, usually between 2 and 24 weeks. WIP does encourage volunteers to coordinate their travel plans with other volunteers in order to coordinate transportation to the assigned project.

Cost: Program fees are based on the length of stay and range from $1,025 to $2,835. The program fee includes orientation, lodging, and project-related expenses. Volunteers are responsible for their travel to Ghana, food, and in-country transportation. Many volunteers offset fees by fundraising for WIP, which is a registered nonprofit organization.

Getting Started: WIP accepts volunteers year-round via a registration form on their website. They provide a volunteer guide prior to departure and an informal orientation upon arrival. No interview is necessary.

Needed Skills and Specific Populations: While WIP recruits volunteers with business skills, they do not require these skills in their volunteers. Volunteers must be at least 16 years old unless accompanied by a parent; there is no maximum age limit to volunteer with WIP. WIP would be happy to attempt to accommodate volunteers with disabilities, though it may be difficult to do so in Ghana. Families are welcome to volunteer with WIP, especially mother-daughter teams.

Are You at All "Creative"?

By Elizabeth Eva Lampman

Women in Progress (WIP)

On the first morning of my internship at the large one-room office of Women in Progress in Accra, Ghana, the cofounder of the organization, Renae, asked me, "Are you at all 'creative'?" She asked as if it was a shot in the dark, as if creativity were some rare genetic trait that she definitely doesn't possess. I was elated to hear her question. I imagine my mom and dad grinning in response to this question while remembering the countless hours I spent in the craft room from the time I was old enough to cut and glue. I didn't really hesitate with fabricated modesty. I've finally learned to identify creativity as one of my strengths in interviews and personal statements, so I simply said, "Yeah, I am." She responded by pulling out some new beads and explained that the beads are great, but the women need a design for how to use them in jewelry. Beading! I couldn't believe my good fortune to have the opportunity to pursue one of my hobbies for the benefit of this women's organization.

So over the next few days, I created designs for how to use these new beads in jewelry. What's so exciting is that all of these beads (even the glass ones) are handmade out of recycled materials. One of the Women in Progress bead makers recently discovered that she could make beautiful, almost iridescent beads by cutting, coloring, and rolling recycled water bottles. The beads are electric teal and indigo and roughly half an inch in length. And what's best about this project is that Renae said, upon looking at my beaded creations, "I am so glad you're working on this. Your jewelry designs mean that the women can start earning money a whole year sooner." Wow, what an amazing feeling I had as I continued stringing beads, that my creativity bumped this project up an entire year.

I am loving my time with Women in Progress. I've been putting in much more than eight hours a day but it doesn't feel like it. At the end of every day I feel tired yet accomplished. The fact is, I know that what I'm doing supports the hard work of so many women who are responsible for their families' and their own livelihoods. I know I'm making a difference. And what a joy to have a supervisor who encourages me to do what I do best . . . to be creative!

Work and Volunteer Abroad (WAVA)

Tower House
67–71 Lewisham High Street
London SE13 5JX
United Kingdom
+44 20 8297 3278
E-mail: smordarski@workandvolunteer.com
Website: www.workandvolunteer.com

Project Type: Community Development; Construction; Education; Medical/Health; Natural Conservation (Land); Natural Conservation (Sea); Orphans

Mission Statement Excerpt: "To give its diverse clients . . . the chance to experience meaningful travel that engages them deeply with their host communities."

Year Founded: 2010

Number of Volunteers Last Year: 500

Funding Sources: None

The Work They Do: Work and Volunteer Abroad offers placements in both community-based and conservation volunteering programs. Community-based volunteers can work with one of approximately 50 community-focused programs, including child care in orphanages, centers for children with disabilities, construction projects, female empowerment programs, medical volunteering, and teaching in both primary and secondary schools. For example, volunteers might help orphans with their homework, teach computer skills, or help build hospitals. In WAVA's conservation volunteering programs, volunteers can work in one of roughly 20 projects, ranging from environmental initiatives to marine conservation and projects involving animals. Examples of conservation volunteer projects include caring for wildlife, educating local communities about conservation, and monitoring specific species.

Project Location: WAVA's projects take place around the world, in South and Central America, Europe, Africa, Asia, and

Australasia. Volunteer accommodations are in a local lodge, hostel, or volunteer house, or with a host family.

Time Line: Projects take place throughout the year, from a minimum of two weeks to a maximum of one year.

Cost: Program fees begin at $100 per week and go up by the length of the volunteer project. The program fee includes airport pickup, accommodations, and food on work days, but does not include international airfare or the return trip to the airport.

Getting Started: Prospective volunteers should apply at least 12 weeks before their intended departure date; start dates for specific programs are available on the WAVA website. Before departure, volunteers must have a phone interview with a WAVA staff member, as well as a conversation with a member of the WAVA team who has visited the project. Some projects may also require a resume and/or references. A predeparture information packet is available, as is a nonmandatory predeparture briefing in London. Volunteers also receive an on-site orientation to the project and the local culture, and they can communicate with past volunteers through the organization's social networking site, www.wavaengage.com.

Needed Skills and Specific Populations: In general, the only requirement is that volunteers speak English; some projects do require that volunteers also speak Spanish. Volunteers must respect cultural differences, and "a friendly, outgoing personality and a sense of humor will go a long way." WAVA volunteers must be at least 18 years old, but there is no maximum age limit. WAVA is committed to equal opportunities for volunteers, including volunteers with disabilities. Families are welcome to volunteer with WAVA as long as all members meet the age requirements.

WorldTeach

Center for International Development, Harvard University
79 John F. Kennedy Street
Cambridge, MA 02138
(617) 495-5527 or (800) 4-TEACH-O; Fax: (617) 495-1599
E-mail: info@worldteach.org
Website: www.worldteach.org

Project Type: Community Development; Economic Development; Education; Youth

Mission Statement Excerpt: "WorldTeach partners with governments and other organizations in developing countries to provide volunteer teachers to meet local needs and promote responsible global citizenship."

Year Founded: 1986

Number of Volunteers Last Year: 467

Funding Sources: Volunteer contributions and partner contributions

The Work They Do: Volunteers teach English to students of all ages, depending on the needs of the country and host institution. In some countries, volunteers may also teach math, science, computer skills, and HIV/AIDS awareness. Volunteers work as full-time teachers and are employed by their host schools or sponsoring institutions in their placement countries. Most volunteers live with host families or on the school campus, and they participate fully in the lives of their host communities.

Project Location: Volunteers can work in American Samoa, Bangladesh, Chile, China, Costa Rica, Ecuador, Guyana, the Marshall Islands, Micronesia, Namibia, Panama, Poland, Rwanda, Tanzania, and South Africa. Host institutions may be public or private primary or secondary schools, public or private universities, vocational schools and institutions, community resource centers, local organizations, or government agencies. Placement depends on the needs of the host communities and the location in which volunteers can be of most use to their host countries. Educational resources available to volunteers depend on placement and vary widely from country to country. Volunteers may live with local families, share houses with other local or foreign teachers, or, in some cases, have their own apartments. Volunteers in some countries live in traditional houses without running water or electricity; others have apartments with many modern amenities. Wherever volunteers are placed, they are likely to have their own furnished bedroom and access to a bathroom and a kitchen or cafeteria.

Time Line: WorldTeach offers short-term, eight-week summer programs that depart in June, and long-term, 6- to 12-month programs with varying departure dates throughout the year.

Cost: Program fees vary by location and range from $1,000 to $5,990, with the exception of the Marshall Islands, American Samoa, Micronesia, and Bangladesh programs, which have no program fee and are fully funded. Each program fee covers international round-trip airfare from a gateway city within the United States to the country of service, room and board, health insurance, emergency evacuation, visa and predeparture materials, and in-country orientation and training. Long-term teaching volunteers receive a small monthly living stipend that is usually equivalent to what local teachers earn.

Getting Started: All application materials and instructions can be found online at WorldTeach's website. All candidates must submit two letters of recommendation, and applicants for long-term teaching programs are required to interview with a WorldTeach volunteer who has completed a program. Admission to some of WorldTeach's programs, especially the fully funded programs, can be competitive. Admissions decisions are made on a rolling basis within two to three weeks of the receipt of a completed application, and final application deadlines are typically three months before the program departure date. WorldTeach provides intensive in-country orientation for every program: 7 to 10 days for summer programs and three to four weeks for long-term programs. Orientation includes training in the host country's language, instruction on teaching English as a foreign language, a teaching practicum, discussions of the host country's history and culture, informational sessions on health and safety issues, exploration of the region, and group-building and social activities. Orientation is led by the in-country field director as well as by orientation assistants, who are usually current volunteers who have already begun their work.

Needed Skills and Specific Populations: Volunteers for the long-term programs must be college graduates; volunteers for the summer programs must be at least 18 years old; fluency in the English language is required of volunteers in all programs. Because of WorldTeach's minimum age requirement, it is uncommon for families to volunteer with WorldTeach. Volunteers must also be responsible, caring, self-motivated individuals with a strong interest in cultural exchange and teaching. Volunteers do not have to have previous teaching experience or training, but must have genuine and demonstrated interest in teaching. WorldTeach welcomes senior volunteers. Because WorldTeach places volunteers in challenging circumstances in developing countries and with local host families, it may not be able to accommodate volunteers with certain disabilities or serious health limitations, or those who require specialized housing arrangements.

World-Wide Opportunities on Organic Farms (WWOOF) UK

P.O. Box 2154
Winslow
Buckingham MK18 3WS
United Kingdom
+44 1296 714652
E-mail: info@wwoof.org.uk
Website: www.wwoof.org.uk

Project Type: Agriculture

Mission Statement Excerpt: "To get into the countryside; to help the organic movement; to get firsthand experience of organic farming and growing; to make contact with other people in the organic movement."

Year Founded: 1971

Number of Volunteers Last Year: WWOOF does not keep statistics on the number of volunteers, but the UK branch had 4,500 members last year

Funding Sources: None; WWOOF is self-funded

The Work They Do: WWOOF's premise is simple: volunteers help organic growers in exchange for food and accommodations. WWOOF helps link volunteers to growers, and it leaves the details for the individuals to work out for themselves. Therefore, each volunteer experience with WWOOF is unique, but volunteers can expect that they could be involved with any growing- or farming-related activity on an organic farm. In addition to farming, many WWOOF hosts are also engaged in other projects related to sustainable agriculture, including green building, renewable energy, rainwater collection, and environmental education; volunteers may be able to help with these activities as well.

Project Location: Host farms are located all over the world, but volunteers must join WWOOF in the country they wish to volunteer in; joining the UK WWOOF allows volunteers to work on UK farms. Living situations vary widely, as each grower provides accommodations to the WWOOF volunteer.

Time Line: With so many opportunities around the world, there is always a WWOOF host in need of help. The start and end date, as well as the minimum and maximum amount of time the volunteer spends with the grower, are up to the volunteer and the host to negotiate.

Cost: Other than the membership subscription, there is no cost to volunteer. UK WWOOF's membership fee is £20, for which members receive access to listings of grower hosts and four newsletters per year. Volunteers pay their own travel costs.

Getting Started: Applications are available on WWOOF's website. Growers are responsible for providing training and orientation to volunteers.

Needed Skills and Specific Populations: WWOOF volunteers must be at least 18 years old; senior volunteers are welcome to work with WWOOF. Volunteers with disabilities must work with individual growers to determine the feasibility of working on specific farms. Some WWOOF hosts welcome volunteers with children, but this is at their discretion; these families must arrange this directly with prospective host farms prior to arrival.

Judith and a giant zucchini! Judith was a WWOOFer (volunteer) from France who lived in the Redfield Community in Buckinghamshire, England, for several months over the course of a summer. She helped look after organic fruit, veggie, and herb gardens, Jacobs sheep, chickens, and bees. She also helped harvest, cook, and preserve all the wonderful homegrown produce. In return for her boundless energy and enthusiasm, Judith had fresh and nutritious meals provided for her, a room to call her own, learned a lot about organic farming techniques, had lots of opportunities to practice her English . . . and gained 23 friends (fellow WWOOFers) for life. *Photo courtesy of Scarlett Penn/WWOOF*

World-Wide Opportunities on Organic Farms (WWOOF) USA

430 Forest Avenue
Laguna Beach, CA 92651
(949) 715-9500
E-mail: info@wwoofusa.org
Website: www.wwoofusa.org

Project Type: Agriculture; Construction; Natural Conservation (Land)

Mission Statement Excerpt: "WWOOF-USA is part of a world-wide effort to link volunteers with organic farmers, promote an educational exchange, and build a global community conscious of ecological farming practices."

Year Founded: 2001

Number of Volunteers Last Year: Approximately 11,000

Funding Sources: None; self-funded through memberships

The Work They Do: WWOOF-USA provides a network of organic farms willing to host volunteers who wish to learn about sustainable agriculture through hands-on experience on the farms. Volunteers may help in the farms or gardens by planting, weeding, harvesting, and providing animal care. Other opportunities on farms may include tending medicinal plants, construction, green and alternative building, permaculture, and solar energy projects. WWOOF-USA does not provide actual placements, but rather a directory of potential host farms that volunteers can contact directly.

Project Location: WWOOF-USA lists more than 1,400 host farms in all 50 US states, as well as Puerto Rico and the US Virgin Islands. Accommodations vary by host farm.

Time Line: Volunteers are accepted throughout the year. The length of the volunteer experience is directly negotiated between the volunteer and the host farm. Some host farms request that volunteers make multi-month commitments, while others accept weekend volunteers. Most participants volunteer for four to six hours per day.

Cost: The membership fee to join WWOOF-USA is $30 per person or $40 to also receive the Host Farm Directory in the postal mail. Volunteers receive free room and board from their hosts, but they are responsible for their own travel to the farms.

Getting Started: Prospective volunteers should join WWOOF-USA and obtain the host farm directory. Volunteers can join WWOOF-USA either through the organization's website or by downloading, completing, and mailing in an application with a check. Any orientation or training is left up to the individual host farm.

Needed Skills and Specific Populations: Individual volunteers must be at least 18 years old. Some host farms will accept volunteers under that age, as long as they are volunteering with someone over 18. Senior volunteers are welcomed. Some host farms may be able to accommodate volunteers with disabilities. In general, no previous experience or skills are needed, though some individual host farms may have their own requirements. WWOOF cannot help international volunteers with visas.

Wyoming Dinosaur Center (WDC)

110 Carter Ranch Road
P.O. Box 868
Thermopolis, WY 82443
(800) 455-DINO or (307) 864-2997; Fax: (307) 864-5762
E-mail: wdinoc@wyodino.org
Website: www.wyodino.org

Project Type: Archaeology; Museum; Scientific Research

Mission Statement Excerpt: "Providing the best paleontological experience by being a scientifically recognized institution that is educational, engaging, and enjoyable for visitors of all ages."

Year Founded: 1993

Number of Volunteers Last Year: Approximately 350

Funding Sources: Private enterprise

The Work They Do: WDC offers Dig-for-a-Day programs, which allow participants to help discover, collect, and document Jurassic Period dinosaur fossils. Excavation work at the WDC's two main quarries has yielded well-preserved bones of camarasaurus and diplodocus dinosaurs. All activities assist in current scientific research projects, which provide valuable information concerning the environment that existed in the area more than 140 million years ago.

Project Location: The dig sites are located 15 minutes from the WDC on Warm Springs Ranch at the northern end of Wind River Canyon in Wyoming. Participants usually stay at local hotels.

Time Line: As the project name indicates, this is a one-day program. WDC runs the Dig-for-a-Day program from late spring through early fall, Monday through Friday. The day begins at 8:00 AM, ends by 5:00 PM, and includes a 30-minute lunch break. If needed, participants can return to the WDC on one of the hourly tour buses earlier than 5:00 PM.

Cost: The program fee for Dig-for-a-Day participants is $150 per adult and $80 per child. WDC requires a $50 deposit per person, which is refunded if the dig is canceled because of inclement weather. Participants who cancel a reservation at least 30 days before the project date will receive a full refund. The program fee includes lunch, but participants are responsible for all other expenses, including travel, accommodations, and other meals.

Getting Started: Prospective participants must call the WDC at the number listed above to register in advance. Participants undergo an orientation at the start of the day that discusses the geology and paleontology of the work site as well as digging and data-collection procedures.

Needed Skills and Specific Populations: Individuals must be at least 18 years old, but children younger than that age may participate if accompanied by an adult; families are welcome to participate. Participants must be able to work outdoors, walk on uneven ground, and be able to withstand high temperatures, although shade and water are always available. Participants with disabilities can work in the museum's preparation lab, stabilizing and cleaning bones for study and display. Certain disabilities can be accommodated in the field, although the appropriateness of this will be determined on a case-by-case basis. The WDC also offers a Kid's Dig program on select days throughout the summer for children ages 8 to 12, wherein kids hunt for fossils, participate in a dig in the dinosaur quarry, work in the molding/casting lab, and participate in an educational scavenger hunt in the museum.

YMCA Go Global

5 West 63rd Street, 2nd floor
New York, NY 10023
(888) 477-9622 or (212) 727-8800, ext. 4316,
ext. 4334, or ext. 4328
E-mail: itracy@ymcanyc.org, cruzj@ymcanyc.org, or
chiu@ymcanyc.org
Website: www.internationalymca.org

Project Type: Community Development; Youth
Mission Statement Excerpt: "YMCA Go Global is a voluntary
service and capacity-building program that places adults
(18+) from the United States & Canada with YMCAs and
community organizations/NGOs around the world."
Year Founded: 2000
Number of Volunteers Last Year: 32
Funding Sources: Foundations and individual donors
The Work They Do: YMCA Go Global volunteers partner with
YMCAs in other countries to assist those organizations in
their work. Work done by volunteers may include teen leadership, health care, education, social work, community
development, and many other fields. Specific examples of
volunteer opportunities with YMCA Go Global include
serving as camp counselors in Ecuador and Italy, helping
with social work and HIV/AIDS awareness projects in South
Africa, and helping with English instruction in Thailand.
Project Location: YMCA Go Global currently has volunteer
programs in South Africa, Philippines, Colombia, India,
Chile, Peru, Thailand, Senegal, China, Singapore, Brazil,
Ecuador, Ghana, Spain, Gambia, Taiwan, Cambodia,
Italy, South Korea, the Dominican Republic, and Nepal.
Applicants may provide YMCA Go Global a list of three
preferred countries, but the organization's staff members
make the final decision on volunteer placement. Housing
varies by host country, but volunteers typically stay in
cabins, apartments, with a host family, or in other similar
accommodations.

Time Line: YMCA Go Global offers one-month to two-year placements. Placements are available throughout the year.

Cost: YMCA Go Global charges a $900 program fee. Food (at least two meals per day), accommodations, and, in some countries, a small stipend are provided to the volunteer by their host YMCAs. Volunteers must provide their own international airfare.

Getting Started: Prospective volunteers can download an application from the International YMCA's Go Global website. Application deadlines are typically in the season before departure; for example, volunteers who wish to depart in the summer will have an application deadline in the spring. Volunteers must conduct an interview by phone or in person and may need to attend a predeparture orientation in New York City. YMCA Go Global also offers an in-country briefing and orientation sessions upon arrival in the host country and language lessons as necessary.

Needed Skills and Specific Populations: Volunteers must be US citizens 18 years of age or older; there is no maximum age. There is no language requirement for YMCA Go Global's placements, with the exception of volunteer sites in Latin America, which ask that volunteers have at least a moderate proficiency in Spanish. Some sites may be able to host volunteers with disabilities.

Youth Challenge International (YCI)

555 Richmond Street W, Suite 313
P.O. Box 1205
Toronto, ON M5V 3B1
Canada
(416) 504-3370; Fax: (416) 504-3376
E-mail: generalinfo@yci.org
Website: www.yci.org

Project Type: Community Development; Economic
Development; Education; Medical/Health; Youth
Mission Statement Excerpt: "Building communities and leaders
through global youth development."
Year Founded: 1989
Number of Volunteers Last Year: 125
Funding Sources: Government and foundation support, as well
as private donors
The Work They Do: Youth Challenge International's programs
are focused on meeting the needs of youth affected by
poverty, especially in the areas of leadership, health, and
livelihoods. Volunteers carry out a range of tasks in support
of this mission, including organizing trainings, promoting
literacy, teaching employability skills workshops, constructing educational facilities, facilitating health education
classes, and organizing small- and large-scale substance
abuse and health outreach events.
Project Location: YCI operates programs in Tanzania, Ghana,
Guatemala, Costa Rica, Nicaragua, Uganda, and Guyana.
Field conditions vary greatly by project, but volunteers
should expect to live and work within a 4- to 10-person
team environment and in basic conditions that include
shared rooms and a local diet. Volunteers in Central and
South America should expect to have no access to the
Internet and to have poor cell phone reception. Accommodations also vary by project, as housing is usually provided
by the host community, and may include group housing or
homestays.

Time Line: YCI operates projects year-round, lasting from 3 to 12 weeks.

Cost: Program fees begin at $2,500 for 3 weeks and range up to $3,900 for a 12-week project. Program fees include accommodations and food but do not include international travel to the placement site.

Getting Started: Applications are available on YCI's website and should be completed three to six months in advance of a project's start date. Prospective volunteers will need to complete a 30-minute phone interview with YCI. YCI offers a predeparture orientation via online conference calls and independent study, as well as an in-country orientation and training once volunteers arrive.

Needed Skills and Specific Populations: Volunteers are accepted into YCI based on their motivation, aptitude, and attitude, and are then placed in a program based on their past travel, work, education, and volunteer experience, as well as their own interests. YCI only accepts volunteers between the ages of 18 and 30 who are Canadian, US, or EU citizens and who can communicate in English. YCI welcomes volunteers aged 18 to 30 with disabilities on projects; in the past, YCI has placed volunteers with visual impairments, speech impairments, and mobility disabilities on projects. Potential volunteers with disabilities are reviewed on a case-by-base basis to ensure YCI and YCI's partners can appropriately accommodate the specific disability. Because of their age limitations, YCI does not place families of volunteers.

Youth International

1112 Sam Cook Road, Unit 1
Gravenhurst, ON P1P 1R3
Canada
(416) 538-0152; Fax: (416) 538-7189
E-mail: info@youthinternational.org
Website: www.youthinternational.org

Project Type: Agriculture; Community Development; Construction; Education; Natural Conservation (Land); Orphans; Youth

Mission Statement Excerpt: "Youth International opens the doors for young people to actively explore and discover a broader perspective on the world while developing a deeper understanding of who they are and what their place is within that world."

Year Founded: 1997

Number of Volunteers Last Year: 95

Funding Sources: Mostly self-funded, with a few private donors

The Work They Do: Youth International sponsors projects that include, for the most part, physically challenging manual labor, though some teaching positions are also available. Specific examples of Youth International's projects include renovating orphanages and schools, teaching English, carrying out conservation projects in the rain forest, and helping the poor in Mother Teresa's clinics.

Project Location: Youth International has an Asia program, with projects located in Thailand, India, and Vietnam, as well as a South America program, with projects located in Bolivia, Peru, and Ecuador. About half of the accommodations are in homestays, with the rest in hostels or tents. Youth International's goal is for volunteers to live and travel as the residents of the country of service do; conditions are often rugged and may lack in basic comforts and amenities.

Time Line: Youth International places volunteers from September through December and February through May. Volunteer programs last for 12 weeks.

Cost: Youth International's program fee is $9,900, which covers virtually all of the volunteer's costs, including all flights, visas, all overland transportation, program activities, and food and accommodations.

Getting Started: Applications for Youth International's programs are available on its website, or they can be mailed or e-mailed to prospective volunteers. Applications are followed up with a phone interview within one week. The three-day orientation begins in Estes Park, Colorado, or alternate locations in the United States. It is completed in-country and lasts three days.

Needed Skills and Specific Populations: Volunteers must have a high school diploma. Senior volunteers can work with Youth International, but the organization's efforts are focused on people aged 18 to 25. Volunteers with disabilities are welcomed, with the caveat that some program areas cannot adequately accommodate all disabilities. Families are not restricted from volunteering with Youth International, but the program does focus on volunteers within a specific age range, not families.

Index by Project Cost

$500–$999

$1,000–$1,999

$3,000+

Index by Project Length

Less Than One Week

One Week

Two Weeks

Three or Four Weeks

Two to Six Months

Six or More Months

Index by Project Location

Asia/South Pacific

Europe

Mexico

Middle East

Index by Project Season

Index by Project Type

Administrative

Catalina Island Conservancy, 77
Cheyenne River Youth Project (CRYP), 81
Farm Sanctuary, 126
Fundacion Aldeas de Paz (Peace Villages Foundation), 139
Habitat for Humanity International's Global Village, 209
Hands Up Holidays, 211
Holy Land Trust (HLT), 216
Mercy Ships, 259
ProWorld Volunteers, 291
Theodore Roosevelt Medora Foundation, 318
United Action for Children (UAC), 324

Agriculture

ACDI/VOCA, 1
CHOICE Humanitarian (Center for Humanitarian Outreach and Inter-Cultural Exchange), 88
CNFA, 93
Concordia International Volunteers, 99
Farm Sanctuary, 126
Foundation for Sustainable Development (FSD), 131
Global Citizen Year (GCY), 151
Global Service Corps (GSC), 174
Global Volunteer Network (GVN), 179
Go Differently, 201
Institute for International Cooperation and Development (IICD), 225

International Student Volunteers (ISV), 231
Jatun Sacha, 242
National Cooperative Business Association Farmer-to-Farmer (FTF) Program, 261
National Trust Working Holidays, 263
Operation Crossroads Africa (OCA), 275
Outreach360 (formerly Orphanage Outreach), 277
Sunseed Desert Project, 311
Sustainable Harvest International (SHI), 313
Via International, 332
Volunteers for Peace (VFP), 350
Volunteers Without Borders (VWB), 357
Winrock International, 362
World-Wide Opportunities on Organic Farms (WWOOF) UK, 373
World-Wide Opportunities on Organic Farms (WWOOF) USA, 375
Youth International, 383

Archaeology

Adelante, 6
African Conservation Trust (ACT), 8
Caribbean Volunteer Expeditions (CVE), 73
Concordia International Volunteers, 99
Earthwatch, 115

Construction

Economic Development

Historic Preservation

Human Rights

Museums

Natural Conservation (Land)

Natural Conservation (Sea)

Orphans

Scientific Research

Social Justice

Trail Building/Maintenance

Women's Issues

Youth

Disability-Friendly Organizations

Family-Friendly Organizations

Senior-Friendly Organizations

Also from Chicago Review Press

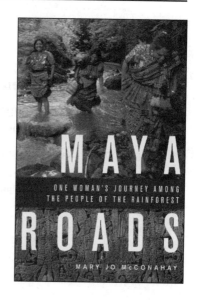

Maya Roads

One Woman's Journey Among
the People of the Rainforest

Mary Jo McConahay

978-1-56976-548-7

$16.95 (CAN $18.95)

"[An] extraordinary travel memoir."
—Laura Fraser, author of *An Italian Affair* and *All Over the Map*

"From enchanted jungles at the center of the Americas all the way to military roadblocks and nightmare massacres, [McConahay is] the best sort of guide. . . . I cannot imagine a better chronicler of this time and place."
—Richard Rodriguez, Peabody Award winner for *PBS NewsHour* and author of *Brown: The Last Discovery of America*

Mary Jo McConahay draws upon her three decades of traveling, working, and living in Central America's remote landscapes to create a fascinating chronicle of the people, politics, archaeology, and species of the rainforest, the cradle of Maya civilization. Captivated by the jungle's magnificence and mystery, McConahay brings to life the intense beauty, ancient ruins, and the resilience of the Maya as well as the horrific violence, increased drug trafficking, and transformation of the Lacandón people. *Maya Roads* is a unique tale of a woman's adventure and the adaptation and resolve of a people.

Invisible China

A Journey Through
Ethnic Borderlands

Colin Legerton and Jacob Rawson

978-1-55652-814-9

$24.95 (CAN $27.95)

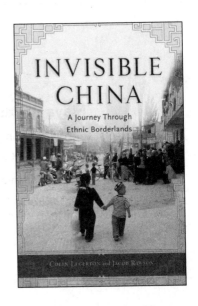

"This odyssey—spanning 14,000 miles—details China's rich diversity in a narrative jeweled with dazzling descriptions. . . . A spectacular achievement."

—Publishers Weekly

In this eloquent and eye-opening adventure narrative, Colin Legerton and Jacob Rawson, two Americans fluent in Mandarin Chinese, Korean, and Uyghur, throw away the guidebook and bring a hitherto unexplored side of China to light. They journey by bus and train to the farthest reaches of the country to meet the minority peoples who dwell there, talking to farmers in their fields, monks in their monasteries, fishermen on their skiffs, and herders on the steppe. As they enjoy an alcohol-fueled dinner with Ewenki village cadres that becomes a heated discussion of human rights, discuss with aging hajjis the Chinese government's razing of their mosque and burning of their Qur'ans, and hike around high-altitude Lugu Lake to farm with the matriarchal Mosuo women, they uncover surprising facts about China's hidden minorities and their complex position in Chinese society.